I0800236

IMAGES
of America

JONESBORO

AND ARKANSAS' HISTORIC NORTHEAST CORNER

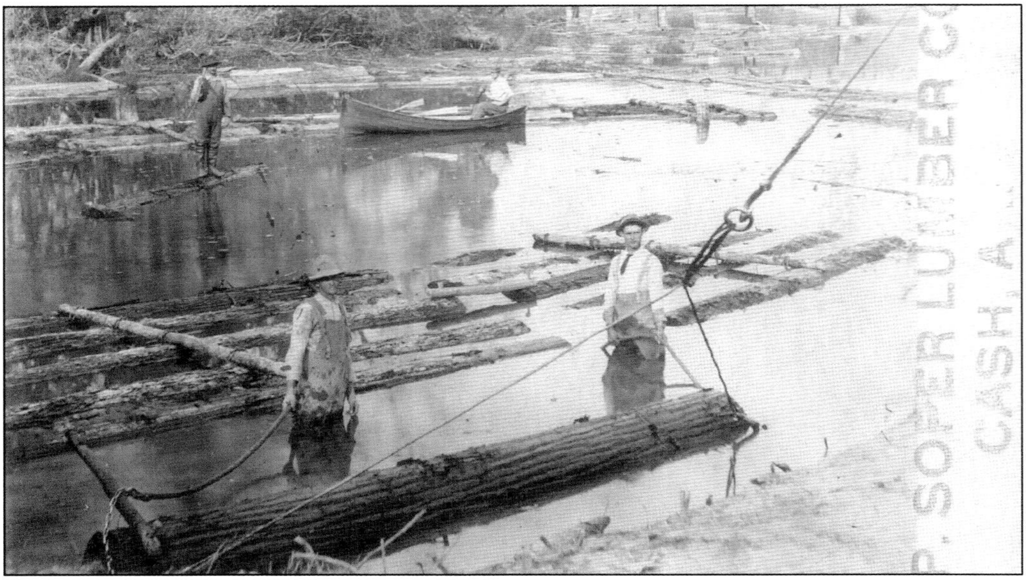

Cash, Arkansas, 1909—seen above—offers a snapshot in time of the labor that went into clearing the vast hardwood forests that once covered much of Craighead County. The logs had been cut and stored in the pond until ready to process into lumber and other wood products. The man working in the water, guiding the cable attached to the log, is wearing a tie. Delaplaine, a community in southern Greene County, was part of the timber boom in the area at the turn of the 20th century. The load of axe handles being hauled on this wagon was likely to be shipped by rail to a distant factory and was among the many products milled from the once abundant hardwood forests.

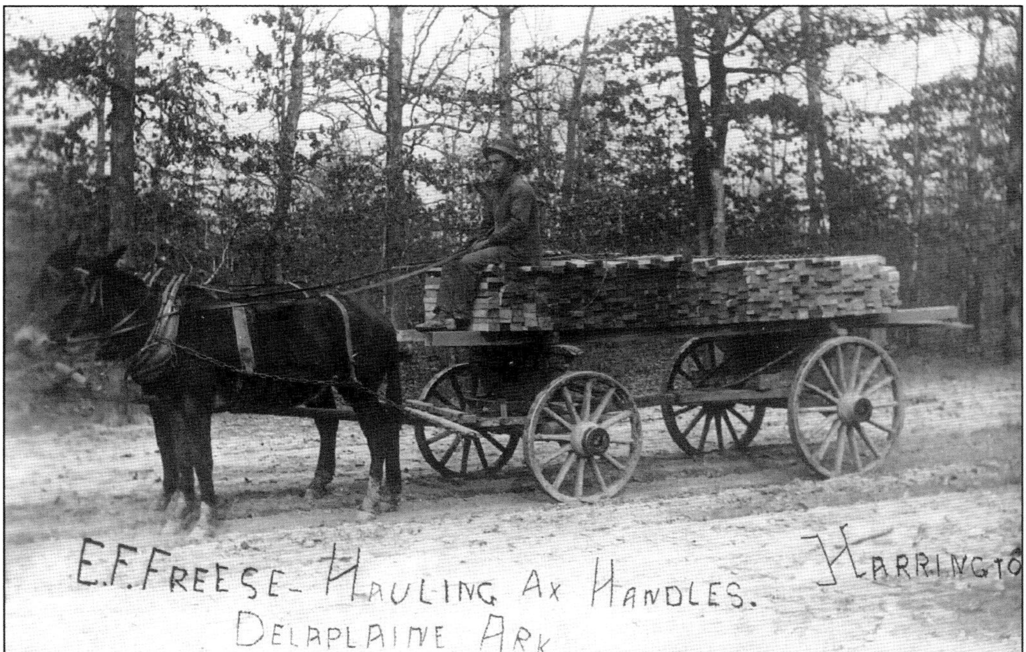

IMAGES
of America

JONESBORO
AND ARKANSAS' HISTORIC NORTHEAST CORNER

Ray and Diane Hanley

ARCADIA
PUBLISHING

ISBN 978-0-7385-1947-0

Published by Arcadia Publishing
Charleston, South Carolina

Printed in the United States of America

Library of Congress Catalog Card Number: 2001097589

For all general information contact Arcadia Publishing at:
Telephone 843-853-2070
Fax 843-853-0044
E-mail sales@arcadiapublishing.com
For customer service and orders:
Toll-Free 1-888-313-2665

Visit us on the Internet at www.arcadiapublishing.com

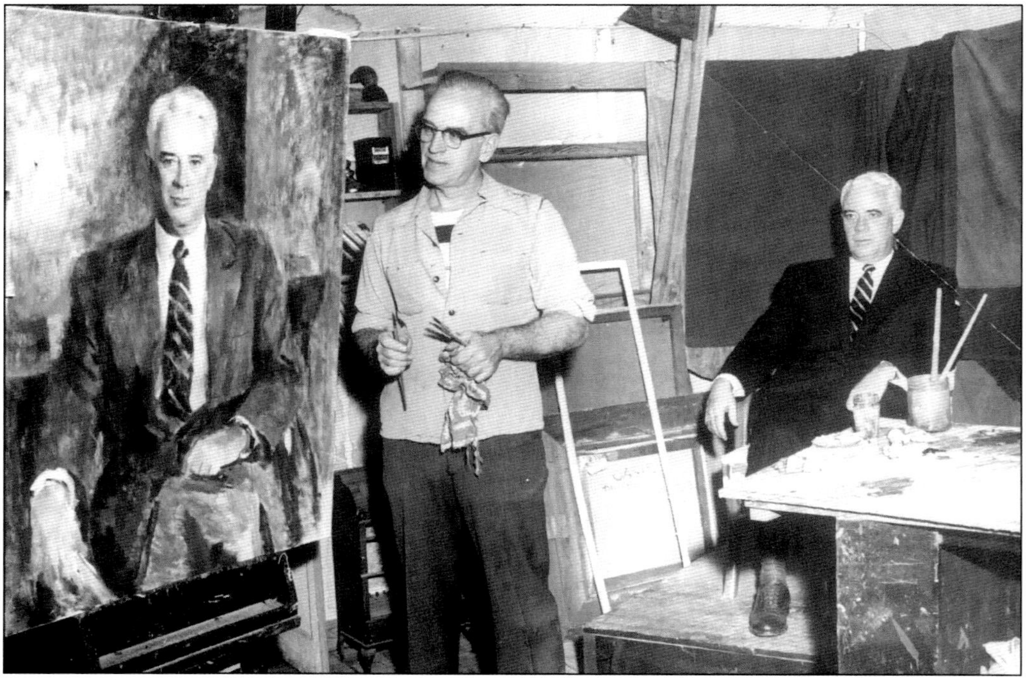

Francis Cherry was an obscure Jonesboro Chancery Judge in 1952 when he launched an underfunded campaign for governor against incumbent Sid McMath. With the aid of such events as a "talkathon" on a Little Rock radio station (literally talking on air for 24 hours), and attempting to raise funds with a "dollars for decency" pledge, he kept a promise to answer "any and all" questions. Cherry won, but his tenure was cut short when he was defeated two years later by Orval E. Faubus. In this photo, taken in 1955, Cherry was having his portrait painted to hang in the State Capitol, with those of other past governors.

CONTENTS

ACKNOWLEDGMENTS

This book, though it bears the names of the authors, is possible only because of the contributions of a number of people who make their homes in Craighead, Clay, and Greene Counties. For help with research in Clay County, we sincerely thank Mrs. Una Pollard of Piggott for her research, along with Jim Poole of Piggot State Bank, Chuck Haywood of Spokane, Washington (formerly of Clay County), and Barbara McKeel and Geraldine Wagster of the Rector Public Library. In Greene County the services of Bettye Busby of the Greene County Library were invaluable; she is a storehouse of knowledge on her community. The Craighead County portion of the book was made possible thanks to the help of Ruth Ball and Elvis Meilke of the Craighead County Library; they are researchers of the first order. Technical assistance on railroad and train depot questions came from Dr. Bill Pollard of Conway. Many of the photos come from the authors' collection, but the book is also indebted to the photo contributions of the Arkansas State University Museum, the Greene County Library, and the Craighead County Jonesboro Library. A special note of thanks is extended to John Kennte of Child Art Studio—located on historic Pruett Street in Paragould—for sharing his fabulous private collection of historic Greene County photos, to Lynn Ewbank of the Arkansas History Commission for her assistance, and to LeMay Photography of Little Rock for professional photo services. All photo credits appear on page 128.

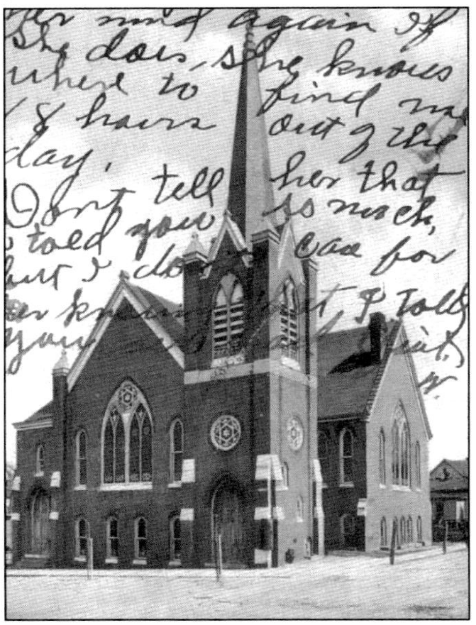

Although the images on postcards show how the world has changed from horse-and-buggy days to the age of space shuttles and computers, sometimes the messages penciled on the back of postcards decades ago suggest that human relations may not have changed all that much. Written on the back and continuing to the front of a card showing the local Methodist Church was a poignant message: "Well Hazel, M and me quit last night, I guess it is for good this time cause I will never ask her for another date, I don't know her real reasons, but I guess she knows her business, hope she is satisfied. M. may change her mind again, if she does, she knows where to find me 18 hours out of the day. Don't tell her that I told you so much but I don't care for her knowing that I told you we had quit." Signed only "W," the card was mailed to New Albany, Indiana, from Jonesboro, 1908.

INTRODUCTION

Arkansas is a diverse state, rich in natural resources, scenery, and history. Some of these riches are known around the world, but much is tucked away in the small towns and side roads of this remarkable state. In most efforts to chronicle Arkansas' past, perhaps one of the areas least covered is the far northeastern corner of the state, including Clay, Greene, and Craighead Counties. Into the early part of the 20th century, this area was a collection of small towns scattered through vast forests of hardwood timber, and it was consequently slower to develop than other areas of Arkansas. Today the region is anchored by the prosperous city of Jonesboro—now some 55,000 strong with Arkansas State University at its heart—helping make the area a vibrant blend of industry, agriculture, and education.

Over the past century, much of the history of this diverse three-county region was captured on photographs and postcards, providing a window into the lives of the men and women who planted the seeds of the culture and economy of the region today. The towns of Jonesboro, Paragould, Corning, Piggott, and Rector—along with a host of smaller communities—all have stories to tell of their founders: of how they were named and perhaps renamed, of fires and floods, boom and bust. The goal of the authors is to capture a cross-section of the area's history as reflected in these images, supported by the collected accounts penned on the backs of postcards and shared with us by people who still call the region home today.

Along with the rest of modern-day Arkansas, the area that would make up these three counties was acquired for the United States when President Thomas Jefferson obtained the Louisiana Purchase from France in 1804. Settlement would come slowly, delayed certainly by one of the strongest earthquakes in U.S. history in 1811. A noted explorer and ethnologist, Henry Schoolcraft recalled in a poem the terror that came with the quake: "The Rivers they boiled like a pot over coals, And mortals fell prostrate, and prayed for their souls." The New Madrid Earthquake, which rang church bells as far away as Boston, changed the area's geography and left its mark on the land even until today. The quake laid waste to much of what was planned by potential settlers to become prime farmland, with parcels sinking as much as 20 feet in some areas. In other locations steep ridges rose up, the channel of the St. Francis River was destroyed, and the natural drainage pattern of the region was changed for decades to come. The federal government had issued bounty certificates to the veterans of the War of 1812 to be redeemed for land in the area, but much of it proved unusable in the aftermath of the massive earthquake.

Hesitant for fear of more earthquakes, the first four settlers in the area that became Craighead County and Jonesboro bravely paddled small boats down the St. Francis River from the Indian village of Chillicataw, located at what is today Kennett, Missouri. Upon arrival at a spot on the river denoted as Deep Landing, a man named Rittenhouse and his wife decided to begin work on a cabin while the other two pioneers returned upriver to Chillicataw for additional supplies.

Upon returning weeks later, they found a completed cabin but with Mr. Rittenhouse dead beside it, a bullet lodged in his head. Mrs. Rittenhouse was found nearby, beheaded—presumably by Indians. Needless to say, this first foray's tragic ending put a damper on the dreams of other settlers for some time thereafter.

The first white settler to make a permanent mark on the area was Daniel Martin, who located a farm about 6 miles from present-day Jonesboro in 1829. The 80-acre bounties given to veterans of the War of 1812 were often bought and sold several times, helping to bring more settlers who spread out over the area that makes up present-day Clay, Green, and Craighead Counties. In an area that otherwise more closely resembles the flat, swampy delta, the dominant geographic feature is Crowley's Ridge, named for pioneer settler Benjamin Crowley. Running for a length of 150 miles north from Helena through northeast Arkansas and varying in height between 250 and 500 feet, the crescent-shaped ridge was created over the centuries by the shifting Mississippi River and perhaps enhanced by the upheaval of the 1812 earthquake. Because the lands on either side of the ridge tended to be low and swampy—especially after the earthquake—settlers were drawn to the heavily timbered ridge; it is upon this high ground that cities like Jonesboro in Craighead County and Paragould in Greene County eventually took root and grew.

In 1860, the population of Craighead County was around 3,000, but 40 years later in 1900, it had swelled to almost 20,000—with some 4,500 people residing in Jonesboro. While Jonesboro was emerging as the leading city in the region, the growing railroads, timber industry, and agriculture also brought jobs and population to such communities as Paragould in Greene County and Corning, Piggott, and Rector in Clay counties. By the time the year 1900 had rolled by, the residents and visitors to the area were discovering a means of communication that was sweeping the nation, the picture postcard. As evidenced by this book, the postcards that came out of northeast Arkansas, especially in the first two decades of the 20th century, left an invaluable record of the day-to-day lives of the people calling it home.

Commercially-produced picture postcards in the United States had their start in 1893, when they were first sold at the World's Columbian Exposition in Chicago. Over the next decade the fad swept the nation; *American Magazine* said in 1906: "Postal carditis manias are working havoc among the inhabitants of the United States.... There is no hamlet so remote which has not succumbed to the ravages of the microbe postale universelle." Four years later, in 1910, the same publication said, "Like a heaven-sent relief, the souvenir postal card has come to the man of few ideas and a torpid vocabulary. No invention in recent years has been so gratefully received. To the thousands of weary travelers it gives a means to say, 'See for yourself; I can't describe it.'" The sheer numbers bore out the scope of the fad, for in 1906 the annual consumption of postcards in the U.S. was reported to be almost 800 million cards. Beyond the record of the photos on the fronts of the cards, some of the written messages on the backs offer additional insights into the daily lives of people who worked hard to build their communities and care for their families. It is because of this postcard craze, which faded after World War I, that we today have many of the views of dusty, small-town streets and farm life in northeastern Arkansas during the first score of years of the 20th century.

It is the authors' hope that these snapshots from the past will stimulate awareness of the fascinating history of Arkansas' northeast corner—the story of the land, its people, what has and hasn't changed—and encourage those working to maintain the cultural and natural resources of the area for generations to come.

One

Clay County

The rivers of northeast Arkansas played a vital role in the early settlement of the area because travel by boat was often the only way to penetrate what was once an intractable wilderness of primeval forest and swamps. The first European settlers almost certainly entered the area by water, paddling their boats down the St. Francis River that divides today's Clay County from the Missouri boot heel. As evidenced by this 1909 postcard for the river town of St. Francis, boats like the *Ethel B* were still important at that time, although the railroads would soon end the romance of the river.

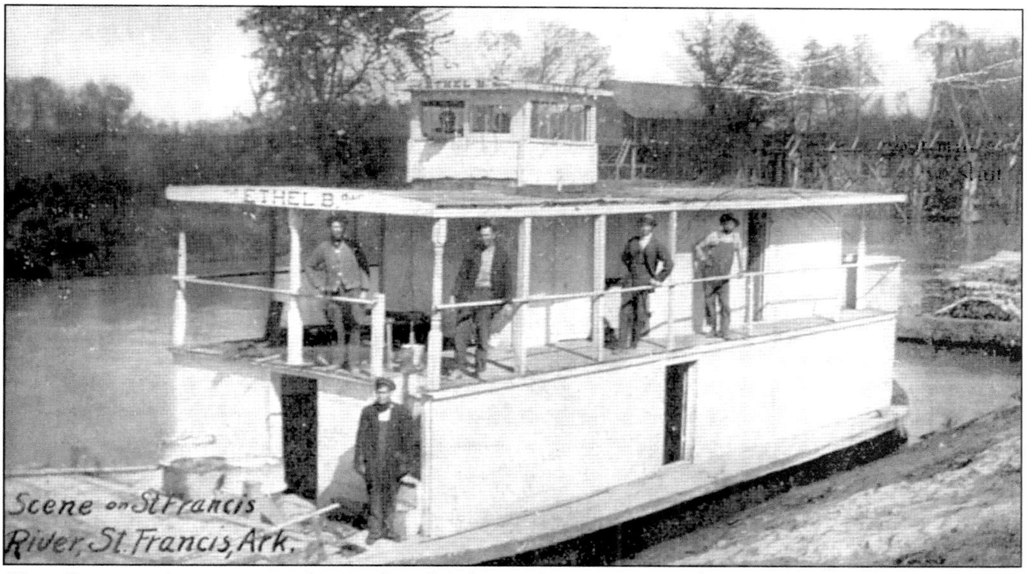

Clay County, the most northeasterly of Arkansas' counties, is also one of the state's youngest counties. Formed by the state legislature in 1873, it was taken from parts of Randolph and Greene Counties and was initially called Clayton County. The county was named for Powell Clayton, a controversial figure who had been a Union soldier in the Civil War and was the state's reconstructionist governor from 1871 to 1877. Dislike of reconstruction in general and the man in particular led to the renaming of the county as simply "Clay," but in honor of the beloved Southern statesman Henry Clay.

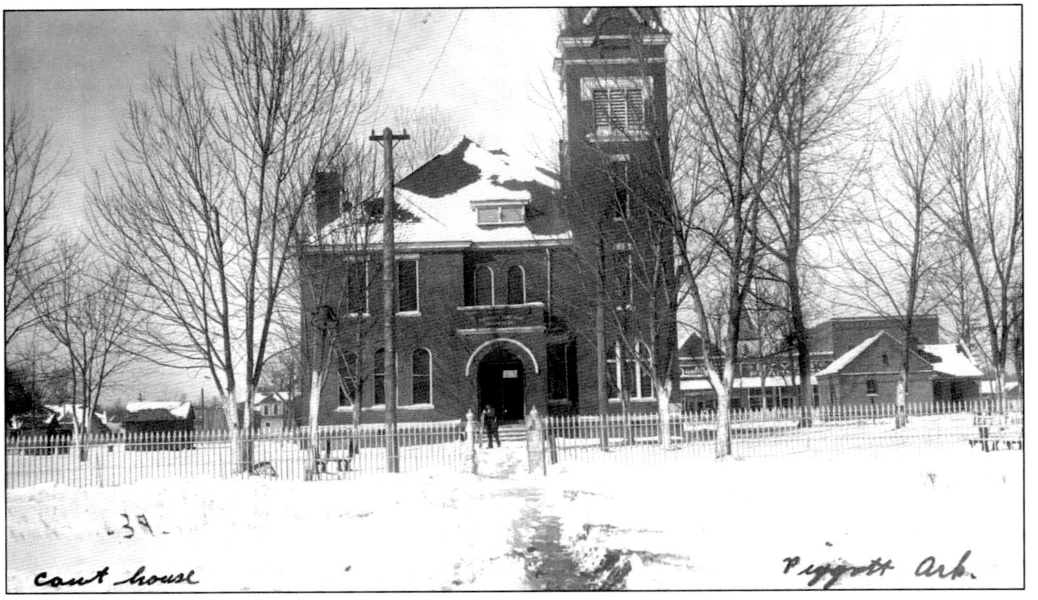

Out of Arkansas' 75 counties, Clay County is one of ten to have two distinct county seats and two courthouses. As county governments were forming in the late 1800s, the state's rivers were often flood-prone, with unreliable ferries and no bridges, so that access to a single county seat was cut off for many. Even if the distance from the edge of the county to the seat was more than a reasonable wagon ride, two county seats were formed. The eastern district of Clay county found Piggott designated as its seat; its *c.* 1890s courthouse is seen above on a 1908 postcard. The card's message sent to a man in Chicago read, "Am in Piggott now and am going to an ice cream supper tonight, wish you could be with me. As ever a faithful sweetheart, Ada." The western district county seat found its home in Corning; the courthouse is seen below in 1907. "I hope you got done harvesting & thrashing by this time. I am working in a sawmill, but things are looking blue, they are talking of shutting down the mill as all the other mills have shut down in the south." Both courthouses were replaced with modern buildings in 1966.

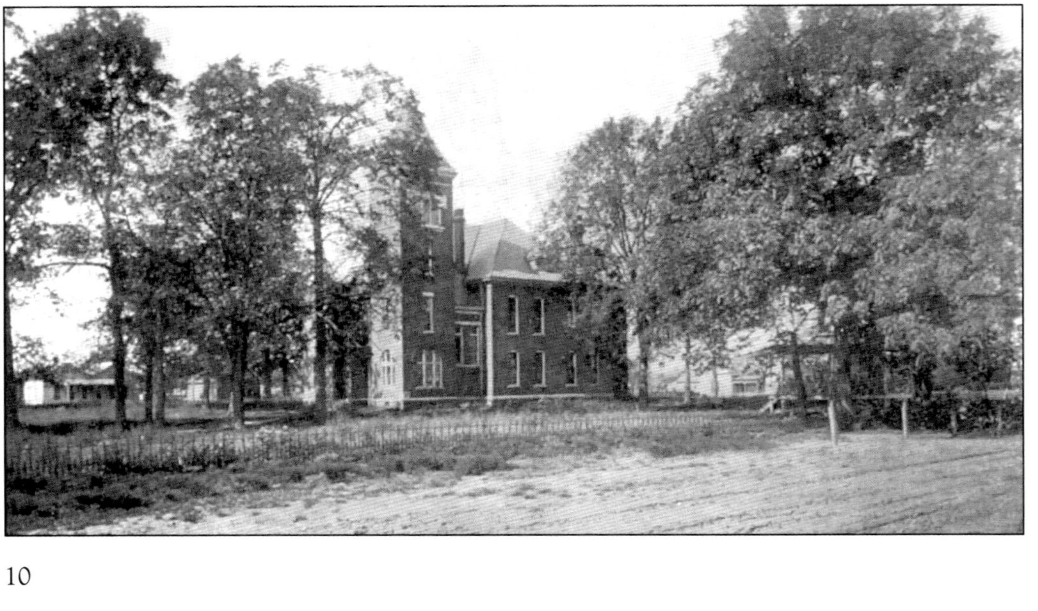

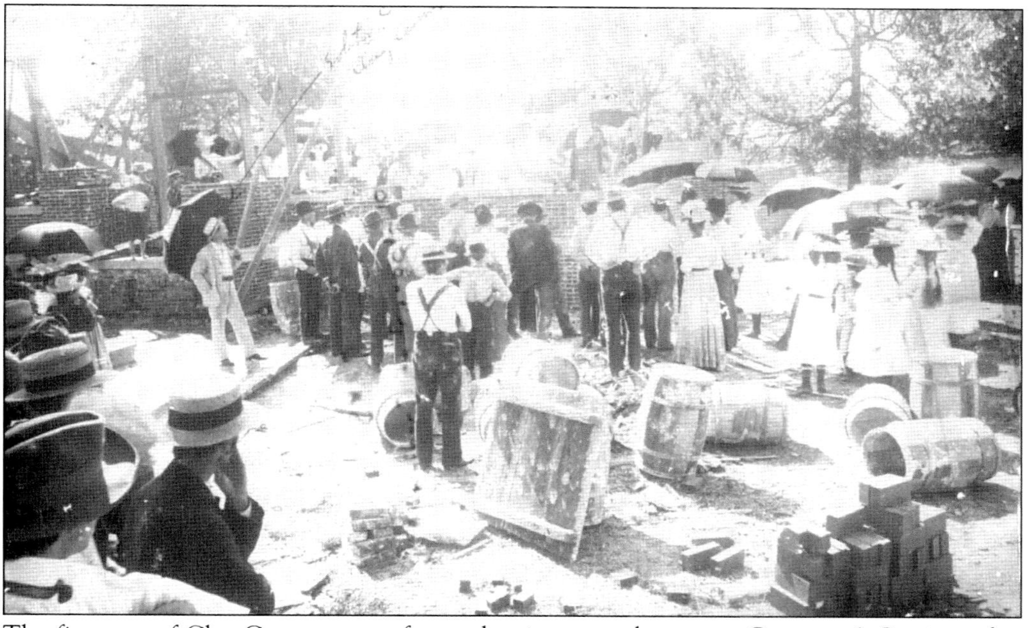

The first seat of Clay County was a former logging camp known as Carpenter's Station, after the man who ran the depot of the St. Louis-Iron Mountain Railroad. In 1873, railroad baron Jay Gould suggested renaming it to honor H.D. Corning, an engineer who helped build the railroad that brought prosperity and settlers. In the 1900 photo above, the citizens were laying the cornerstone for the courthouse seen on the opposite page.

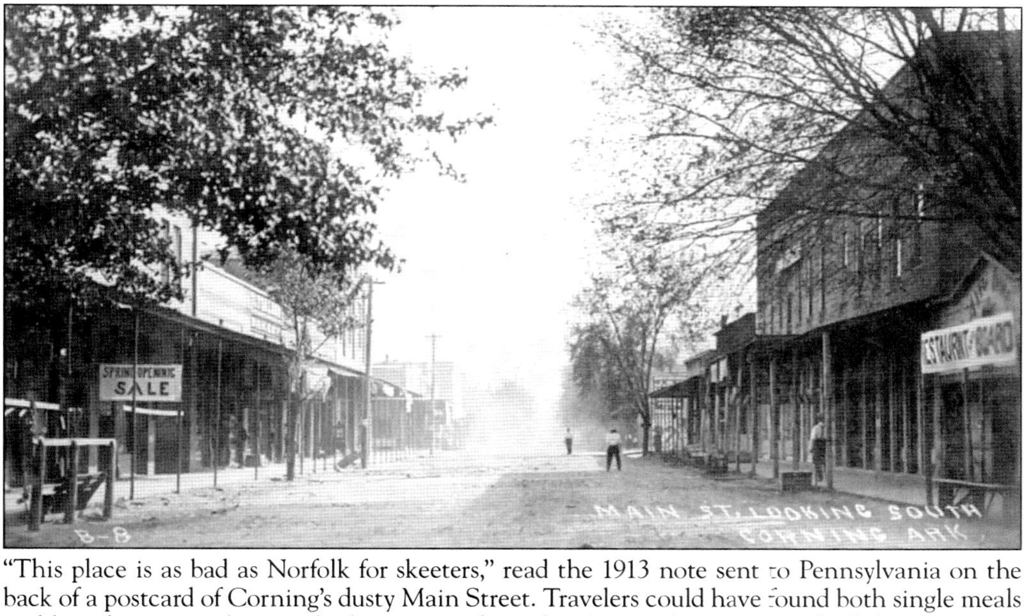

"This place is as bad as Norfolk for skeeters," read the 1913 note sent to Pennsylvania on the back of a postcard of Corning's dusty Main Street. Travelers could have found both single meals and boarding, according to the banner on the right. Across the street on the left, a store was having a "Spring Opening Sale," while further down the street was the City Bakery. At the time, hitching posts for saddle horses and wagon teams were still in evidence, as the automobile was a fairly recent innovation.

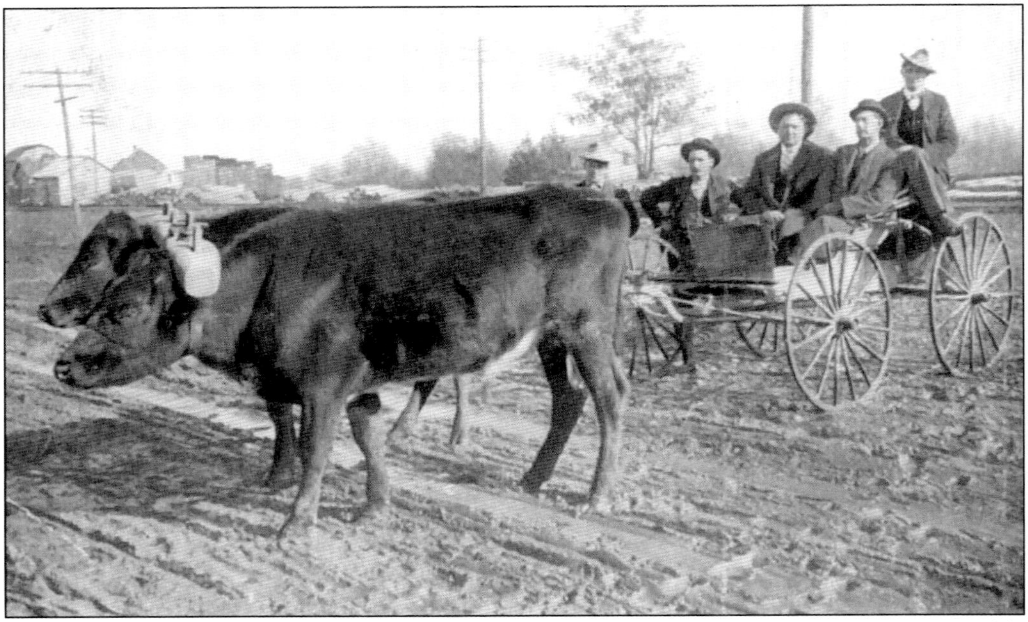

In Corning, as with much of rural Arkansas, early 20th century roads were often impassable after a rain; even in dry weather it took beasts of burden like oxen for some jobs. The oxen that pulled these men into Corning would have been able to do work that horses could not, pulling logs and other loads through the mud.

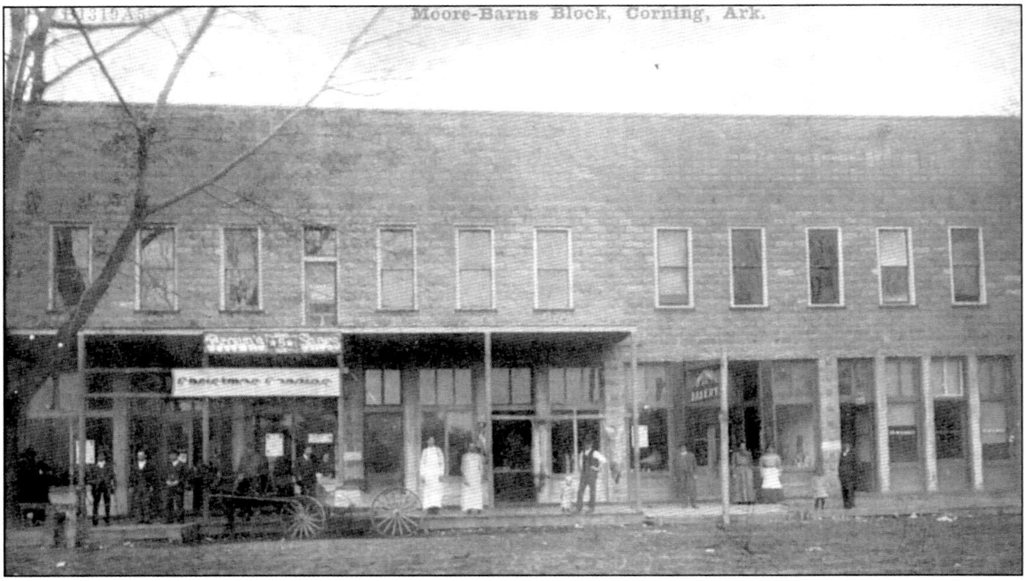

While the Corning visitor from Pennsylvania complained of "skeeters," a 1911 Kansas visitor named Emma found much to like about the little town. "Am here visiting my son Edwin, this is where my husband died in 1909. Weather is beautiful, Town is 2,200 [people], has electric lights, city water works, lumber & Cotton shipped out every day." Surely Emma visited the Moore-Barns block, including the City Bakery on the right and the mercantile on the left, which was promoting Brown's Shoes. The buildings seen here burned in the mid 1990s.

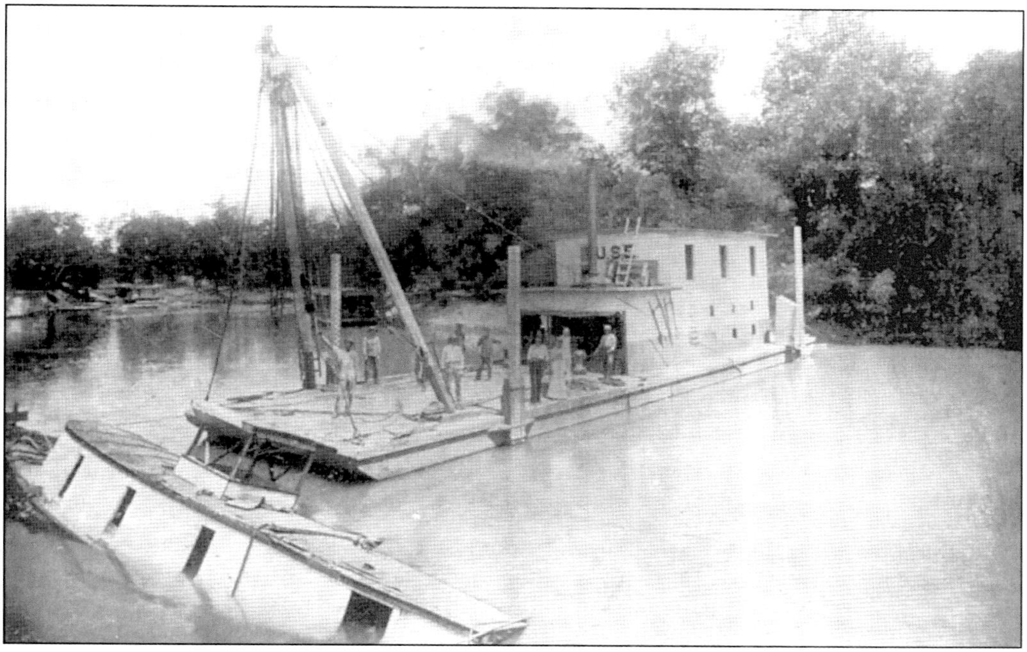

The unreliable roads of Clay County at the turn of the century still warranted dependence on the area's rivers to move certain heavy goods, when speed of delivery wasn't essential. Both of these postcards were mailed by a Corning visitor in 1911, taking note of all the fish she had caught. Indeed, the Black River flowing east of Corning was rich in both fish and boat traffic. The *W.S. Quay*, seen above, was a work boat with lifts used to clear sunken boats, logs, and other obstacles from the channel. Below is seen the *Choctaw* at dock and a stack of firewood ready to load for firing the boat's boilers. The expanding railroads, along with silt filling the river from unchecked land clearing, would soon bring an end to commercial boat traffic on the Black River.

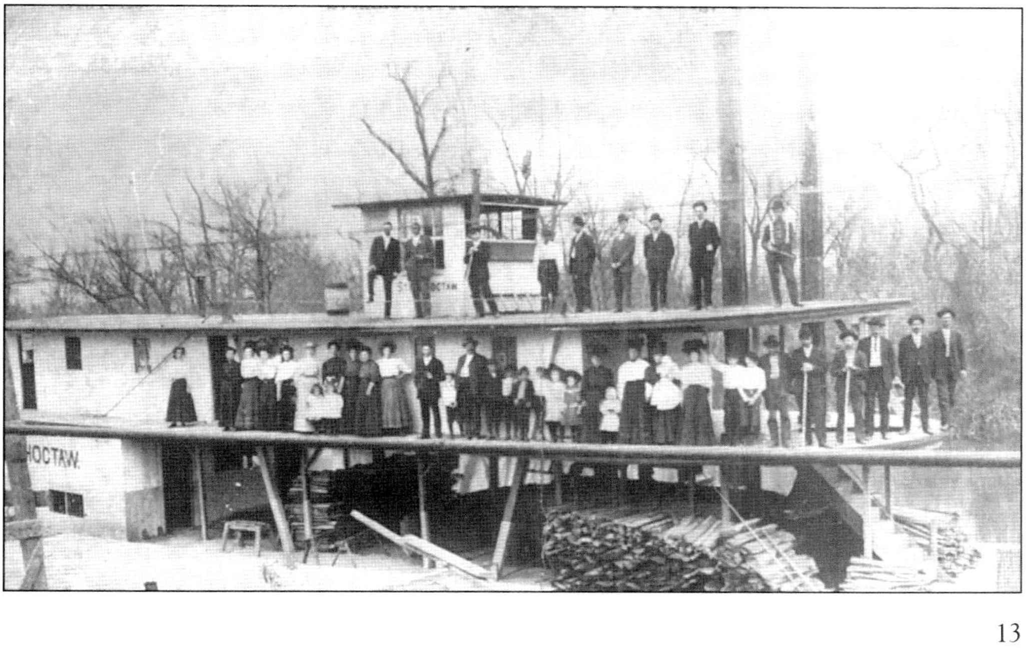

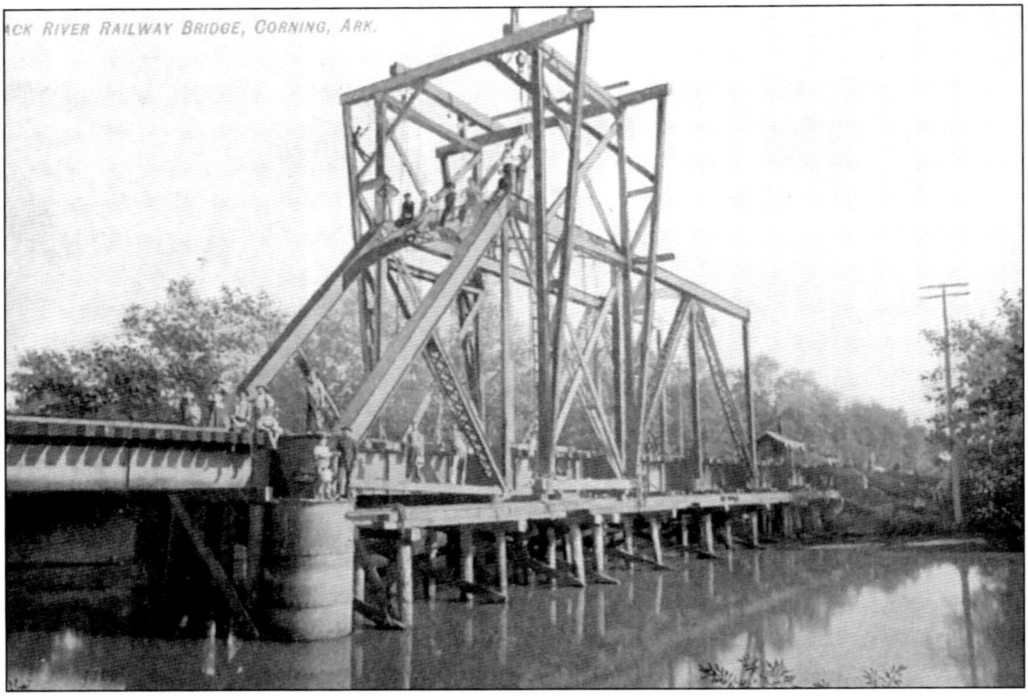

In the waning days of the riverboat era, pilots of the river craft did not have to look far in order to see the cause of the demise of their livelihood. This bridge, erected by the Missouri Pacific Iron Mountain Railroad, crossed the Black River east of Corning. The complex mechanism towering over the bridge, upon which several men are perilously perched, was in reality a movable crane-like device that carried the heavy steel beams that were being used to build—or rebuild—the bridge. Written on the back of a 1913 postcard of the modest train depot in Corning was an Illinois father's message home, while he worked far away in Arkansas: "Please express my light suit to me here and put my razor in with it, try to get it here this week. Tell the boys hello for me." The depot—seen below—where 12 passenger trains a day stopped in 1910, is gone today.

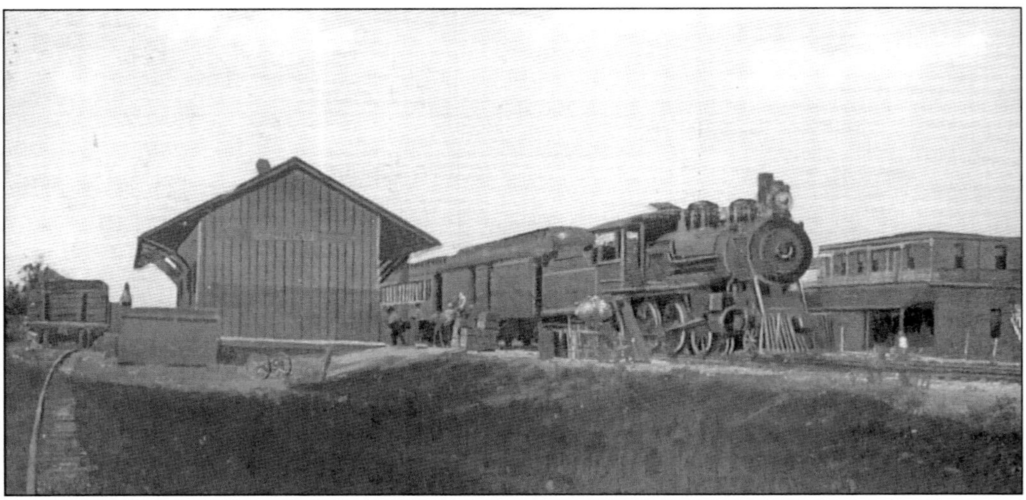

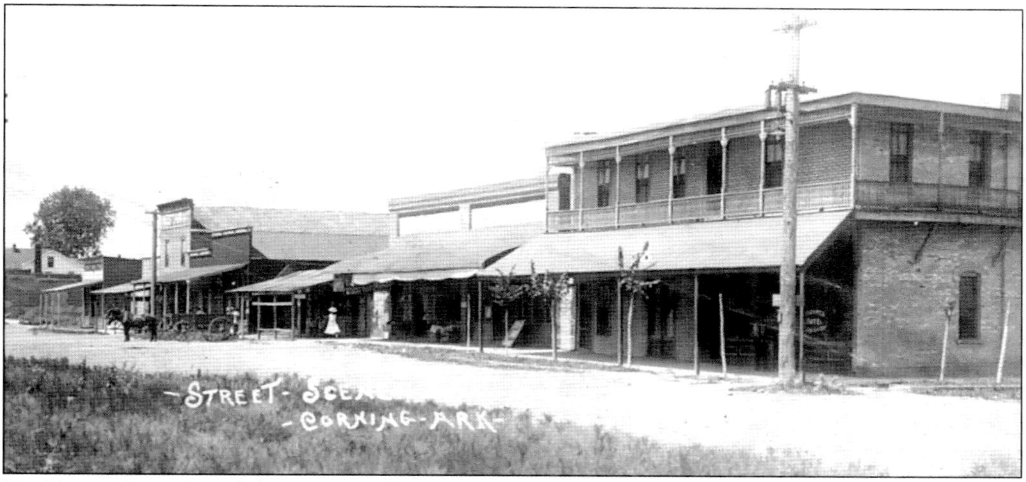

Visible to the right of the train and depot in the photo on the opposite page is the St. James Hotel, seen above on the right. The St. James was the largest hotel in Corning, and its location across the street from the depot brought many guests. The hotel survived long enough to house the first wave of automobile-borne tourists who came down the dusty, rutted roads. It was destroyed by fire in 1926—one man died in the blaze.

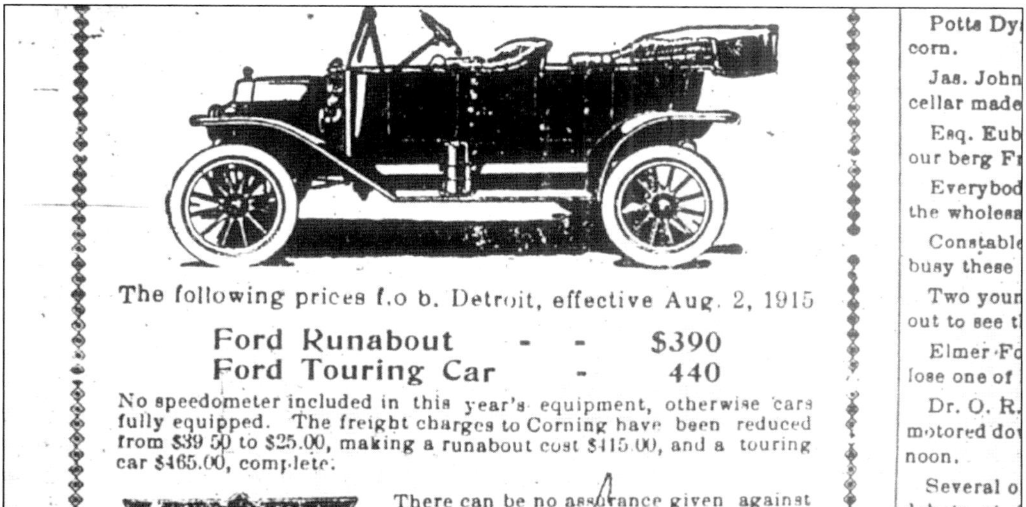

While local ticket agent W.O. Beard was running the bustling Corning train depot, the seeds were germinating for the next leap in transportation technology that would kill off most passenger rail travel. The *Clay County Courier* carried this ad in 1915 for the local Ford dealer, the W.D. Bennett Garage & Machine Shop. The cost of a Ford Runabout was $390, while the Touring Car sold for $440. In great irony, the ad makes note of the fact that shipping charges to Corning had been reduced from $39.50 to $25, due to a discount given by the railroad, which brought automobiles in from Michigan plants.

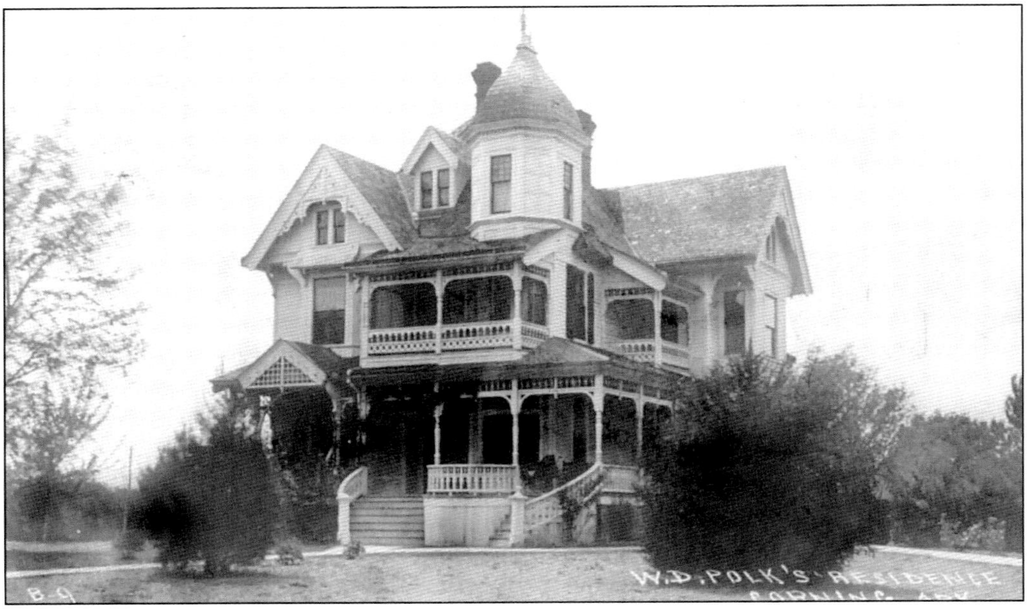

W.D. Polk was among the well-off Corning residents who might have vacationed by train or who perhaps bought a Ford Touring Car from W.D. Bennett. The wealthy banker built this handsome home around 1910. The Polk family lost all their wealth and their home with the coming of the Great Depression and the collapse of the banks. The home was restored in the 1960s but, sadly, burned shortly thereafter.

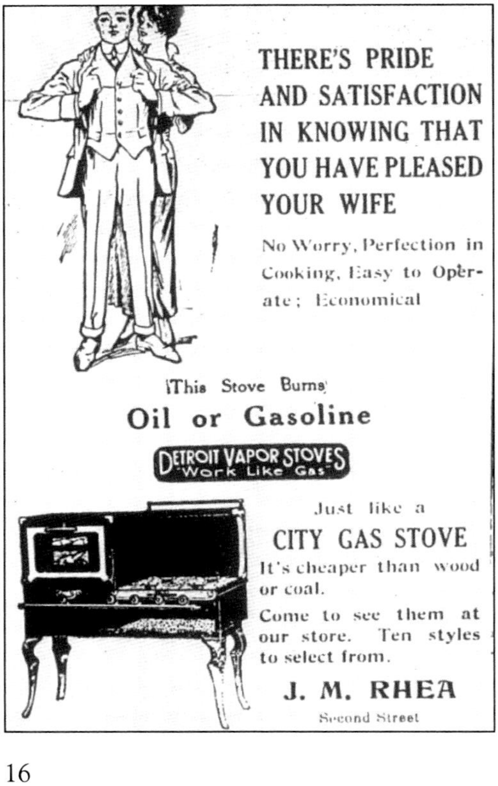

J.M. Rhea was among the 21 merchants that sponsored a 1914 ad in the Corning newspaper, beseeching residents not to patronize mail-order houses like Sears & Roebuck, but rather to shop locally. "That you have a right to spend your money where you please, no one denies, but the practice of spending it out of Corning works an injustice to you in the end just as surely as it injures us at the time you take or send it away. Corning is the financial center of this section from which your living must come. The more money we can keep at home the better will the financial conditions be. If they are good Mr. Workingman will have employment at good wages. Every necessity of life can be bought here at as low a price as anywhere else." In the same paper, Mr. Rhea sought to sell a kitchen stove that could burn either oil or gasoline.

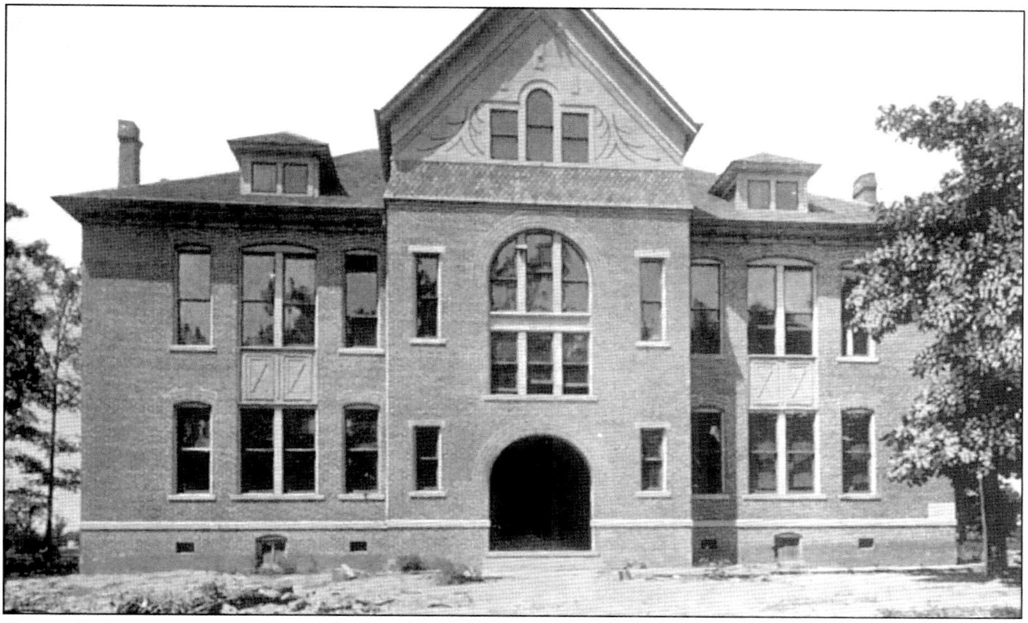

Part of the money spent with local merchants found its way back to support Corning's impressive school building, touted in the article below as one of the state's best. The postcard was mailed in 1908, a year in which Arkansas had more than 5,000 school districts, with the state contributing only $10 per year per student. The school seen above served students of all ages in Corning and had become very crowded by 1940, when it burned down. Some reports attributed the fire to arson, committed by those desiring more modern school buildings; several new schools were then built, thus dispersing the grades.

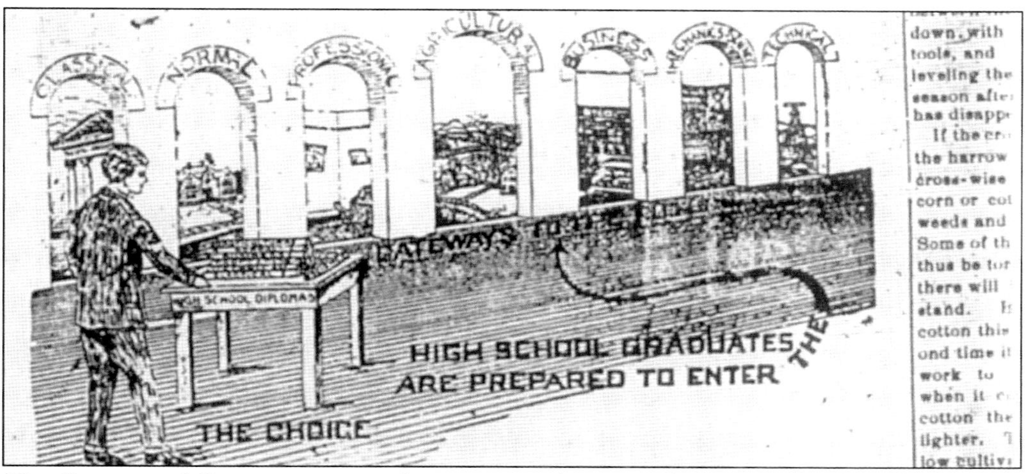

Clay County and Corning in particular put an emphasis on education, as evidenced in part by this illustration that ran on page one of the *Clay County Courier* in 1914. Seeking to improve the low rate of high school graduation in the state at the time, the ad promoted the increased opportunities a diploma would provide: "Over 60% of the successful men in all walks of life have had, at least, a high school advantage. Those who completed high school, the increased average earning capacity is equal to $10 for each day spent in school. Yet barely 15% of the present generation have had high school training."

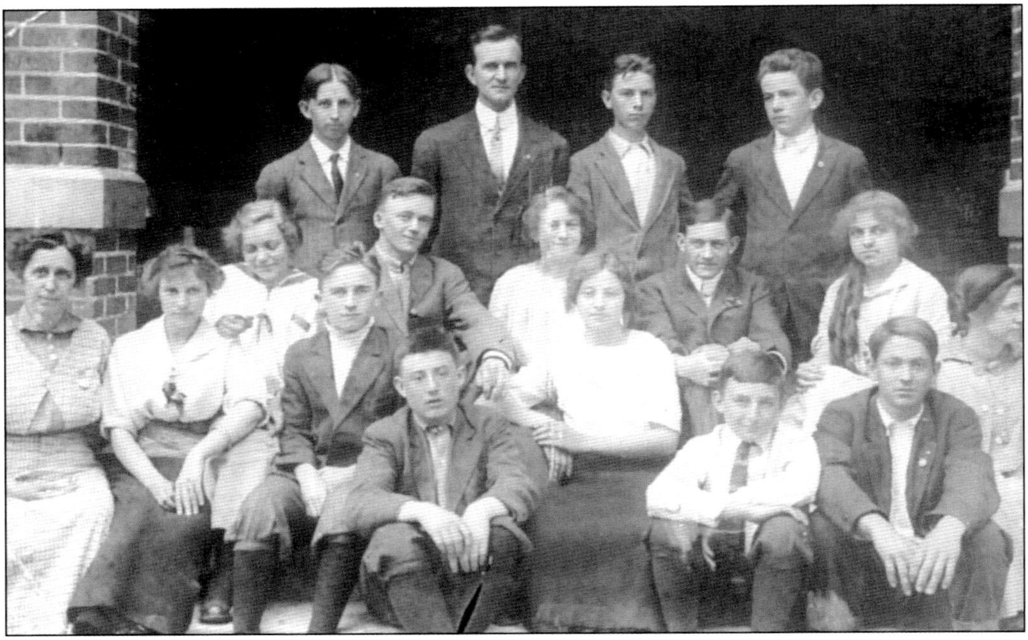

The Corning School was often the backdrop for class photographs, as with these students and faculty posed on the front steps in 1908. All of these young people would have been born in the 1890s and would come to adulthood as the Great War raged in Europe. At the time, Arkansas had 395,000 children enrolled in its public schools, but the average daily attendance was reported at only 255,000, in a time when most young people did not finish high school. In the c. 1910 photo below, the young men of the Corning Military Band posed on the lawn of the school, perhaps preparing for a concert.

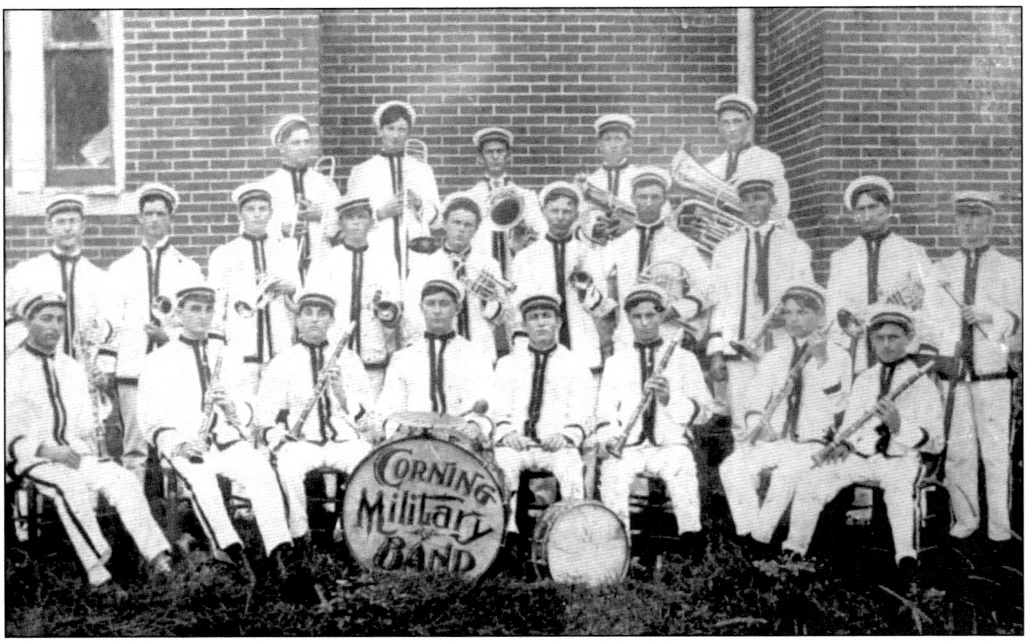

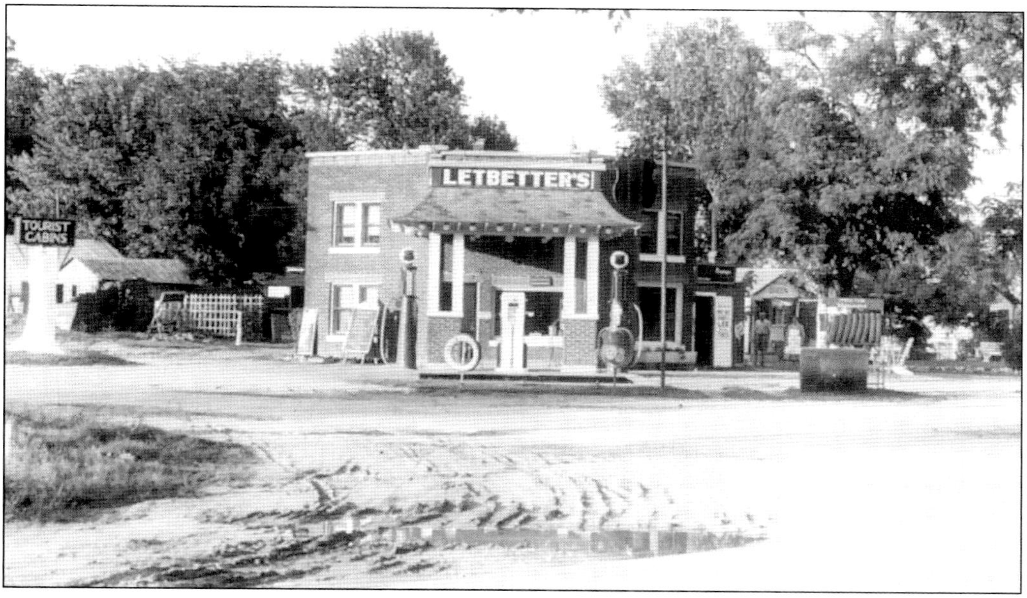

Corning found itself with the great commercial advantage of being in the path of U.S. Highway 67, which had origins as far back as 1800, in the old Southwest Trail that connected St. Louis and Texas. Initially a dirt road and not paved until the 1930s, the highway brought many thousands of automobiles through Corning each year from the 1920s on. One of the businesses that grew up to serve the motorists was Letbetter's Tourist Camp and Gas Station. The Letbetters named each cabin after a character on the popular "Amos & Andy" and "Lum & Abner" radio programs. On the card below, the cabins to the left are named Lum and Abner, and to the right are Brother and Sister Crawford. The gas station served for years as the local bus station, open all hours to serve the many buses passing through Corning. The business was torn down years ago, and the site is occupied today by a fast food restaurant.

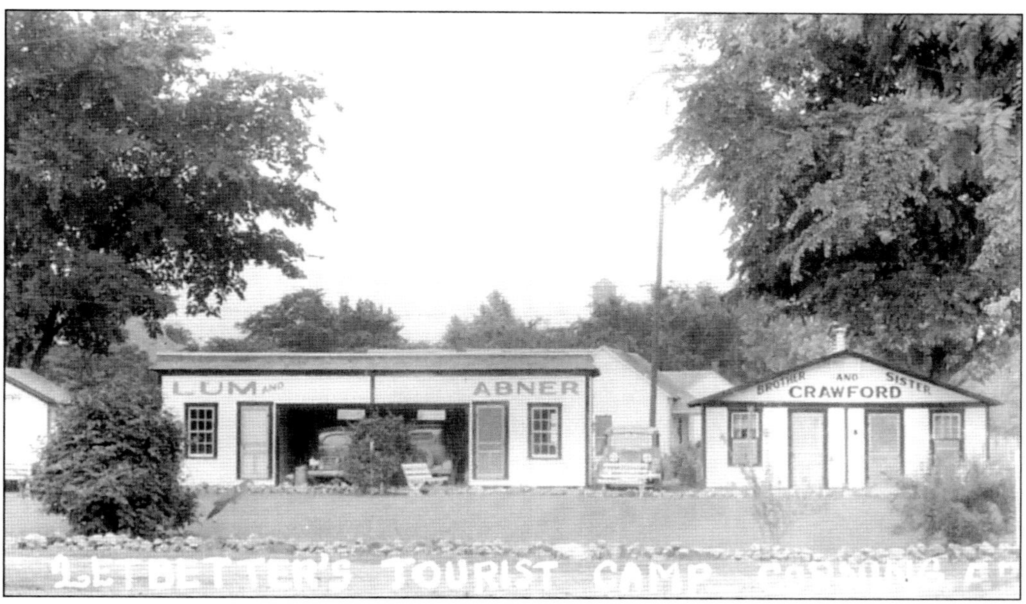

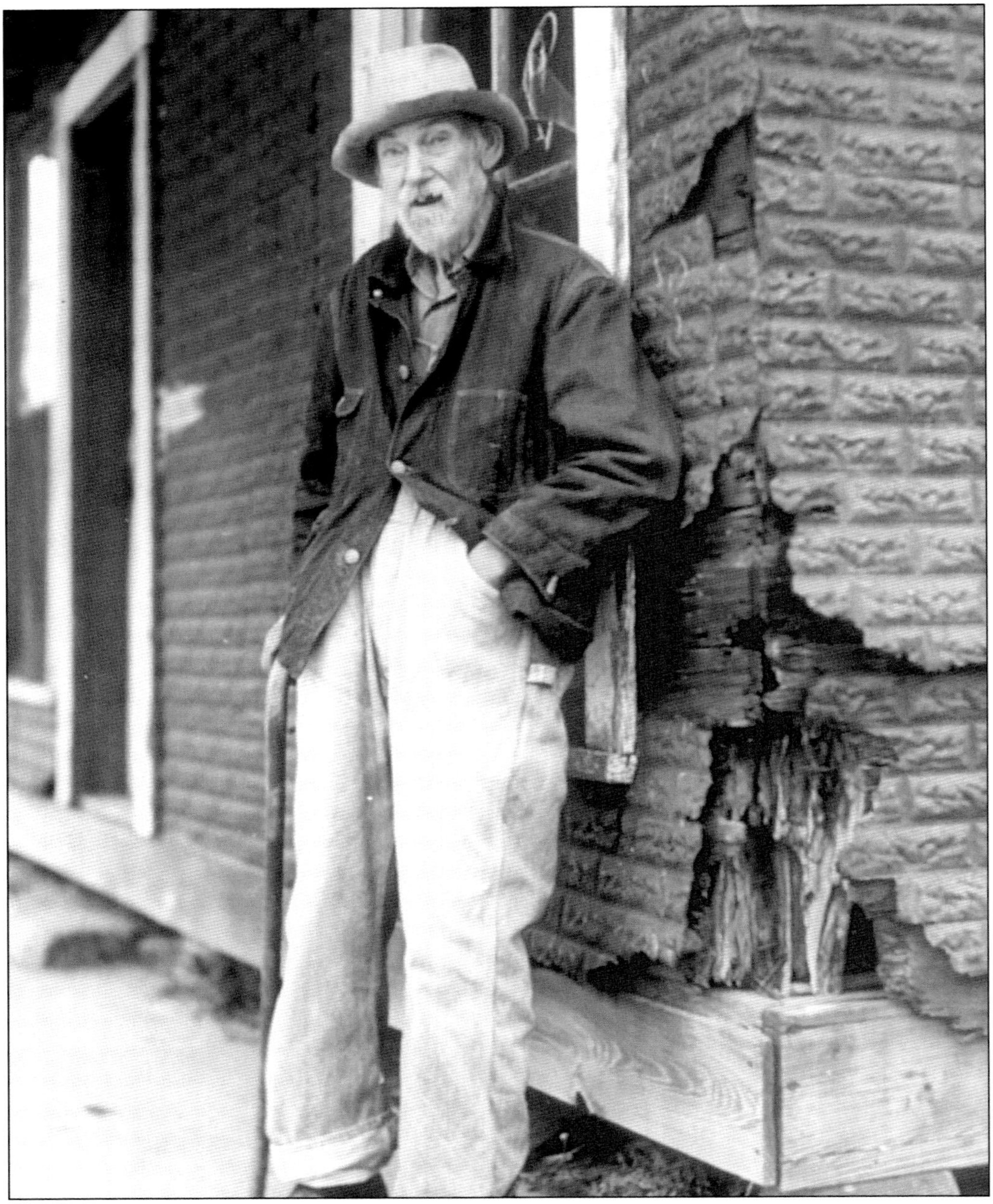

Time has passed in Corning, Arkansas, as it has for all places, but a photographic legacy remains that affords the prosperous little city memories of the people and places that are its history. Sometimes detailed information traveled through the decades with a photograph, but sometimes, as in the case of this photo, one can only wonder. This grizzled, elderly man, who would have been born before the city of Corning existed, paused for a photo in the 1930s on the edge of downtown. With open shoes, missing laces, a walking cane, and few teeth, he was—in some ways, perhaps—as battered by time as the building before which he stands. The reader is left to imagine who he was and where his shuffling steps would have taken him after the photographer walked away.

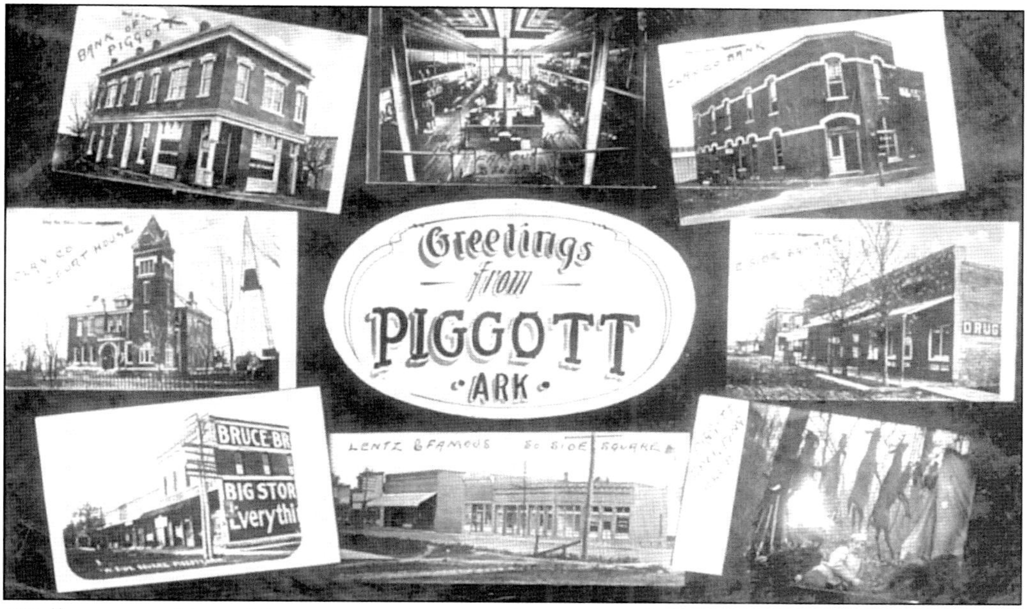

"Well we are seldom sick so you see it is healthy out here," were the words from the eastern district seat of Clay County. The town in part owes its birth to the American Civil War, for Northern troops returned home telling tales of sparsely settled but promising northeastern Arkansas. Doctor James Piggott of Dow, Illinois, led a wagon train of 13 of his neighbors and settled a community first known as Houston, but which would later become the town that bore his name. Featured on this card were the courthouse, the Bank of Piggott, Clay County Bank, a deer camp, and the local business district, 1910.

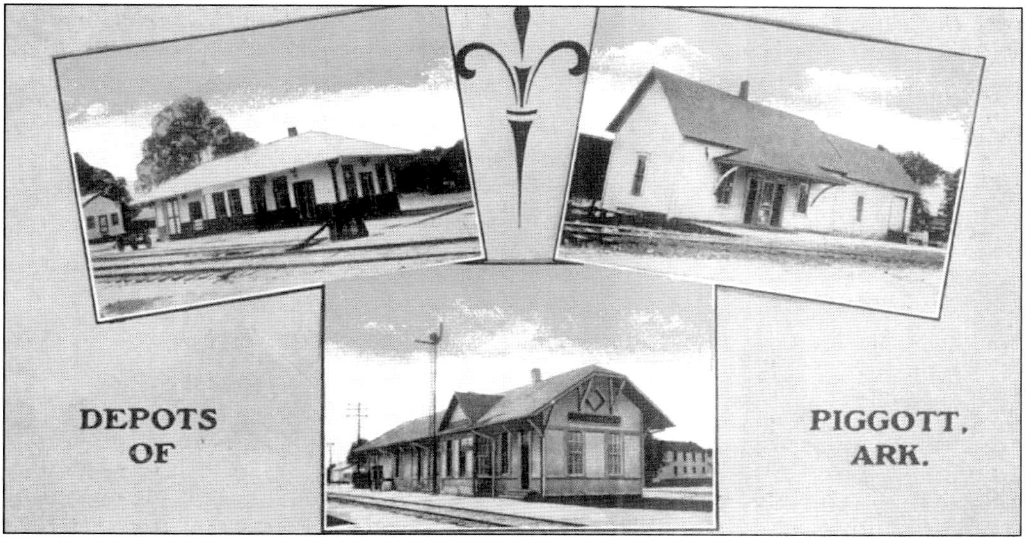

For a town of only 2,000 in 1910, Piggott had an astonishing three train depots. The one pictured at upper left in this view served the Butler County Railroad, while on the upper right is the depot of the St. Louis, Kennett (MO) and Southeastern Railroad. Both these depots were removed years ago. The depot in the lower center belonged to the Cotton Belt Railroad; the railroad is gone today, but the depot still stands, though shortened somewhat.

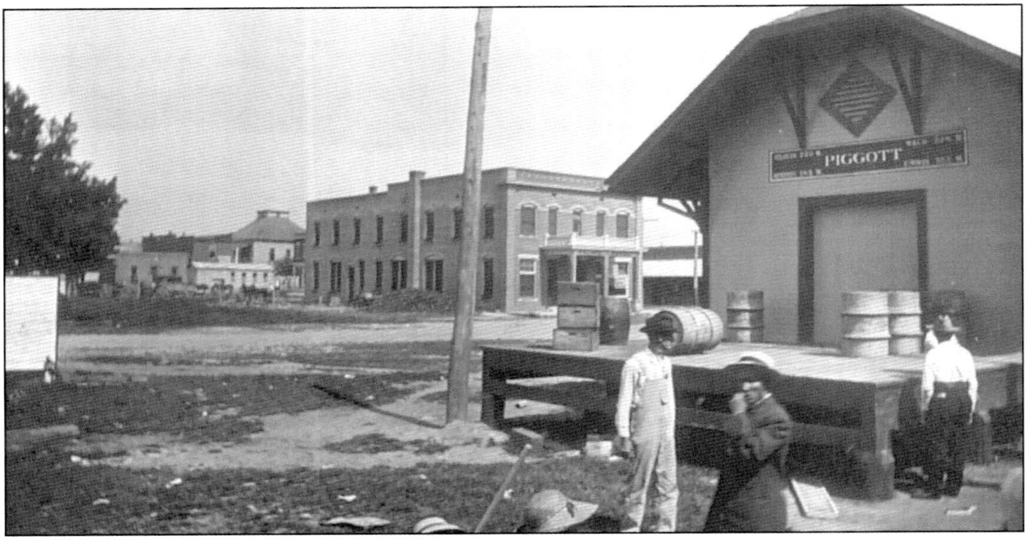

The Cotton Belt depot was a hub for both passenger and freight traffic; the loading dock adjacent to the tracks is seen above, *c.* 1910. In the distance is the Palace Hotel, only a short walk for passengers alighting from one of the numerous daily trains passing through Piggott at the time. The depot closed and moved, but today has been relocated back to its original spot by the tracks, awaiting restoration by the Piggott Chamber of Commerce.

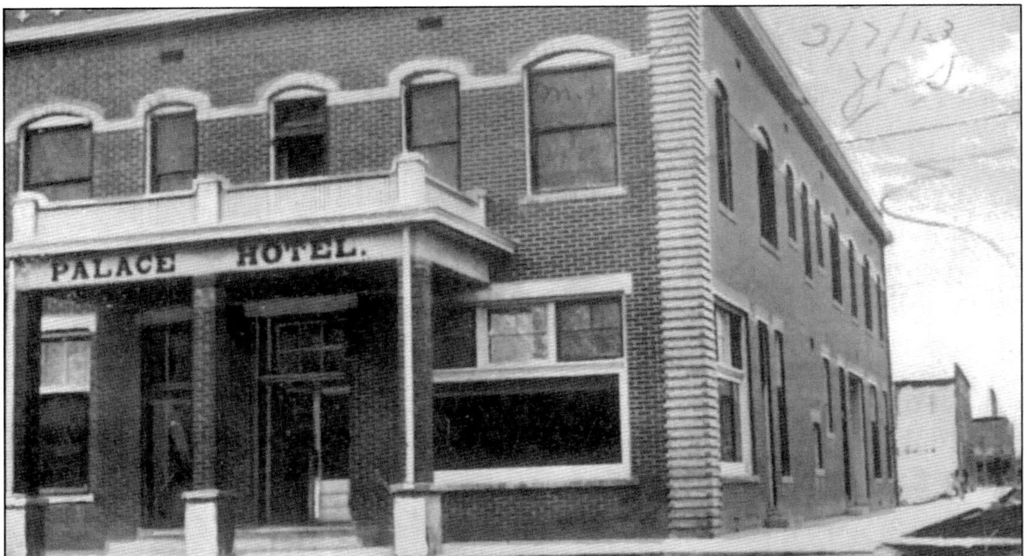

The Palace Hotel, seen near the depot in the card above, housed many of the commercial men passing through Piggott, seeking to sell their wares. Salesmen, or "drummers," disembarked daily from the trains and their heavy sample cases were unloaded for transport, often to the Palace. A newspaper account once said of the Palace, "The character of a place may be pretty well judged by the nature of the hotels it supports.... Piggott is fortunate, having within its confines the Palace Hotel." The hotel had "14 spacious, well-ventilated and neatly furnished guest rooms;" rates were $2.50 without bath, $2.75 with. The structure, lately having housed offices and other businesses, still stands today.

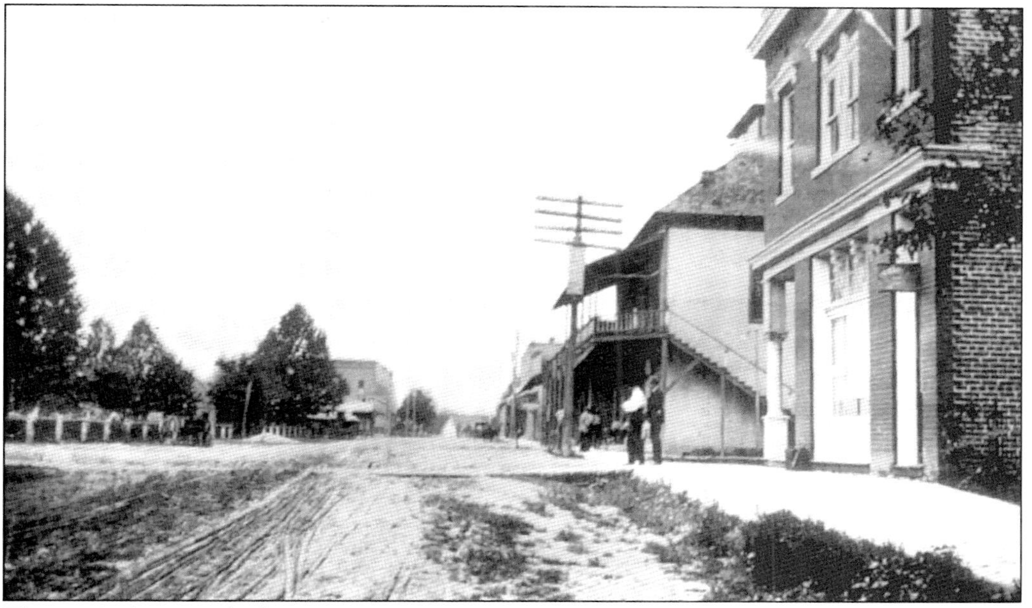

This *c.* 1905 postcard of Piggott's Main Street captured a view across the rutted dirt road from where the court house sat, with weeds growing where they were not worn down by horses and wagons. "Hello Edgar, I got your postcard last night, say, I will write you a good letter about next week," were the words of J.A. Babb to relatives in Missouri.

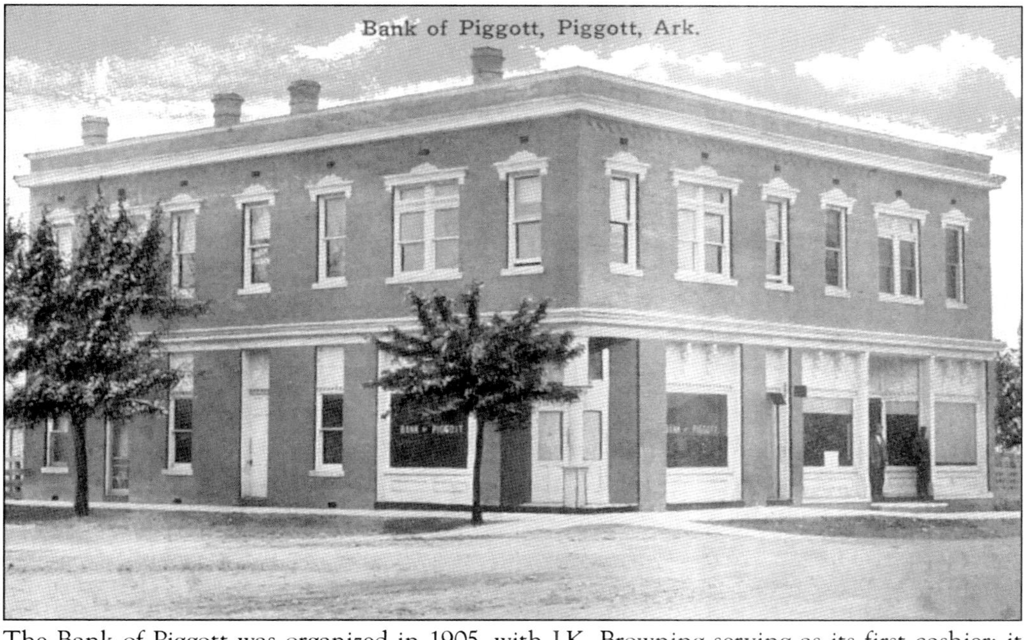

The Bank of Piggott was organized in 1905, with J.K. Browning serving as its first cashier; it moved into this building *c.* 1910. Piggott State Bank, organized in 1930, then moved into the building and remained there until moving to newer quarters in 1974. Though no longer used for banking, the building is restored and still stands among the historic downtown Piggott business district.

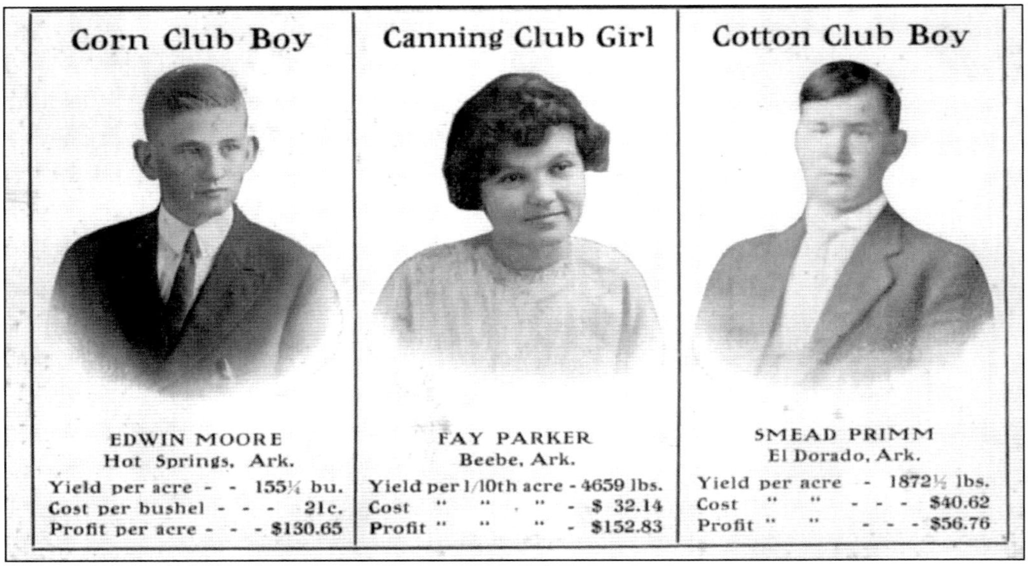

Corn Club Boy	Canning Club Girl	Cotton Club Boy
EDWIN MOORE Hot Springs, Ark.	FAY PARKER Beebe, Ark.	SMEAD PRIMM El Dorado, Ark.
Yield per acre - - 155¼ bu.	Yield per 1/10th acre - 4659 lbs.	Yield per acre - 1872½ lbs.
Cost per bushel - - - 21c.	Cost " " " - $ 32.14	Cost " " - - - $40.62
Profit per acre - - - $130.65	Profit " " " - $152.83	Profit " " - - - $56.76

The Bank of Piggott used this card in 1915, to recognize future farmers of Arkansas. The "Corn Club Boy," "Canning Club Girl," and "Cotton Club Boy" are each listed, along with the remarkable statistics of their agricultural accomplishments, such as Fay Parker of Beebe having raised 4,659 pounds of produce on 1/10 acre. Though the front of the card was cheerful, on the back it was signed by cashier J.K. Browning, advising he had turned over a note to the town constable for collection.

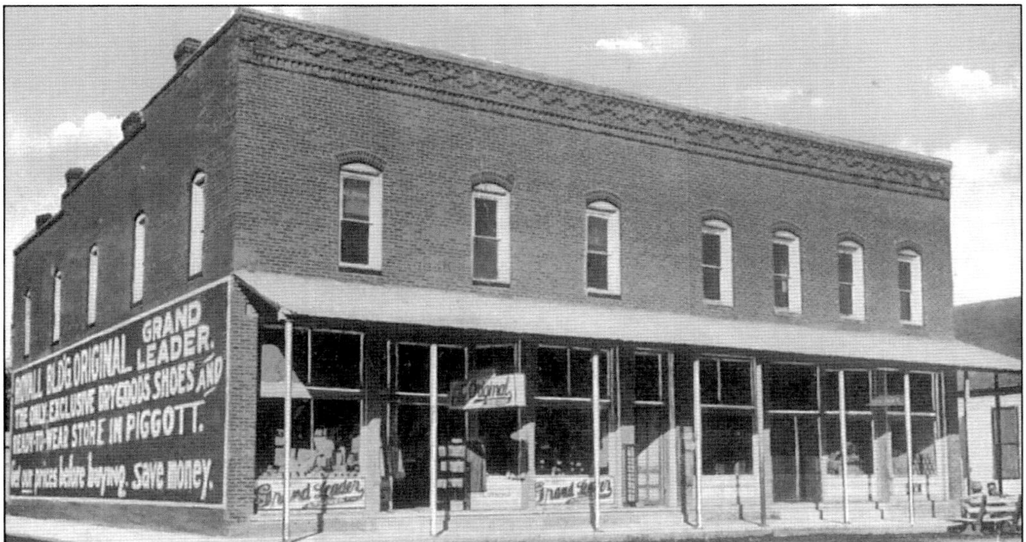

In a town of 2,000, the Grand Leader Store operated in two locations; this one was in the Royal Building. The sign on the end of the building reads, "ROYALL BLD'G ORIGINAL GRAND LEADER, THE ONLY EXCLUSIVE DRY GOODS SHOES AND READY-TO-WEAR STORE IN PIGGOTT. GET OUR PRICES BEFORE BUYING, SAVE MONEY." At one time, a doctor's clinic operated in the upstairs portion of the building, which still stands today and houses Jones Furniture Store.

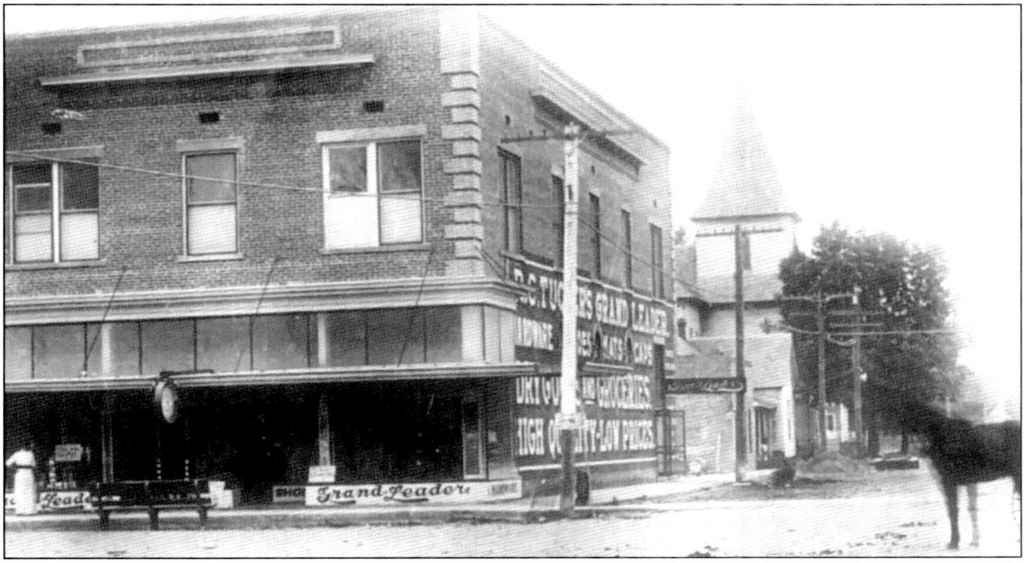

For many years the best-known store in Piggott was the Grand Leader, "The home of high quality, where your dollars do full duty and your trade is appreciated." To shop in the store seen above *c.* 1915, the woman in her long skirt would have had to traverse the dirt street littered with horse droppings before she reached the sidewalk. Once inside, in the Christmas season view below, she would have found a wide selection of boxed dolls on display, among the multitude of hardware and household items. With locations at both Piggott and Pollard, Arkansas, the store advertised on one postcard, "You will find the best place in America to do your trading. Goods of AEROPLANE QUALITY at SUBMARINE PRICES.... Hardware and every thing to eat and wear. NOTHING COUNTS LIKE CASH FOR LOW PRICES—That's why we SELL FOR CASH." The Leader declined to do credit business, unlike some other local merchants. The store was founded in 1913 by R.C. Tucker, after he had sold his interest in the Famous Store, also in Piggott, to M.U. Sowell. The building pictured here still stands.

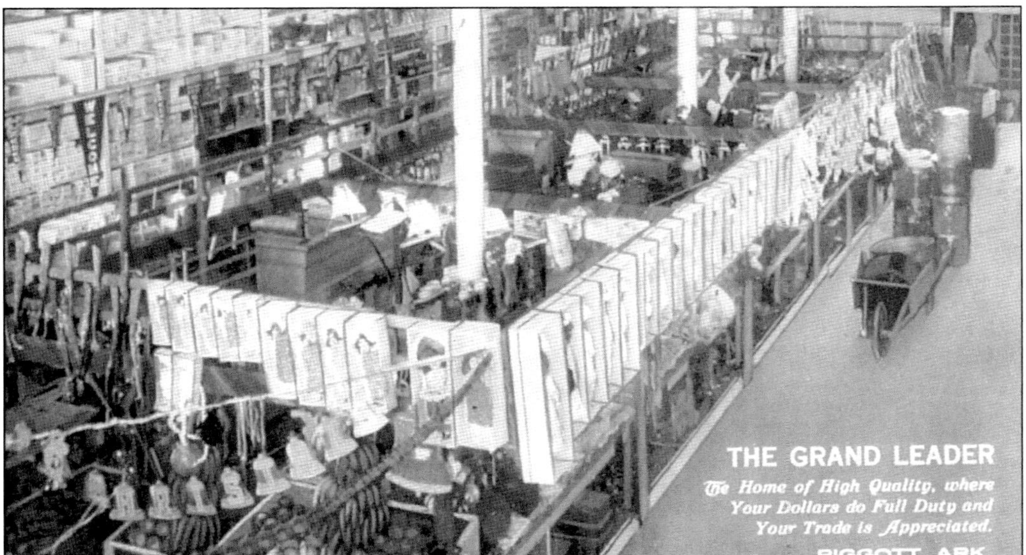

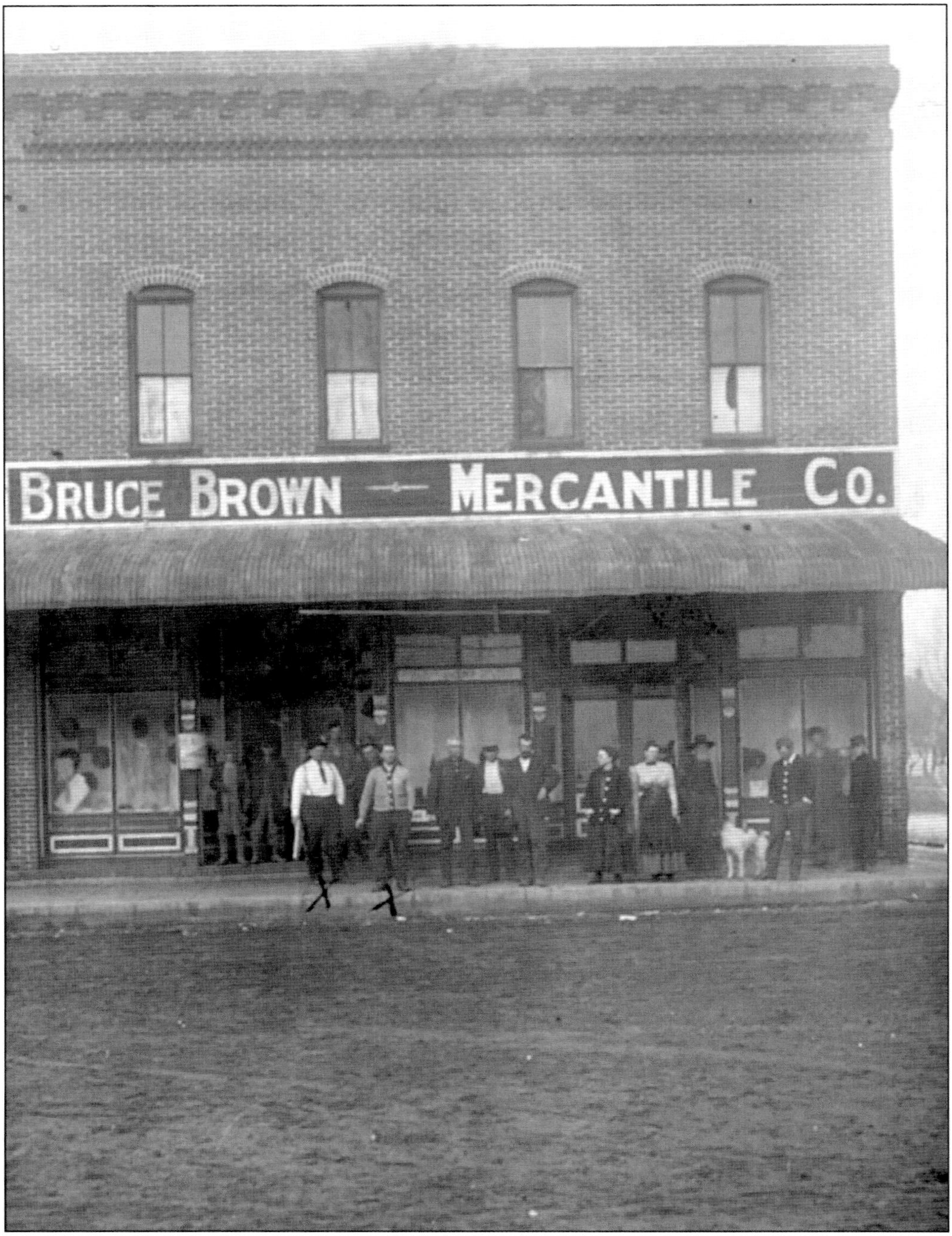

Piggott had a trade area made up of much of eastern Clay County, and it supported several merchants who competed with the Grand Leader. One of these was Bruce Brown Mercantile Company, seen here on a Main Street corner. Posed in front of the store are a group of people and at least one dog, with two men marked by an "x." As noted on the back of the card, this shows "Store where 2 brothers work at Piggott Ark, left Edgar Pierce, right Norris." Most likely, those posed were the owners and employees of the store.

Piggott businessman M.U. Sowell competed with the formidable Grand Leader and other local merchants, using the emblem of a muzzled dog on his envelopes and invoices and proclaiming "You won't get bit if you trade at M.U. Sowell's (Famous Store) General Merchandise." Sowell arrived in Piggott in 1910, and in published accounts by 1920 was called "one of the most enterprising and progressive business men that the town has ever had." In an age before giant discount centers, Sowell stocked merchandise which included "dry goods, clothing, hats, caps, groceries, hardware, harness, furniture, and John Deere farm implements."

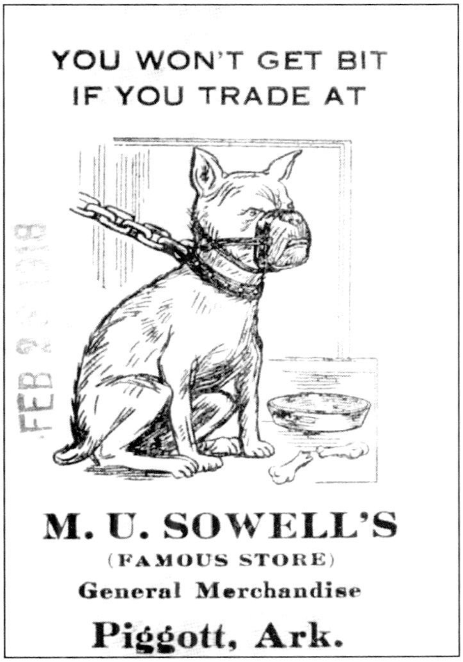

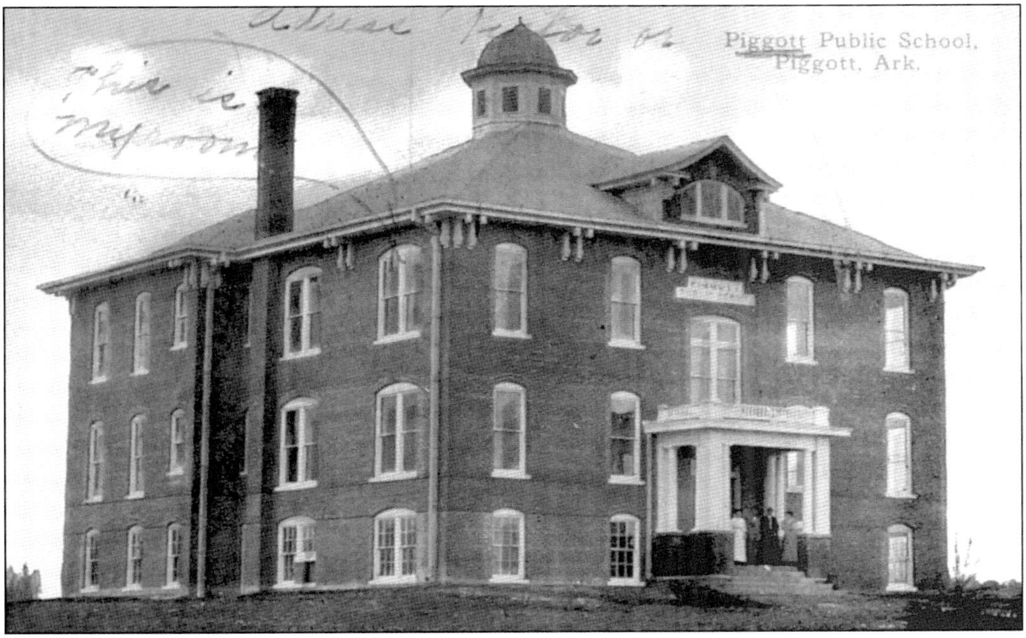

"This is my room" was penned on a card of Piggott's High School, located at Main and Cherry Streets in 1908. "My school began Monday and I think I am going to like it fine," wrote "Ruth," perhaps a teacher or an upper-level student. The state Department of Education would be created in 1911, and limited state funding in the range of $10 per child per year started flowing into schools like Piggott's. Compulsory attendance laws were passed shortly thereafter, but local control of schools found enforcement sadly lacking for many years. This building was torn down in 1954, to make way for a new elementary school.

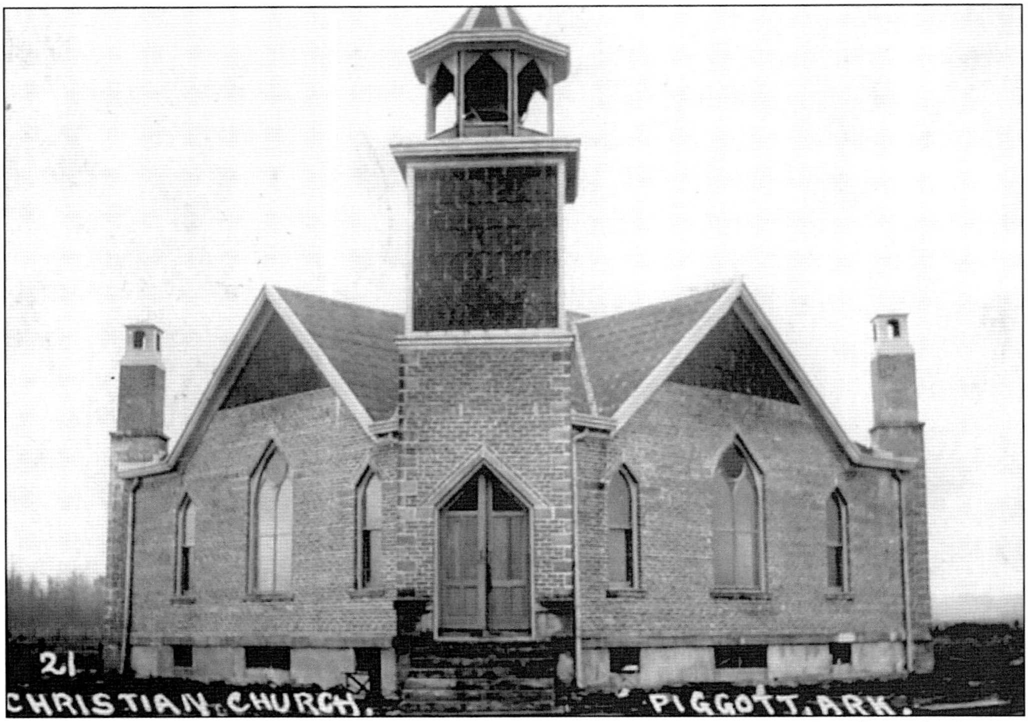

Piggott, as with most small Arkansas towns of the era, boasted a variety of churches, which were used in promoting the benefits of settling in the town. Among the most striking of the churches was the First Christian Church, erected in 1907. With a congregation splitting out of other churches, businessman R.C. Tucker and others helped erect this building, moving the congregation from its quarters in the Odd Fellows Lodge Hall. With many modifications over the years, the new brick house of worship seen here in 1907, served until 1969, when it was replaced with a new church.

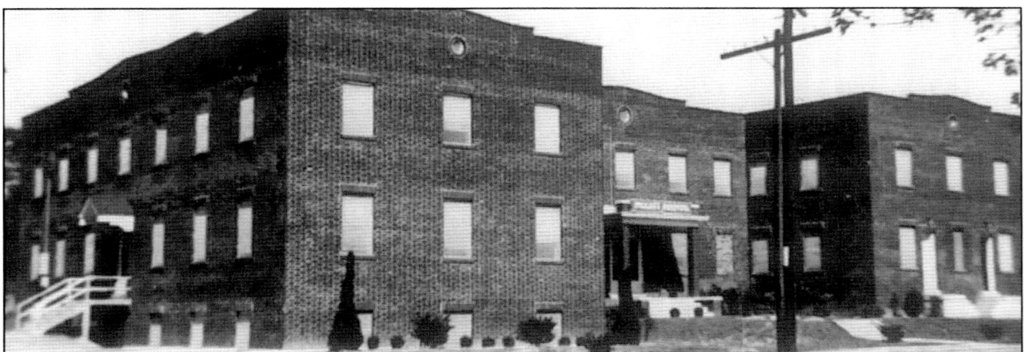

Today this brown brick building stands east of downtown surrounded and shaded by large trees, home to a large medical clinic. At the time of this *c.* 1950 postcard, however, the building was part of the pride of Piggott as the town's own large hospital. Headlined in the local paper as "A DREAM ABOUT TO COME TRUE," the construction in the late 1940s of the 40-room hospital was made possible by bond drives. At that time, Arkansas ranked last among all states in a ratio of hospital beds to residents, having only one hospital bed for each 1,000 people; a hospital for a town such as Piggott was truly an accomplishment.

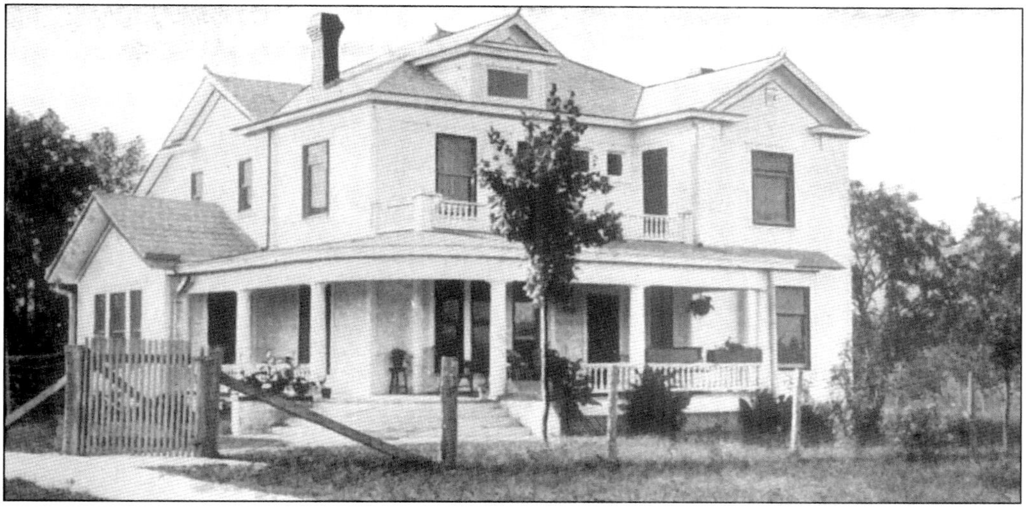

Paul M. Pfeiffer, son of a wealthy chemical company magnate, moved his family from St. Louis to the fertile soil of Clay County in 1913. He settled in Piggott and built this expansive home at 1021 West Cherry, seen above on a postcard made the same year. Pfeiffer parlayed his already substantial wealth into further interests that made him perhaps the wealthiest man in the region, owning at one time some 63,000 acres of farm and timber land. He shared his wealth, however, helping carry much of Piggott through the Great Depression. Rather than give handouts to unemployed men of the area, Pfeiffer gave them jobs, particularly that of painting his house—over and over again. In recent renovations of the home, some eighty coats of paint were uncovered, testimony to the man's generosity. One room of the home was discovered full of quilts, purchased by Pfeiffer to give area women the dignity of earning money for their creations. Pfeiffer's daughter Pauline married famed author Earnest Hemingway in 1927; it was the wealth of his new in-laws that supported the writer while he established himself professionally. Hemingway, a troubled man with a fondness for alcohol, was eventually relegated to a remodeled barn loft behind the house, where he wrote much of *For Whom the Bell Tolls*. Paul Pfeiffer died in 1947. The home and barn have today been restored by Arkansas State University as an historic site that hosts many visitors each year; in the 2001 photo below, the growth of the once spindly oak tree is most evident. (Photo by authors.)

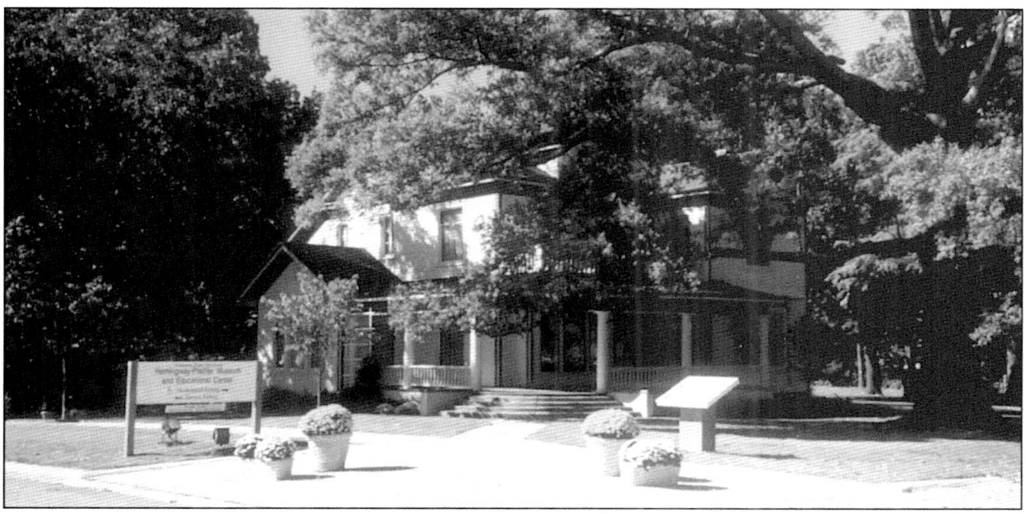

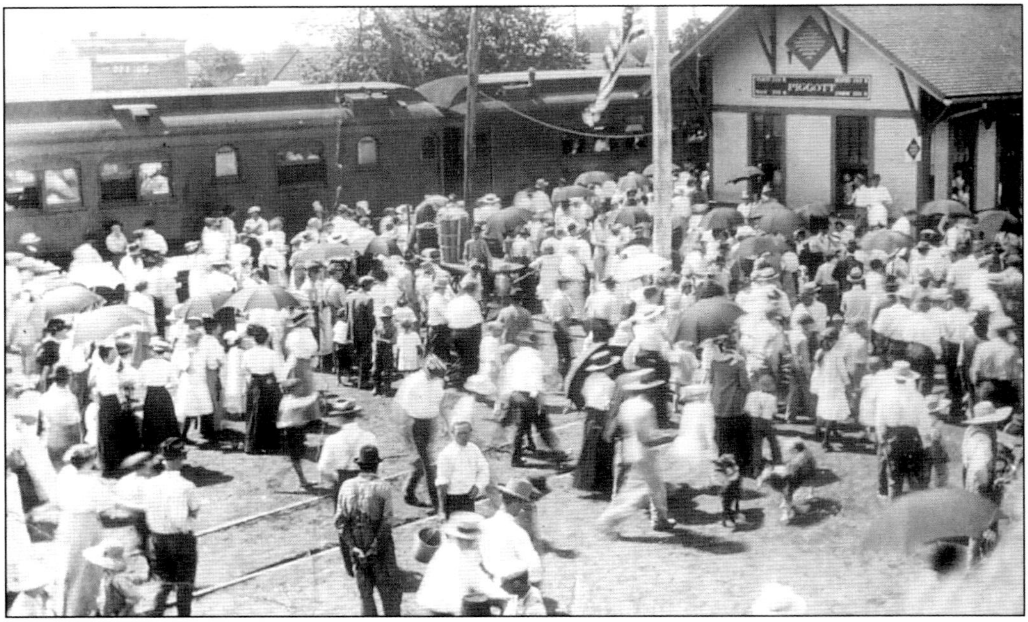

Piggott fostered many values as it grew, including hard work and prosperity, faith proclaimed in its many churches, and also patriotism when called upon. In 1916, with World War I already raging in Europe, the U.S. was attacked on the Mexican border by the forces of rebel leader Pancho Villa. President Woodrow Wilson commanded U.S. Army General "Black Jack" Pershing to raise troops to chase down Villa in the mountains of Mexico. The local militia of Piggott rose to the call, as did the citizens who surrounded the Rock Island depot to see them off to action, likely on the Texas-Mexico border. Though reduced in size, the depot still stands today.

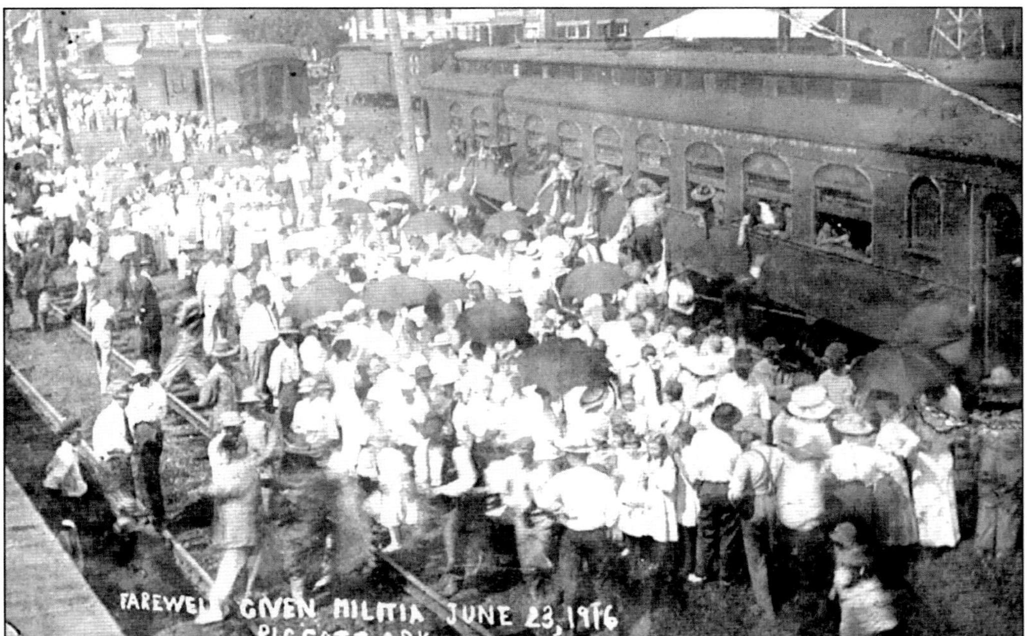

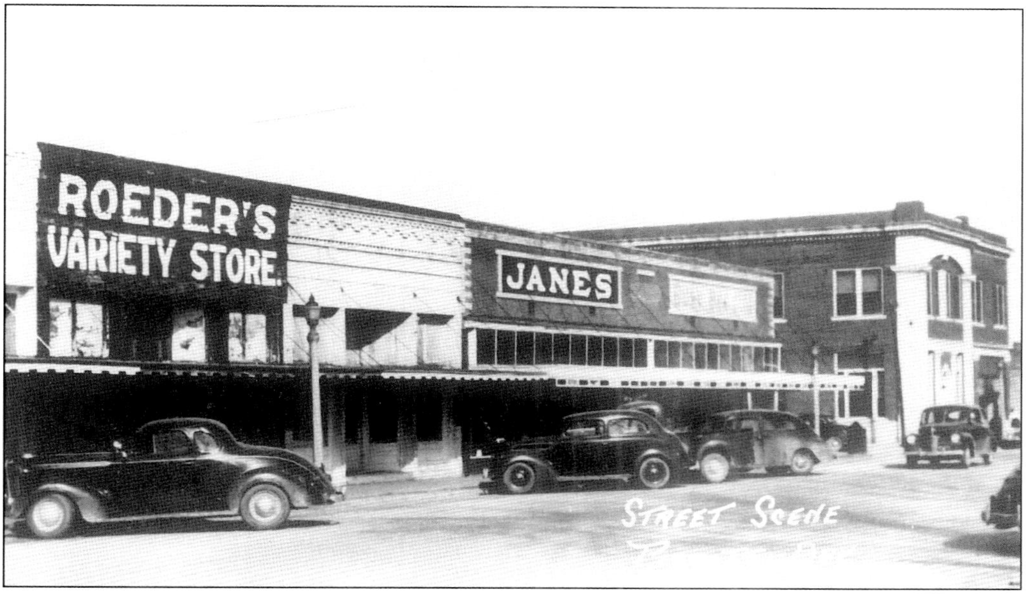

As the 20th century rolled on, the fortunes of Piggott rose, fell, and diversified as the timber industry faded with the clearing of trees and the expansion of farmlands. Today the town remains tree-shaded and attractive, with one of the most intact, vibrant downtowns in the state. Though Roeder's, Jane's, and the Busy Bee are no more, their buildings house other merchants on the square.

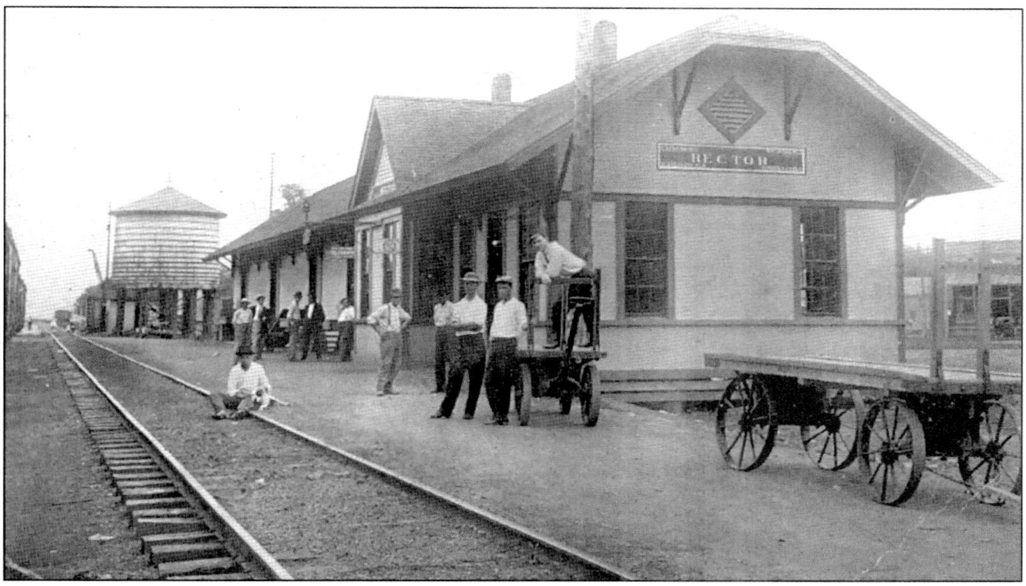

Rector, Arkansas, in the southeastern part of Clay County, was incorporated in 1887, after it grew up around the tracks of the St. Louis Southwestern Railroad. It was named for Henry Rector, Arkansas' sixth governor, who served from 1860 to 1862. By 1910, when this card was made, the Cotton Belt Railroad depot was the lifeline for this town of just over 1,000 people. It served to bring in passengers and freight and to ship out farm and timber products. The depot is gone today.

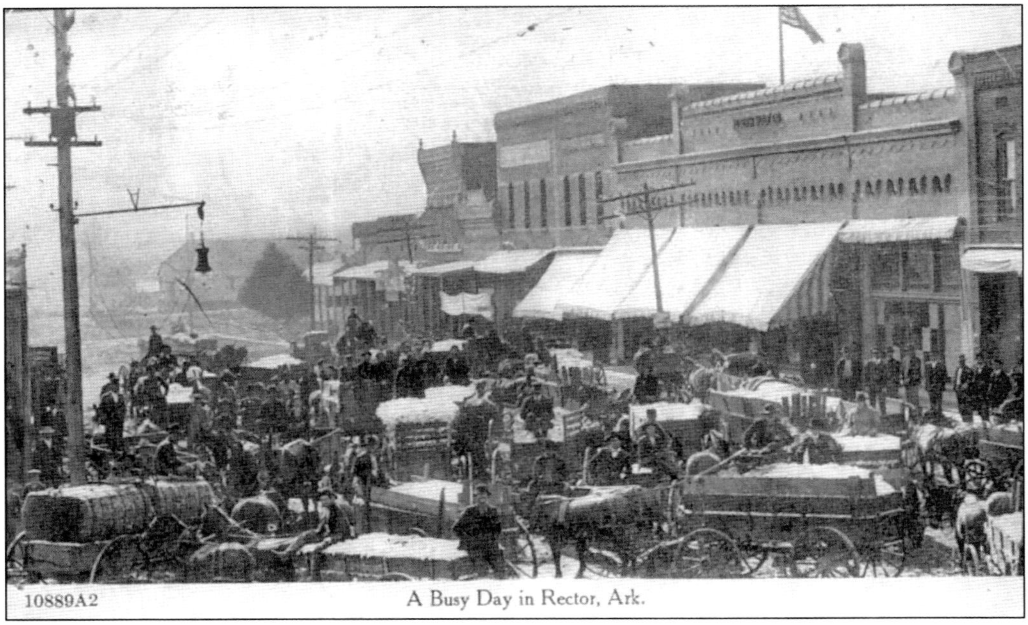

A Busy Day in Rector, Ark.

On occasion, Rector's Main Street was jammed with people, horses, and wagons, often to the delight and profit of the merchants whose small shops stretched for several blocks. The card above from 1908 was taken in the fall, when the cotton crop was being brought in to market, to be sold to buyers who likely came by train. The *c.* 1903 view below finds a much different reason for packed streets: the circus was in town. The parade was coming south from the rail depot where the circus train had unloaded; it was intended to stir interest while en route to the edge of town, where it would perform over perhaps a three-day run. At the head of the parade in the distance are war-bonneted, mounted Indians, while the cage wagon in the center likely bore a lion or tiger, all to the delight of the boys crowding close for a better view. A sign posted on the fence at the lower left offers a hint of upcoming entertainment of a different sort, an October 18 performance at the Opera House—remarkable for a small farm community.

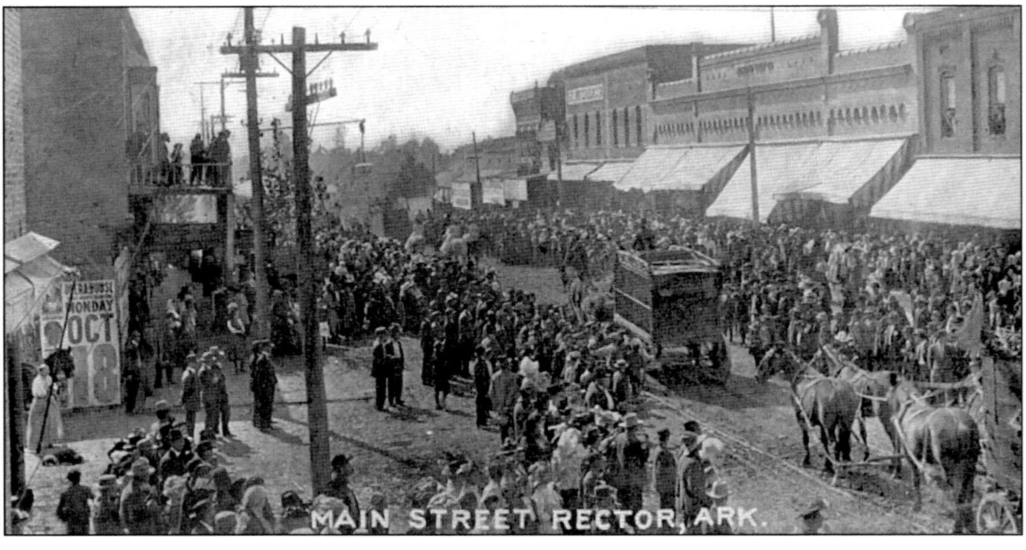

MAIN STREET RECTOR, ARK.

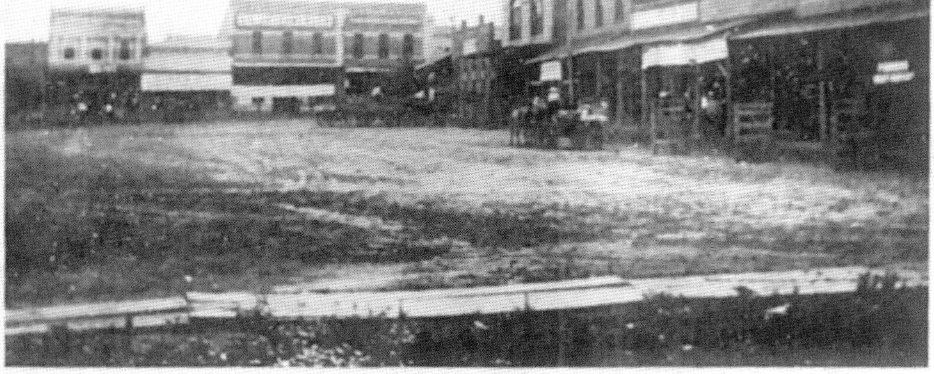

FRONT AND MAIN STREETS, RECTOR, ARK.

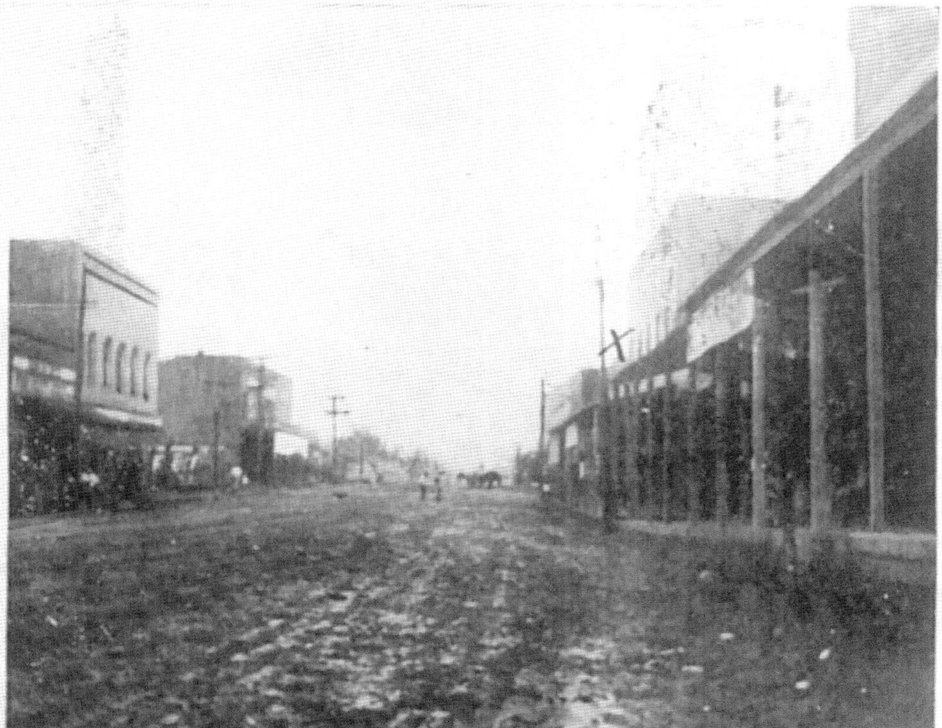

MAIN STREET, SOUTH, RECTOR, ARK.

At other times, Rector found its streets quiet and almost empty, such as in the scenes on this 1909 postcard. Capturing both Main and Front Streets, the message penned to Missouri read, "We moved to 'Okansaw' Tuesday, we have to board as there are no vacant houses. This is the street we board on. Will start to school Monday, it is a three story brick building. They teach everything that they teach in Cairo except domestic science. Instead they teach shorthand, violin, piano and elocution—Buster up to date." Most of these buildings still stand, though some are vacant.

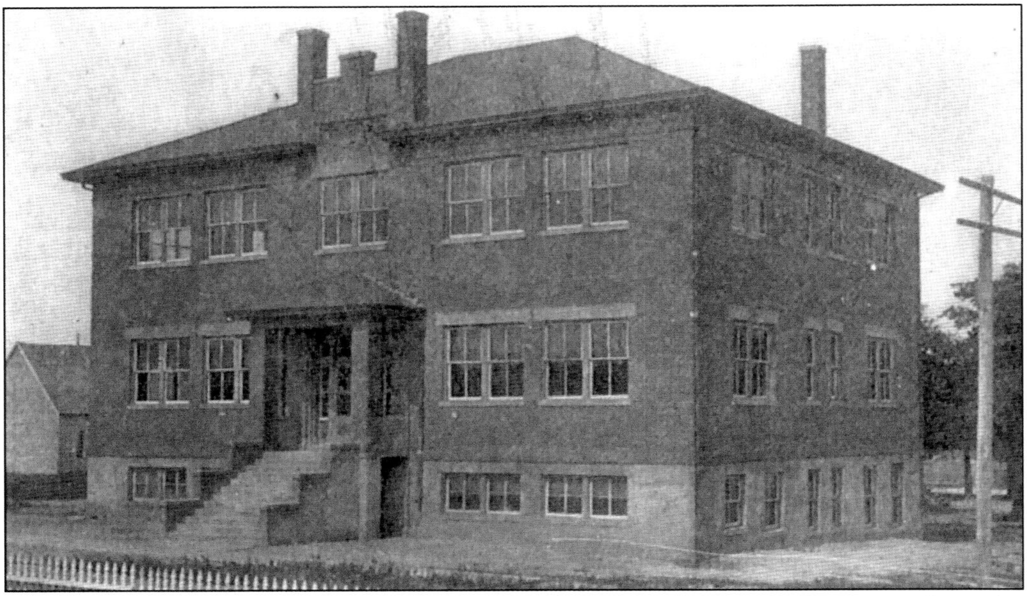

The three-story brick school that was mentioned in the message on the postcard on the previous page was Rector's substantial high school building, seen here in 1914. The sender of the card was in town seeking to buy land, though unsuccessfully; his penciled message to his father in St. Louis reads, "Had all day scouting around Rector. Haven't got anything yet, this hill land such as Crowley Ridge land is poor looking stuff and the bottomland is priced high, am going to leave this burg." The building was razed in 1954.

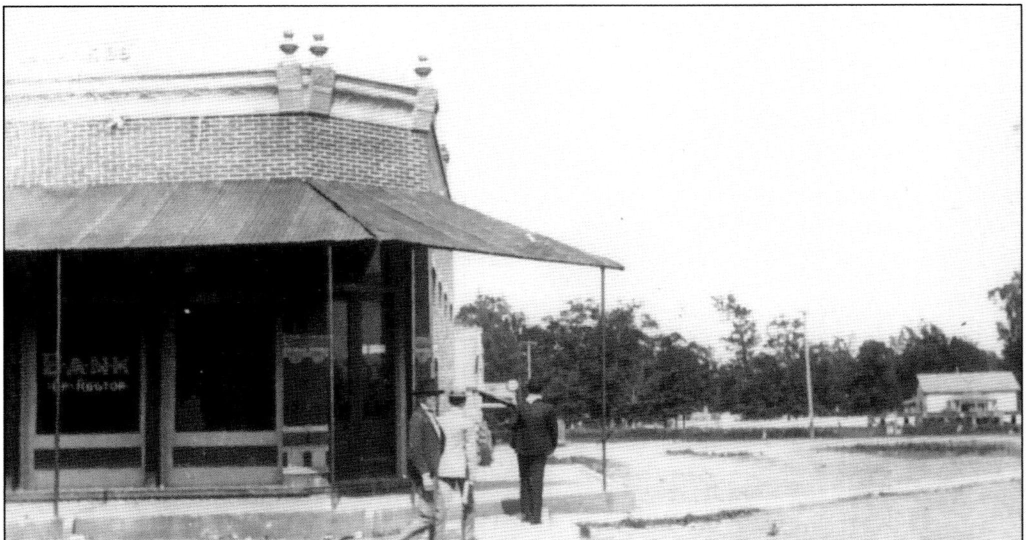

Once newcomers and prospective land buyers settled in Rector, many became familiar with the Bank of Rector, which sat on this dusty corner, having built this building in 1899. In the distance can be seen Motsinger Park, the centerpiece for much of Rector's social activity.

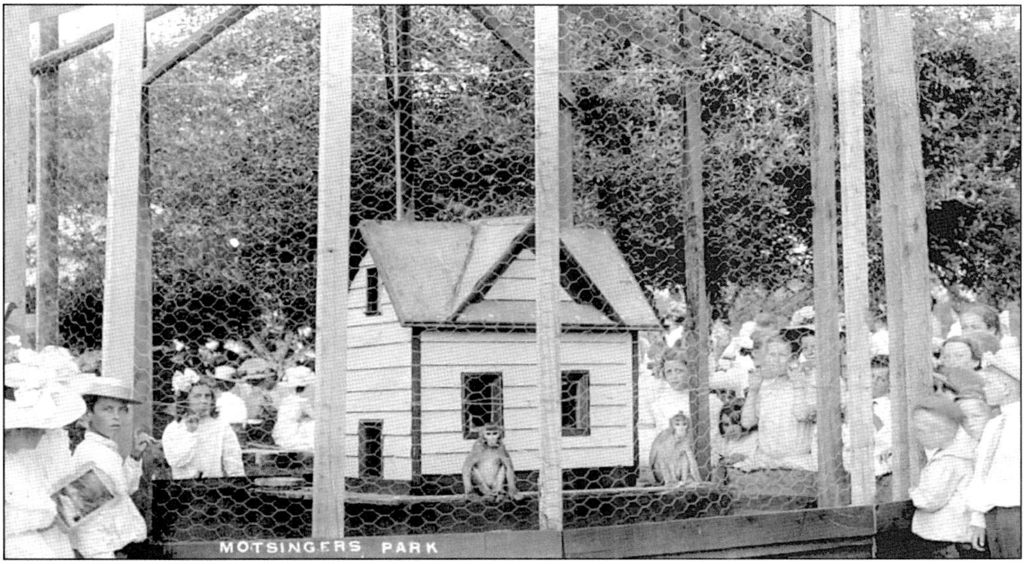

Rector's privately-owned Motsinger Park, located on Rose Hill, housed for some time a private zoo; it had as its main attraction a collection of monkeys, which delighted the local children seen here c. 1910. The project of local jewelry merchant M.J. Motsinger, the park also had a baseball diamond, picnic areas, and statuary throughout the grounds; the facility closed after his death in 1930.

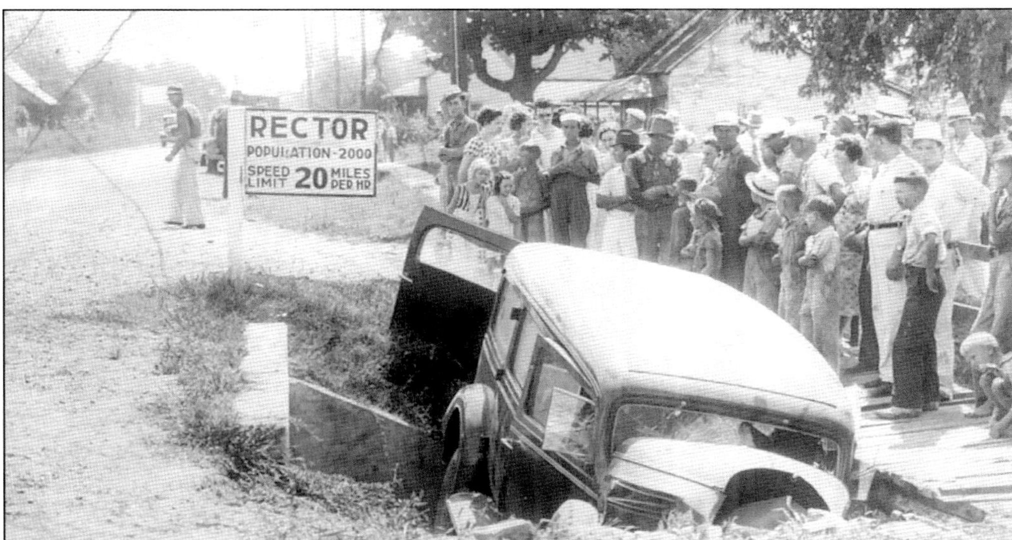

"FOUR DEAD IN AMBULANCE WRECK" was the newspaper headline on July 30, 1936. A Piggott man, Etheridge Staggs, had caught his leg in a gasoline engine attached to a water pump. Dr. George Cone, age 59, provided emergency treatment and then accompanied the injured man in the ambulance, along with a nurse and the man's wife, Ethelmayne Staggs. With 29-year-old driver Clyde Rawlings at the wheel, the speeding ambulance careened out of control coming through Rector and crashed into this culvert at the intersection of Highway 39 and Main Street. All four passengers were killed, and the driver died later.

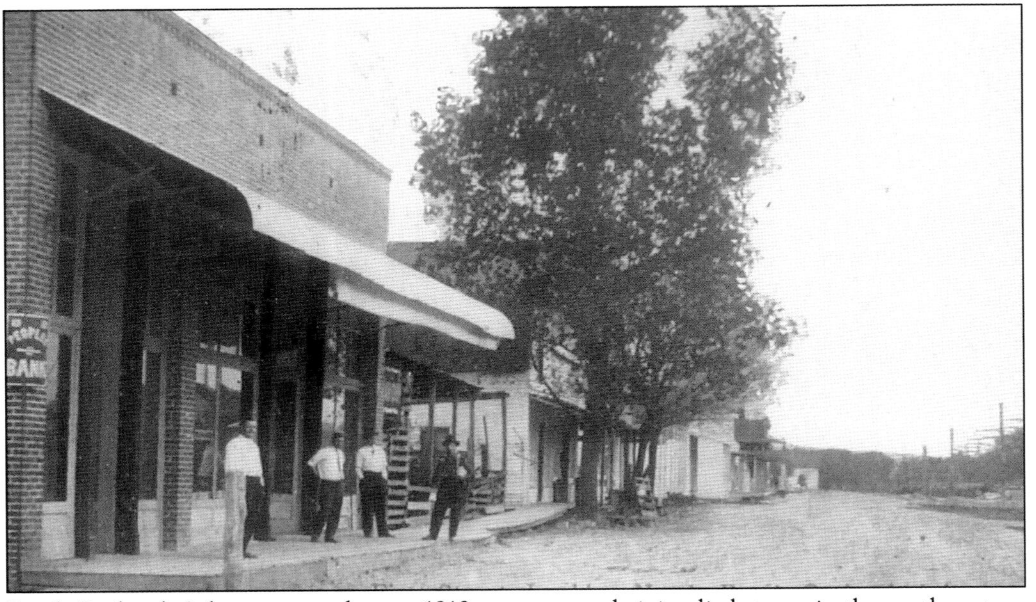

Peach Orchard, Arkansas, seen here *c.* 1910, was once a thriving little town in the southwestern part of Clay County, apparently having been named for the fruit produced in area orchards. The men in the photo are standing on a plank sidewalk above a dirt street outside of Peoples Bank. Today the town consists of a number of homes along Highway 90, though the business block seen here is now gone without a trace.

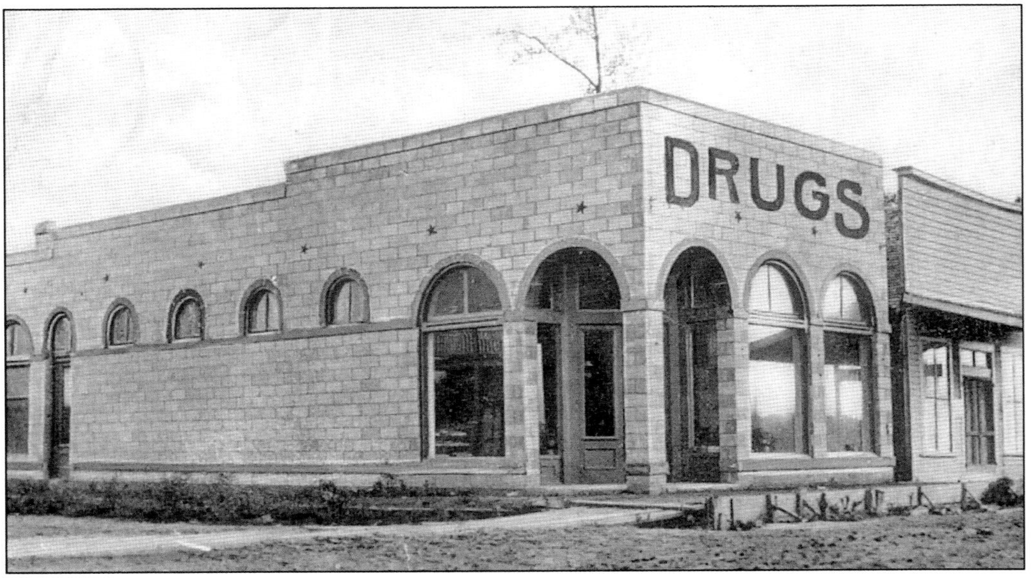

Knobel, Arkansas, named for Missouri Pacific engineer Gus Knobel in the 1880s, is in the southwestern part of Clay County. Here, one can watch traffic pass in front of a turn-of-the-century grocery store that still operates today. In this *c.* 1910 postcard view, the new City Drug Store stands proudly behind a new concrete sidewalk. It was owned by Doctors Cunning and Whitaker, in a practice common at the time, in which physicians would prescribe from among the limited drugs of the day and then have the drug dispensed from their own store.

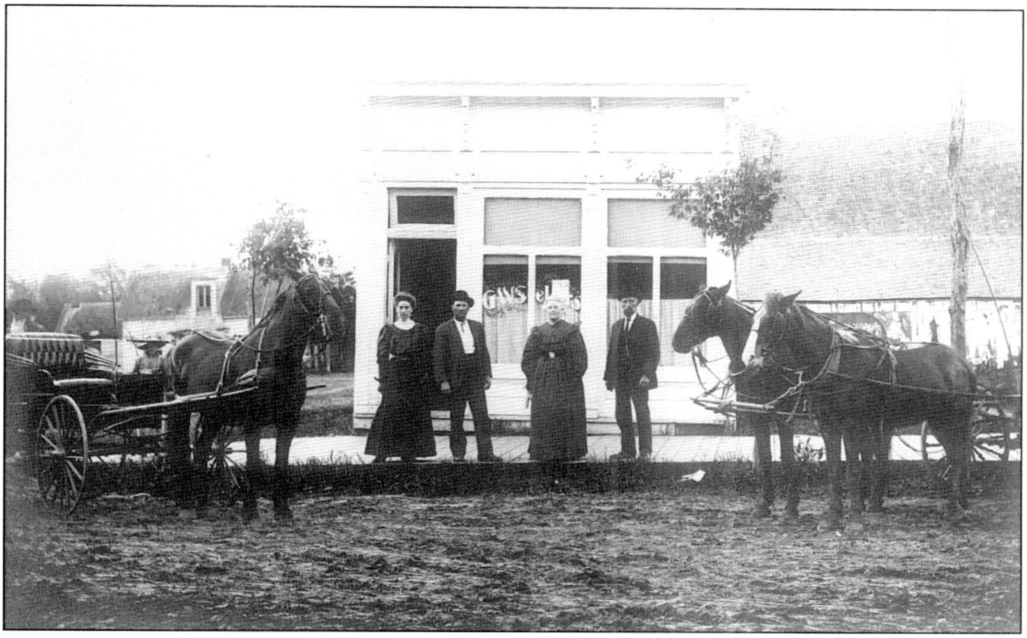

The nearby town of Bridgeport, on the Little Black River, was bypassed with the coming of the railroad. The new town that sprang up beside the new rail line was expected to be a successful venture and, hence, given the name of Success by those who laid it out. Today, it lays a sleepy spot on the map, little noticed except for a sign pointing down a secondary road off U.S. Highway 67.

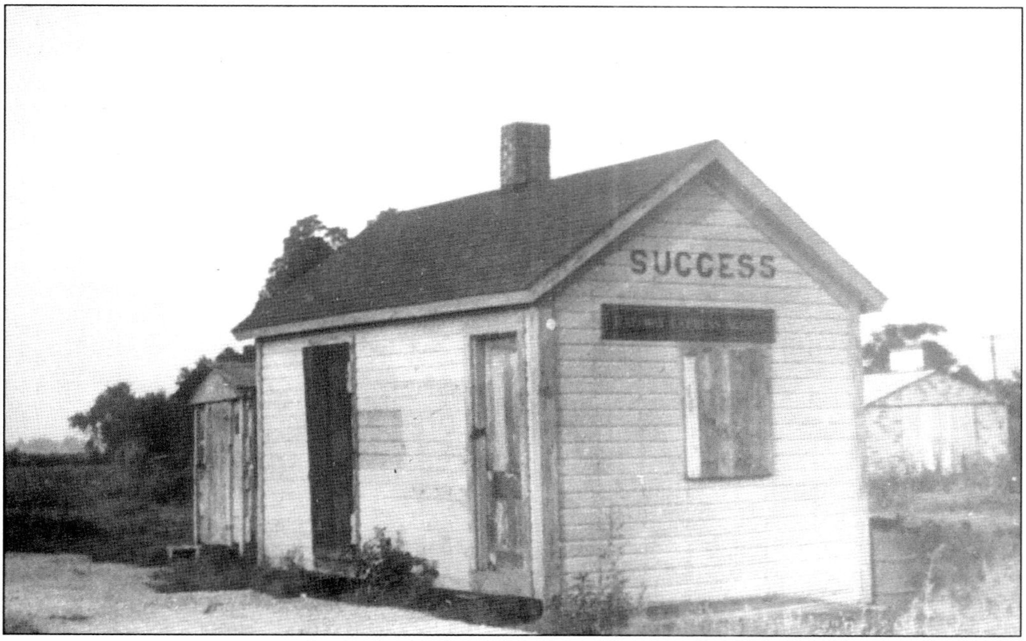

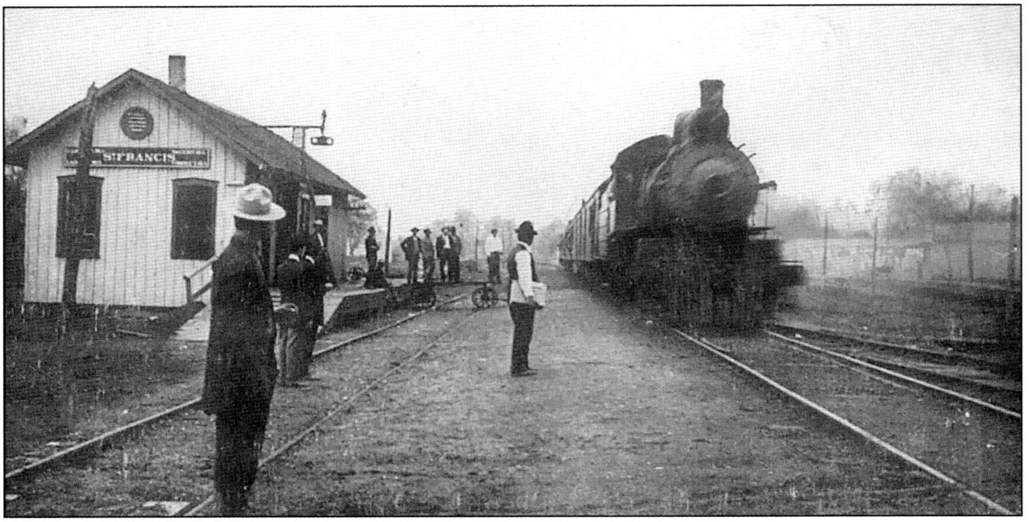

The town of St. Francis, located in the northwestern corner of Clay County, sat on the river for which it was named, and served as a shipping point for lumber and farm products. Like most of the smallest of Arkansas towns, it had a train depot and daily service, evidenced by the locomotive seen here steaming into the station. The town remains, but the depot and the train service are both part of the past.

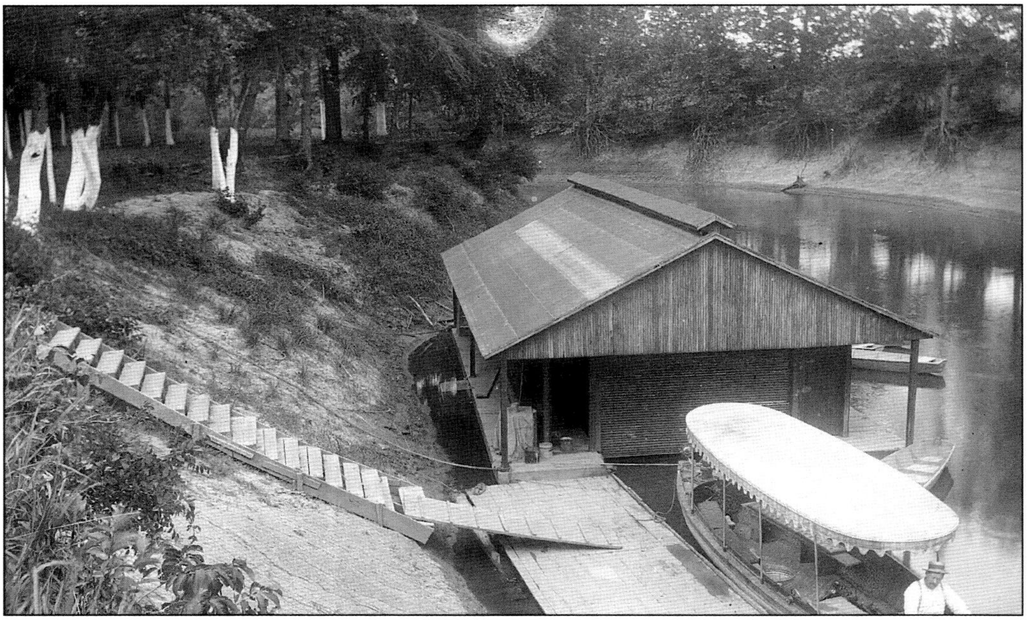

St. Francis was a hub of outdoor recreation with its location on the beautiful St. Francis River. Boat docks and crafts of a wide variety plied the river, including the canvas-topped boat seen here *c.* 1910. Whether for serious fishing or an afternoon with a pretty girl on the slow moving, shady river, the resource has always been one in which Clay County has taken great pride. Although much has changed in Clay County over the past nine decades, the county is today well worth a visit to enjoy the delightful town square of Piggott, to peruse the antique shops of Rector and Corning, or simply to explore the country roads that lace the county.

Two

Paragould and Greene County

By an act of the state legislature in 1833, Greene County was split off from the originally very large Lawrence County in the Arkansas Territory, three years before statehood. It was named to honor Revolutionary War hero Nathaniel Greene, a brilliant leader of the militia serving George Washington in numerous battles. Greene issued personal IOUs to contractors to furnish troops with supplies, since the revolutionary government lacked funds with which to equip the ragtag Continental Army. At the end of the war, General Greene had to sell everything he owned to pay off these debts incurred to help found the United States. In error the "e" was initially left off the end of the county's name, but this was later corrected.

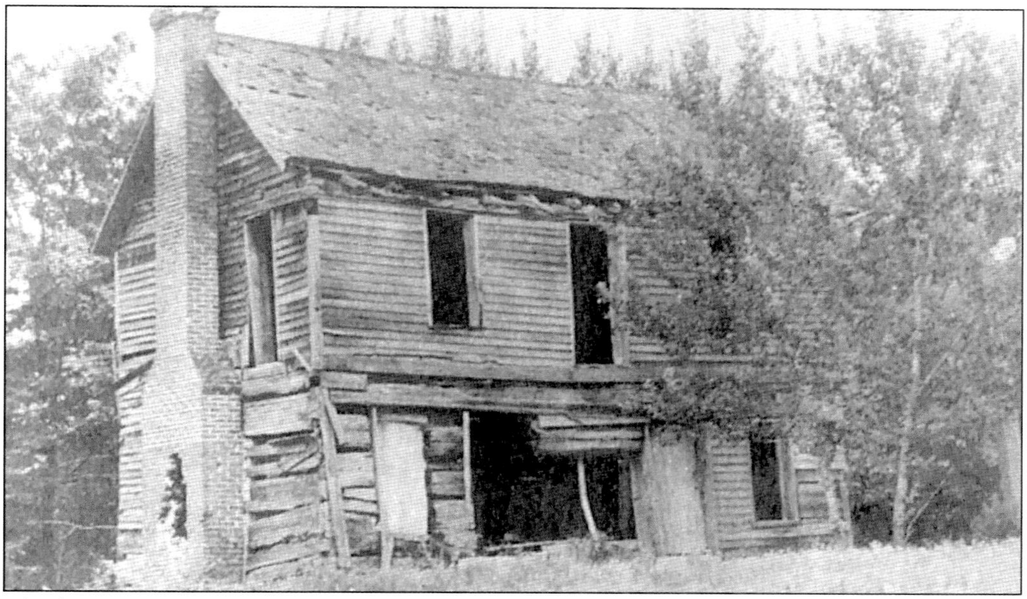

The first permanent settler on Crowley's Ridge in Greene County was Benjamin Crowley, who settled there in 1822, building a fine plantation-style home c. 1832. Over the years, the original log home evolved into a clapboard-sided mansion, and even served as a community clubhouse in the 1930s. Time, neglect, and the elements took their toll, however, and despite valiant citizens' efforts to restore and save the house, it was torn down in the early 1970s.

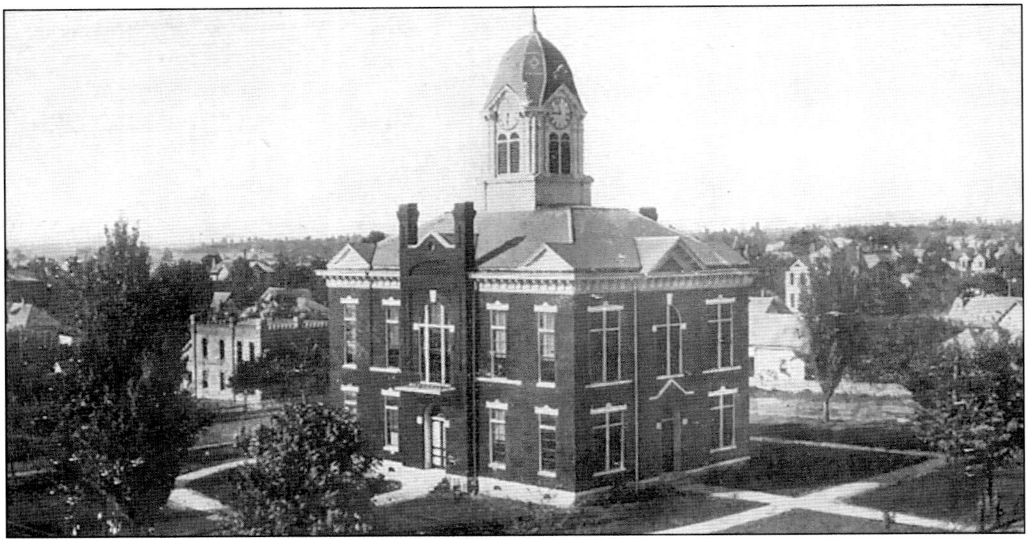

Businessman W.S. Pruett came to Greene County in the 1850s with only $1.50 in his pocket, but he soon met with good fortune. In 1881, he and his partner J.J. Lambert bought up land around the expected junction of two railroads and platted a town with a corporation called the Southwest Improvement Company. The converging tracks belonged to competing railroad men J.W. Paramore and the wealthy business baron Jay Gould; the infant town at the tracks' crossing was named by compromise, combining the names of the two railroad men into "Paragould." In 1884, the Greene County seat was moved from the fading town of Gainesville to thriving Paragould. The new county seat grew rapidly and gained an impressive courthouse by 1888. The city raised an additional $300 above the county's efforts to erect the imposing tower on the building, seen here c. 1910. Local citizens then contributed $700 to add a chiming clock to that tower. For the next 35 years, the clock chimes echoed across town each night to signal the 9 p.m. curfew, which required children to be off the streets and in their homes. As seen below, with the 1911 Children's Pageant on the lawn, the Courthouse was the center of activity for the town.

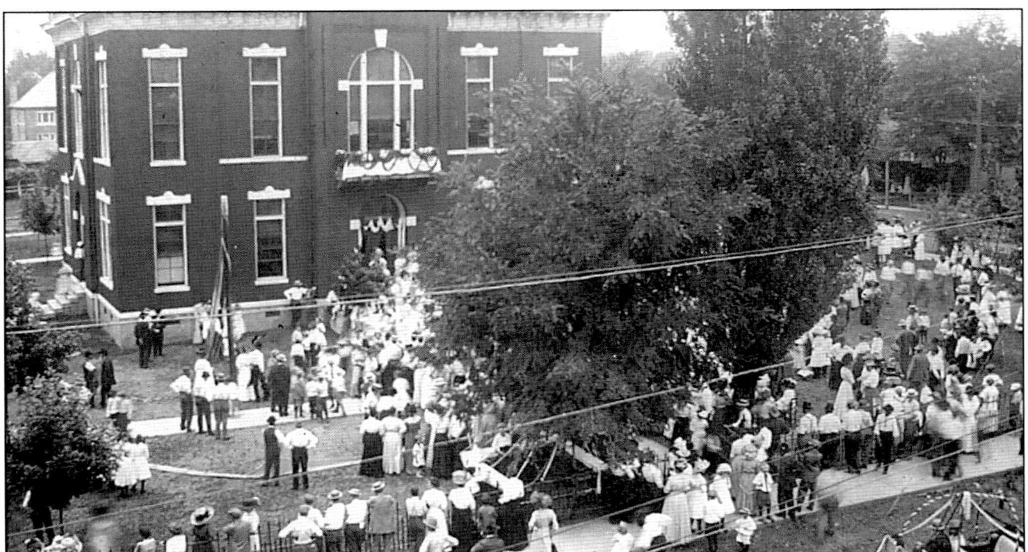

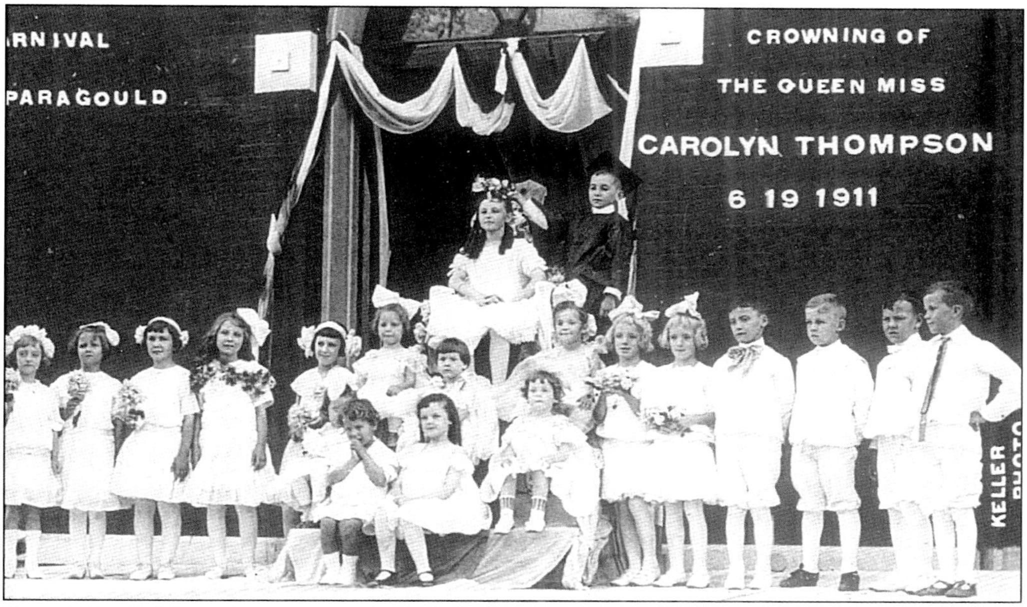

The 1911 Children's Pageant used the courthouse steps as the stage for the crowning of the Queen Miss, the honor that year going to Miss Carolyn Thompson. The city of Paragould is quite proud today to boast that the historic building where these children stood almost a century ago is now being restored to house the area Chamber of Commerce. A new, modern courthouse next door to this building serves as the seat of county government for Greene County.

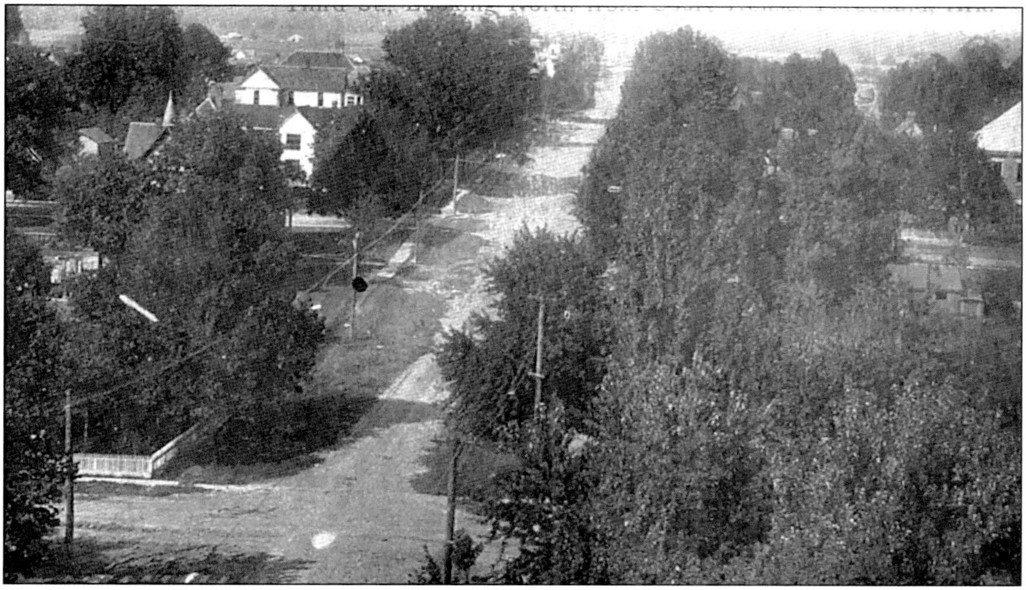

In the golden era of picture postcards, essentially from 1905 to 192C, every town with a courthouse tower had postcard views taken from that high vantage point, which was usually the tallest structure in town. In this case, c. 1908, the photographer had pointed his lens north down Third Street, a dirt thoroughfare lined with large trees and homes. Today the area is much more commercial in nature.

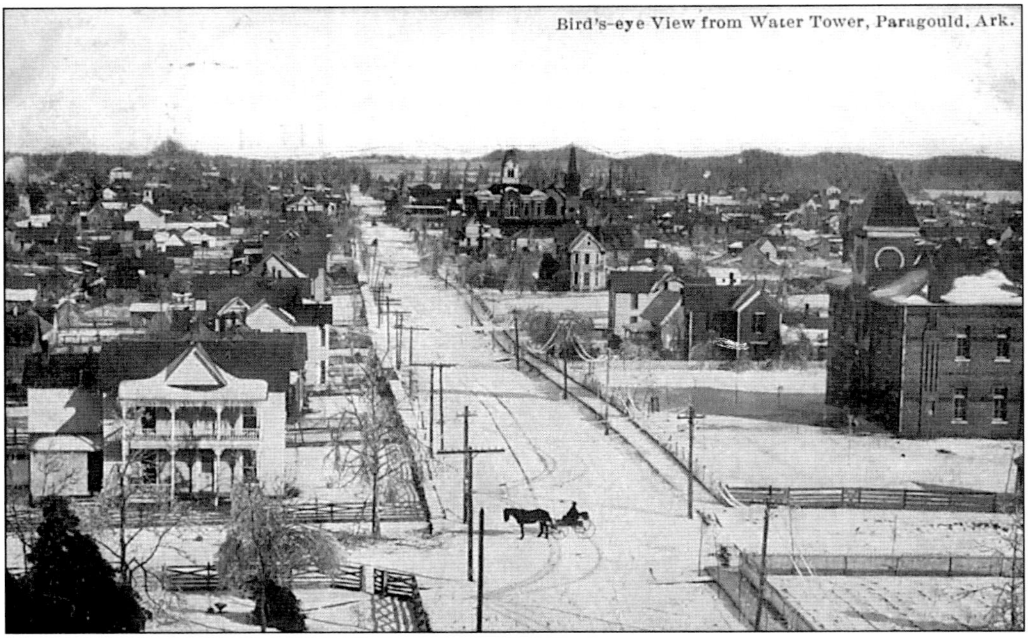

At the beginning of the 20th century, the tallest point in most Arkansas cities, if not the courthouse tower, was a water tower, which also became a common vantage point for photographers. On a cold winter day *c.* 1905, a photographer captured this view from atop the water tower looking toward the imposing courthouse and, further down, the almost empty, snow-covered street. The lone person visible, driving a horse-drawn buggy, perhaps had stopped at the West Side Public School building to the right.

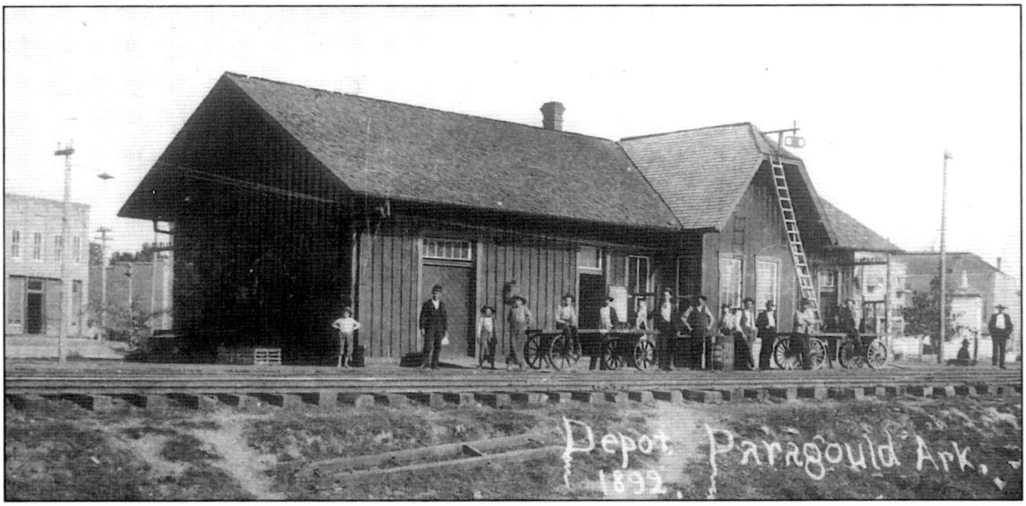

Paragould's birth as a railroad crossroads in the 1880s gave rise initially to a wooden frame depot for the Cotton Belt Railroad, as seen above in 1892, with men and baggage carts seemingly awaiting a train. The railroad helped build the town, initially as a shipping point for timber products from the county, then also for agricultural products and manufactured goods. Into the first part of the 20th century, when roads were poor and unreliable, passenger trains stopped several times a day in Paragould.

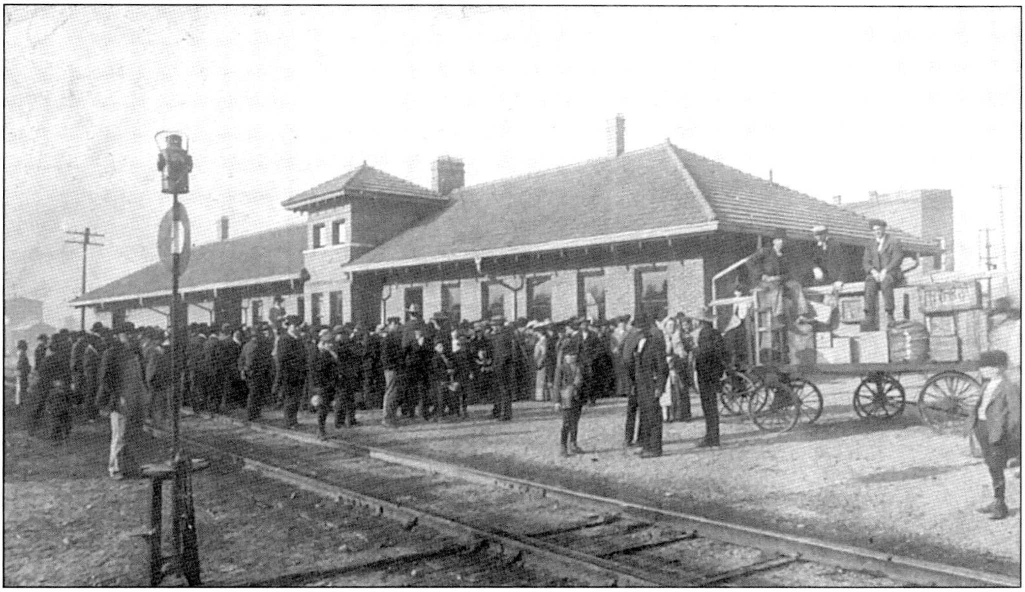

By the time of the 1910 card above, the Paragould depot was a beehive of activity; here a crowd awaits the train, perhaps for the arrival of a special person. Freight is seen stacked high on carts to the right, either taken from a train or awaiting shipment out on the next. In contrast is the card below, mailed in 1913, where only three men are seen standing by the depot on a rainy day. Visible behind the depot is Bertig Brothers Department Store, which would have obtained most of its wares from shipments delivered by trains at the depot. As with the rest of the nation, however, the automobile and modern highways took their toll; the last passenger train left Paragould in 1950. After housing a barbershop for many years, the depot was razed in 1976.

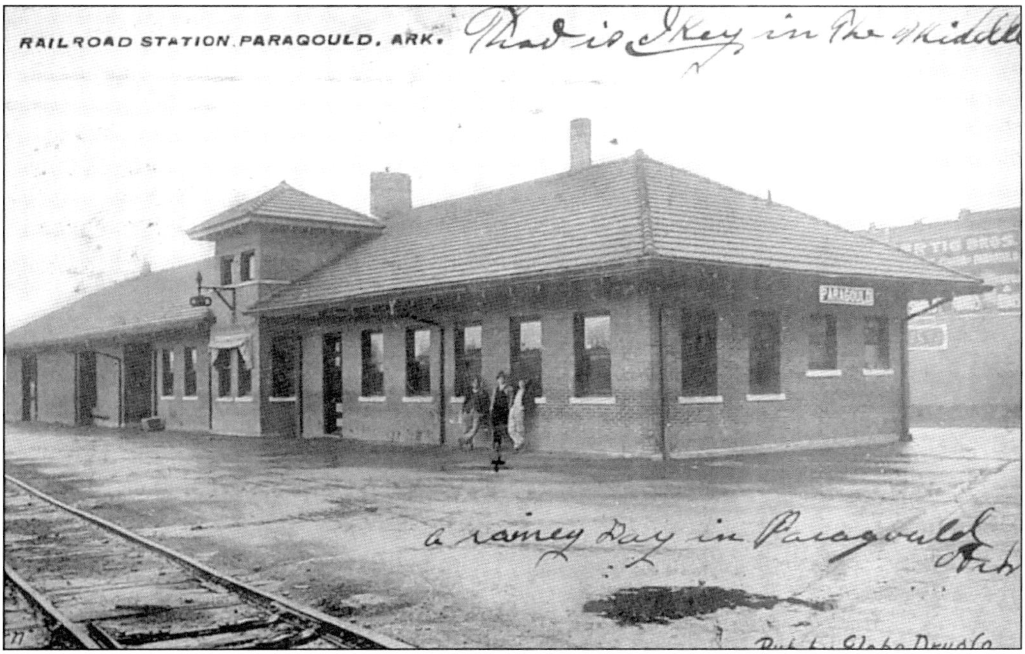

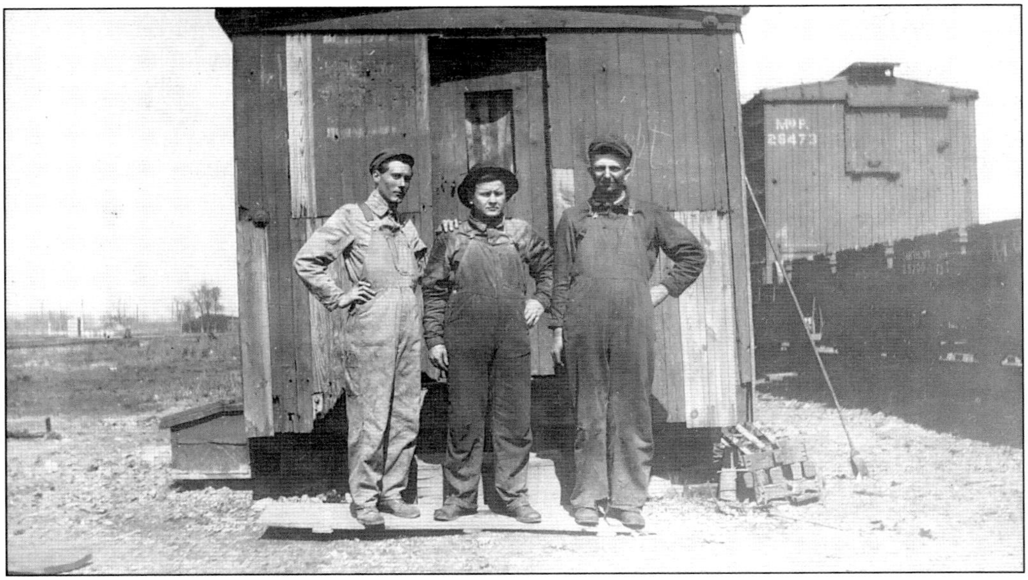

With the busy comings and goings of so many trains, the employees of the railroads had a visible, economically important role in Greene County. The penciled words on the back of this *c.* 1912 card, above, by the McHaney Studio of Paragould read, "Inspector's Shanty & Crew, Paragould." Crews like this would have checked tracks and equipment within their designated areas, with some perhaps living in the "shanty," which appears to be a discarded boxcar minus its wheels. Construction of new rail lines into the great forests and swamps of Greene County was difficult, slow work, sometimes stretching into winter. The postcard below captured what seems to be a group of women, bundled against the cold, visiting a construction crew; logs piled to the side awaited shipment back to the end of the line, also *c.* 1912.

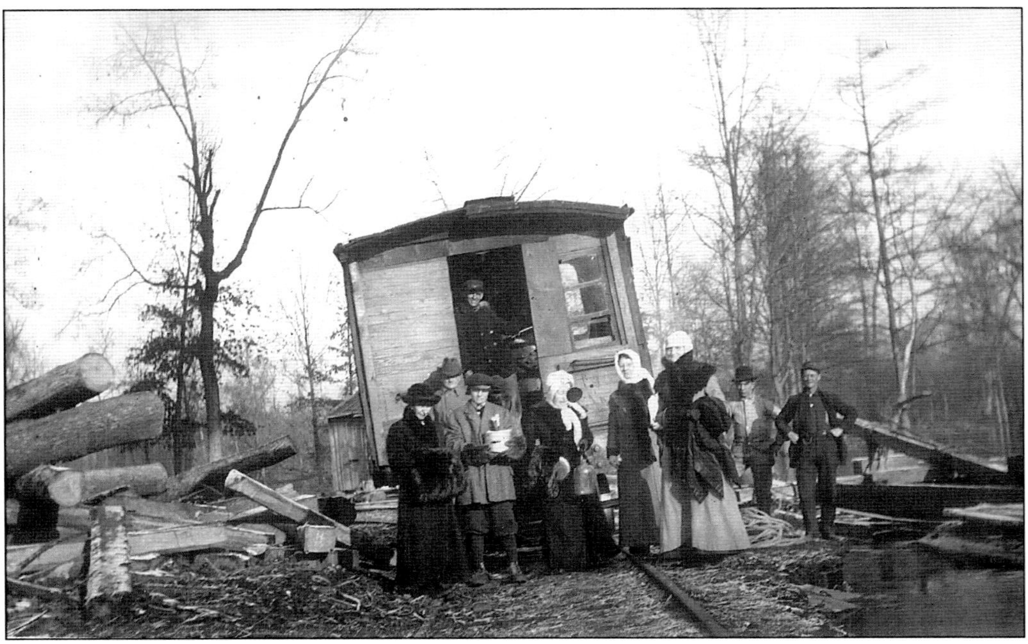

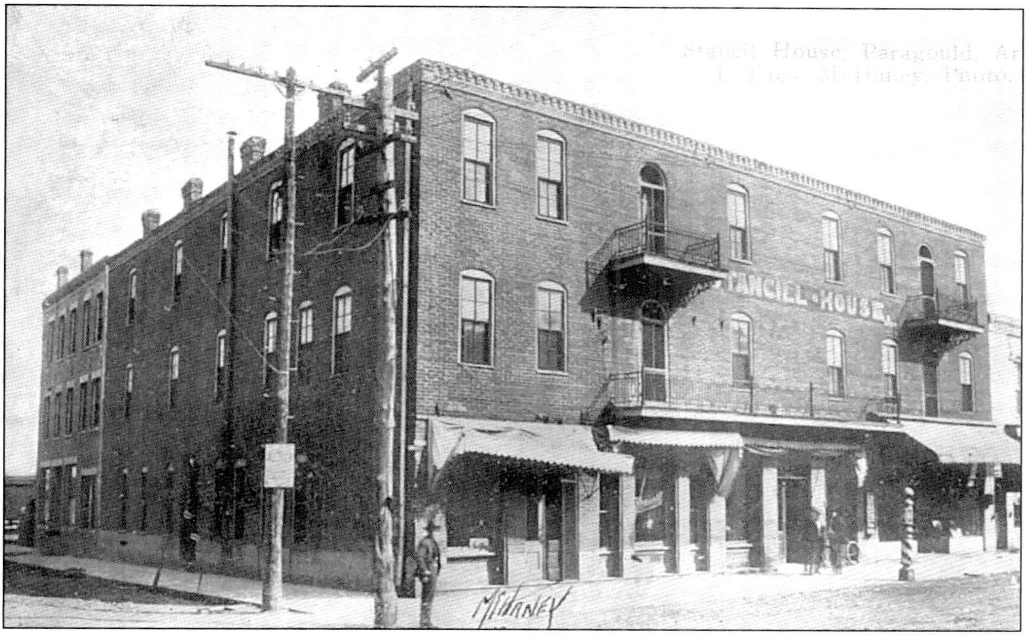

The commerce that developed as the railroads helped build Paragould led to the erection of several hotels. The Stancil House, above, housed many of the passengers and crew from the four passenger trains that stopped in town daily during the early part of the century. The hotel, located at Pruett and Emerson, had 41 rooms, which rented for $1 a day, with meals for 25¢ at the time of this 1912 card. That same year, the postcard below captured the view that guests of the Stancil House would have had when stepping out of the hotel to the left, onto the busy but dusty Pruett Street. In the distance is the train depot, while across the street are a bank and Trice's Furniture Store.

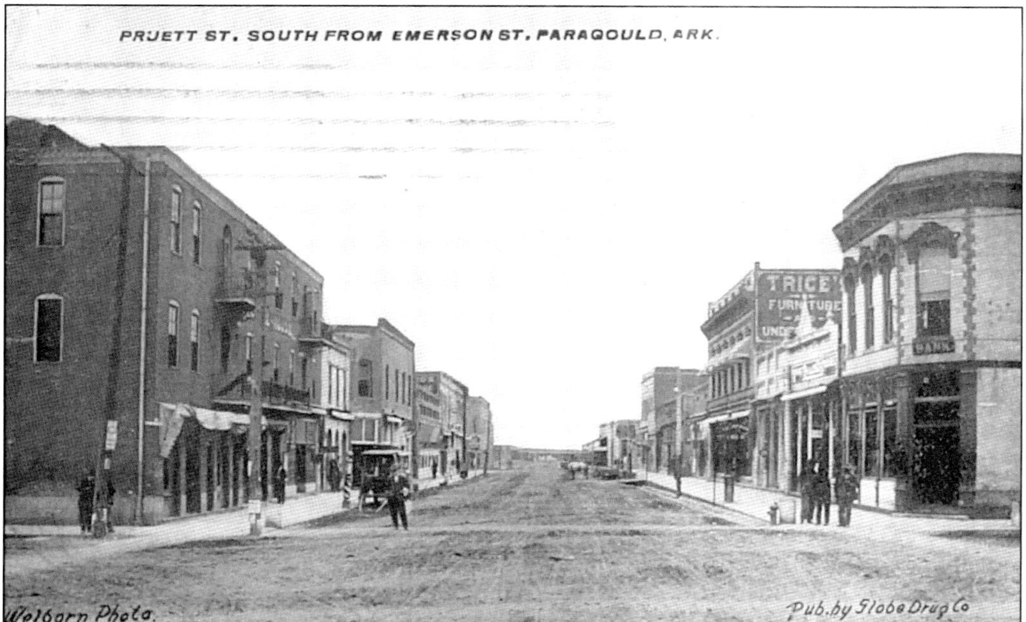

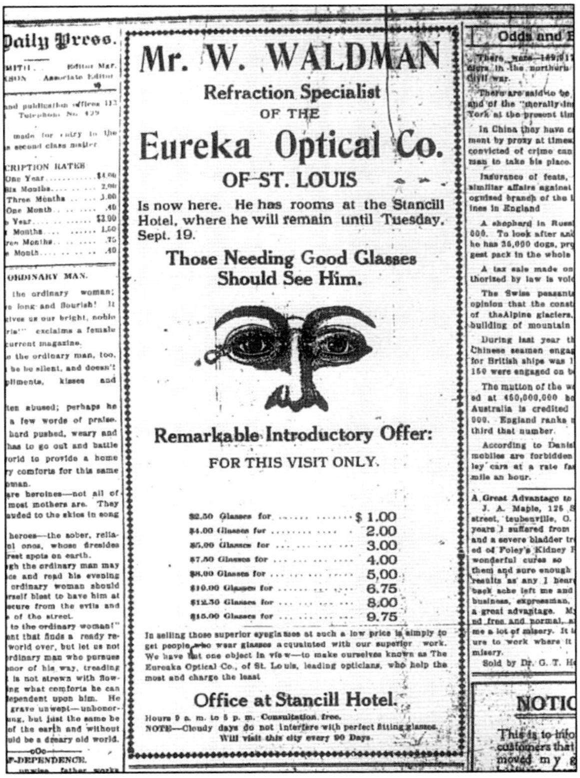

Mr. W. WALDMAN

Refraction Specialist

OF THE

Eureka Optical Co.

OF ST. LOUIS

Is now here. He has rooms at the Stancill Hotel, where he will remain until Tuesday, Sept. 19.

Those Needing Good Glasses Should See Him.

Remarkable Introductory Offer:

FOR THIS VISIT ONLY.

$2.50 Glasses for	$ 1.00
$4.00 Glasses for	2.00
$5.00 Glasses for	3.00
$7.50 Glasses for	4.00
$8.00 Glasses for	5.00
$10.00 Glasses for	6.75
$12.50 Glasses for	8.00
$15.00 Glasses for	9.75

In selling those superior eyeglasses at such a low price is simply to get people who wear glasses acquainted with our superior work. We have but one object in view—to make ourselves known as The Eureka Optical Co., of St. Louis, leading opticians, who help the most and charge the least

Office at Stancill Hotel.

Hours 9 a. m. to 5 p. m. Consultation free.
NOTE—Cloudy days do not interfere with perfect fitting glasses.
Will visit this city every 90 Days.

The Stancil Hotel sometimes served as a place to display and sell the goods and services of traveling business operations. In this case, a newspaper ad sought to sell local residents the eye ware of the Eureka Optical Company of St. Louis. Visiting "Refraction Specialist" Mr. W. Waldman came four times a year, offering eyeglasses at sale prices ranging from $1 to $9.75. The ad noted, "Cloudy days do not interfere with perfect fitting glasses."

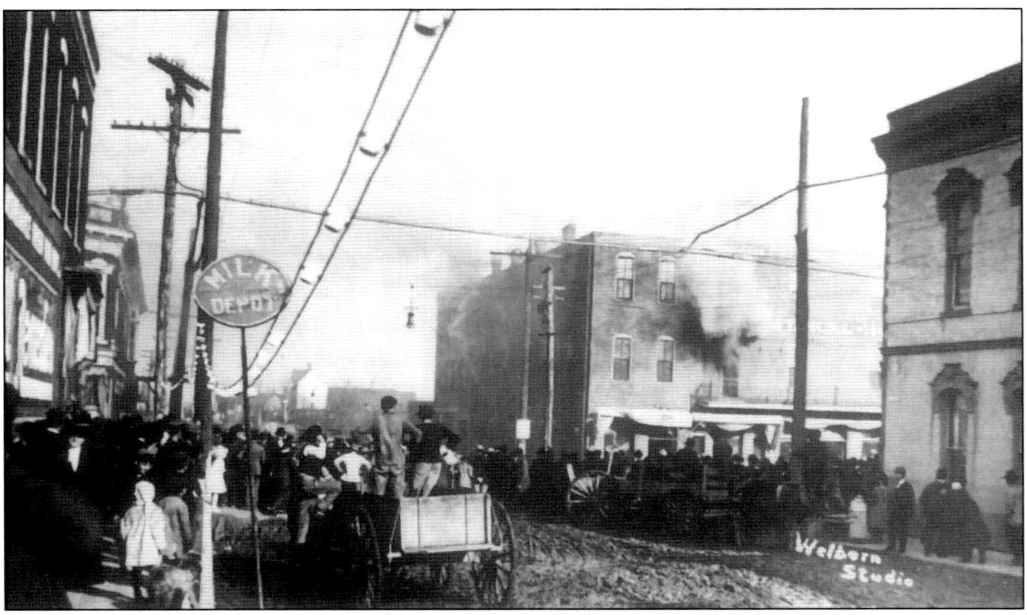

The Stancil Hotel was struck by fire *c.* 1915, a fate common among hotels of the era. It recovered to serve guests but was razed years ago.

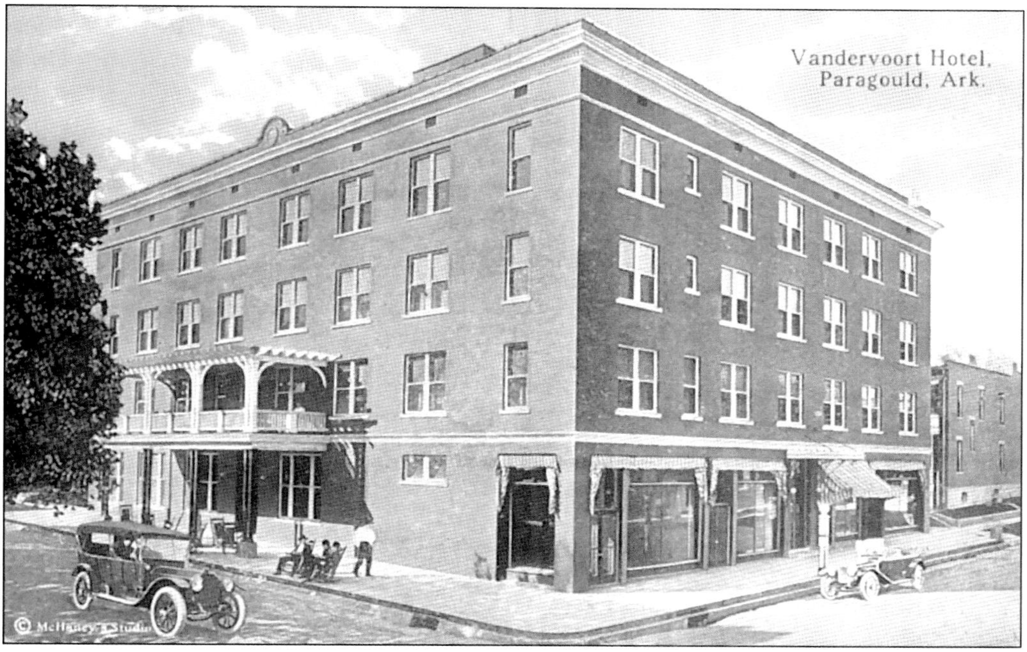

In contrast to hotels like the Stancil, the Vandervoort Hotel at 2nd and West Main was said to be the finest hotel in northeast Arkansas. Built by L.L. Vandervoort and opened in 1915, the hotel boasted a handsome lobby with a skylight, balconies on each floor, and fine food in the Plantation Dining Room. Among the noted guests in the 50 years the hotel stood have been Will Rogers in the 1930s, doing a benefit for local flood victims, and actor Ricardo Montalban in 1950. The image below captured the hotel in the mid 1950s, toward the end of its life; motels on the edge of town had already captured the traveling public's business. The grand hotel was torn down in the 1960s.

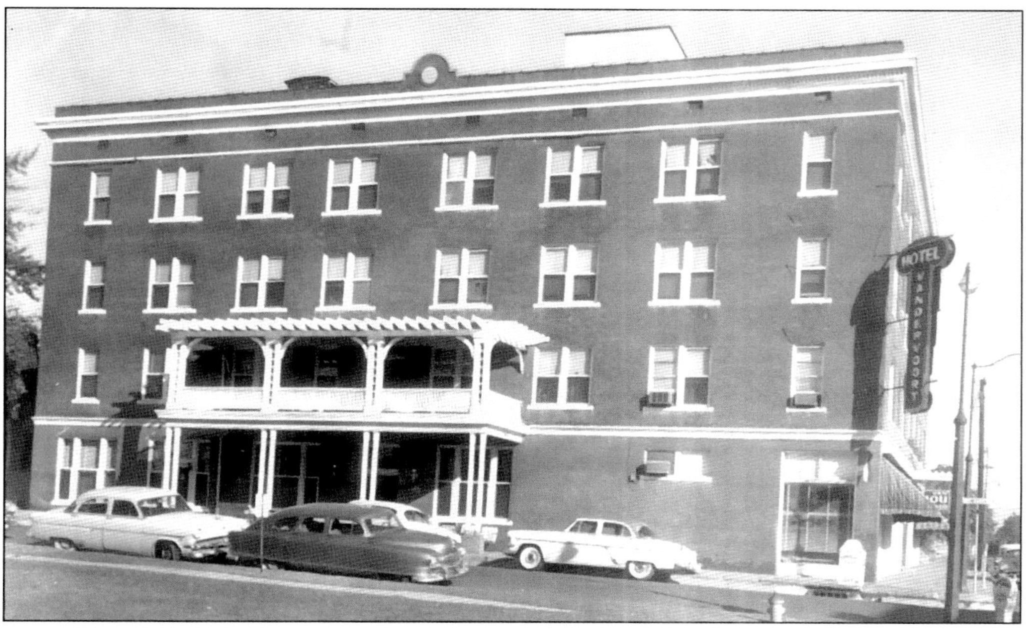

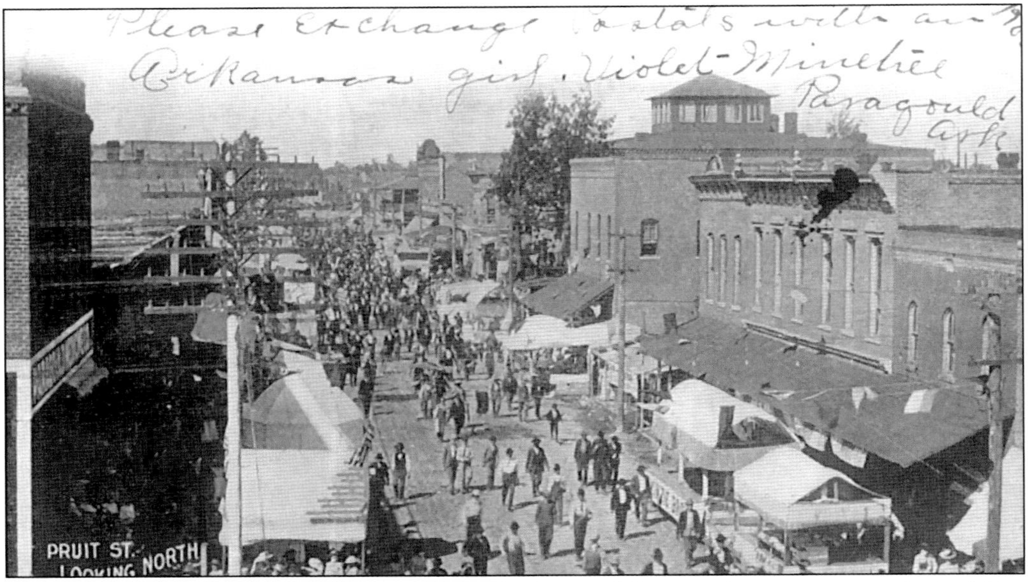

While Main Street was originally intended to be Paragould's major business artery, the inability to extend it led to that designation being shifted to Pruett Street, named for W.S. Pruett, one of the men who founded the town. Running north and south, the long dirt street is seen in this 1907 postcard to be crowded with a parade or march. In an era when messages were not allowed on the backs of postcards, the sender penned on the front, "Please exchange postals with an Arkansas girl, Violet Minetree, Route 1, Paragould, Ark."

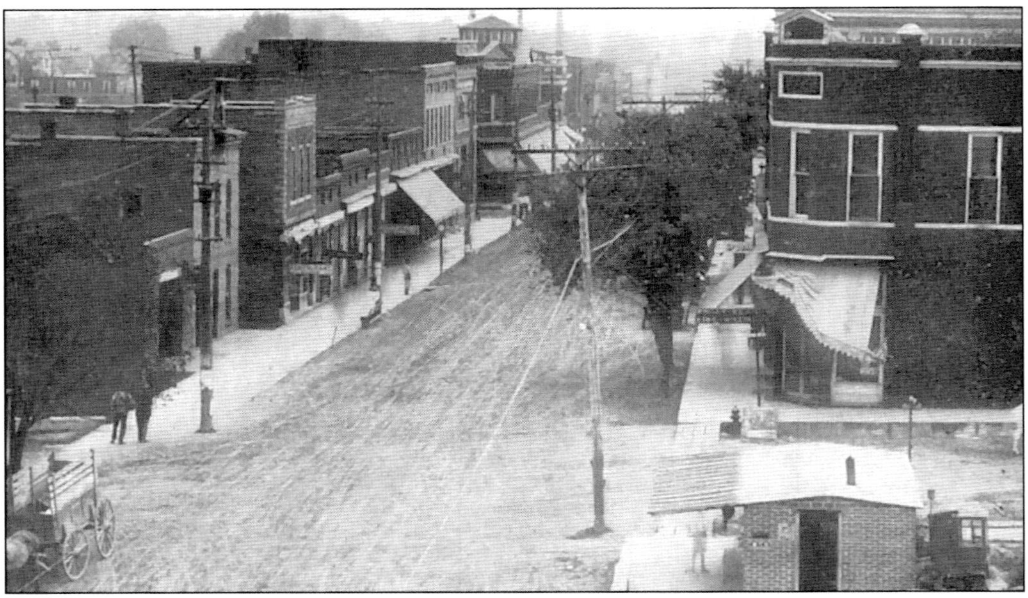

On a quieter day, perhaps a Sunday, the photo for this card was taken from a rooftop at the corner of Poplar Street looking south down Pruett Street, in contrast to the card above. The "x" marked by the sender of the card directs the message, "The wagon you see is a cotton wagon, Ethel you show these cards to Jim, tell him when he writes I will send him some." The bottom floor of the large building to the right housed a millinery store, while across the street was a restaurant.

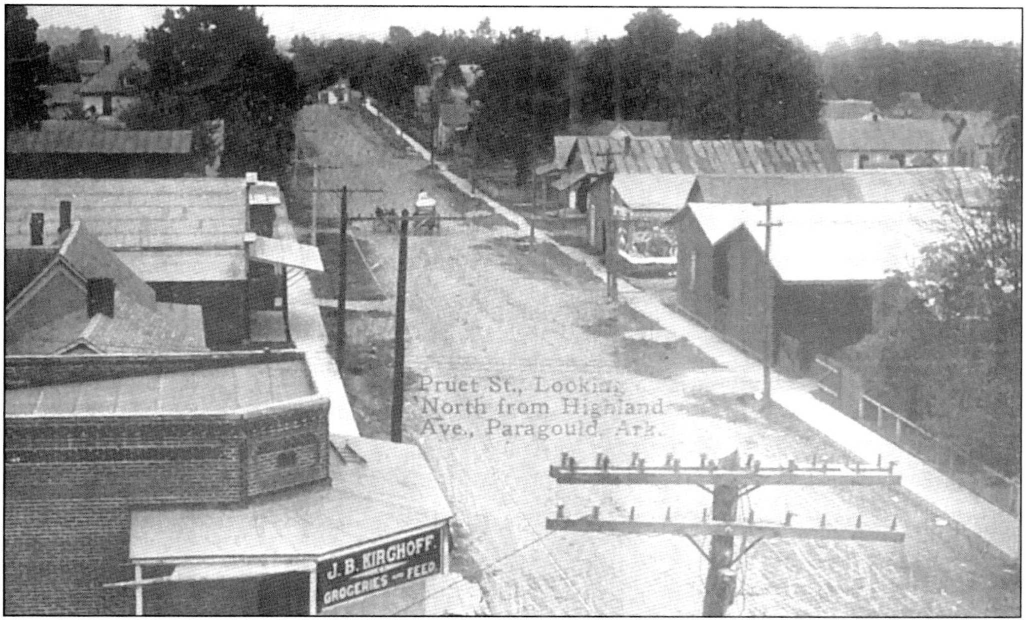

"Sure have been up against hard work. Took a country trip this morning," was the message penned on the back of a c. 1910 card of Pruett Street. The view looks north, toward residential areas on the dirt street, from its intersection with Highland Avenue. In the foreground is seen the corner location of J.B. Kirghoff Groceries and Feed store.

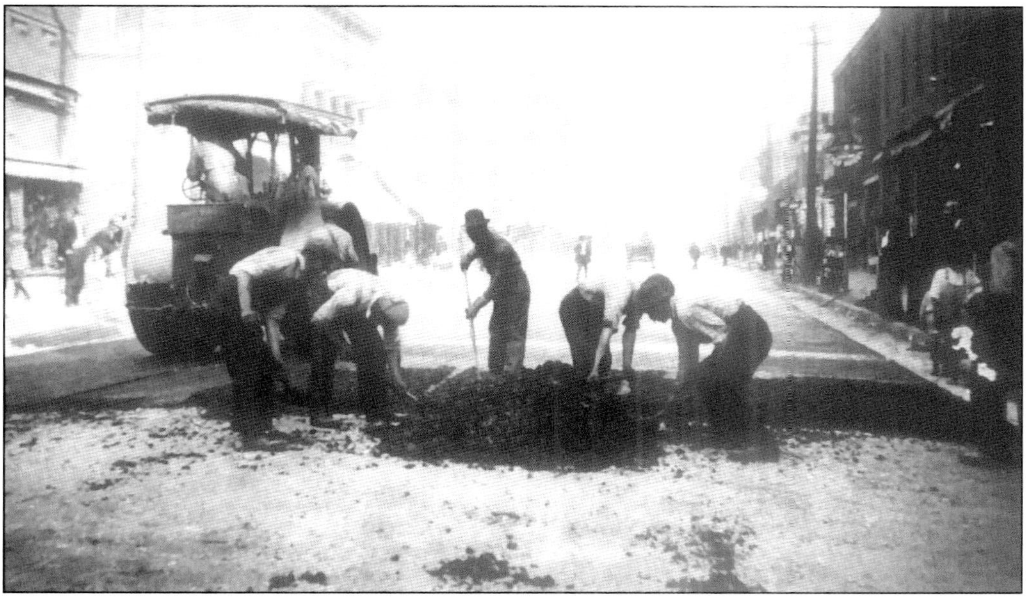

Seen here in 1912, the paving of Pruett Street was among the signs of the first-class city Paragould was emerging to become. The work was backbreaking for the men with shovels, but they were aided by the steamroller once they got the paving material spread out by hand.

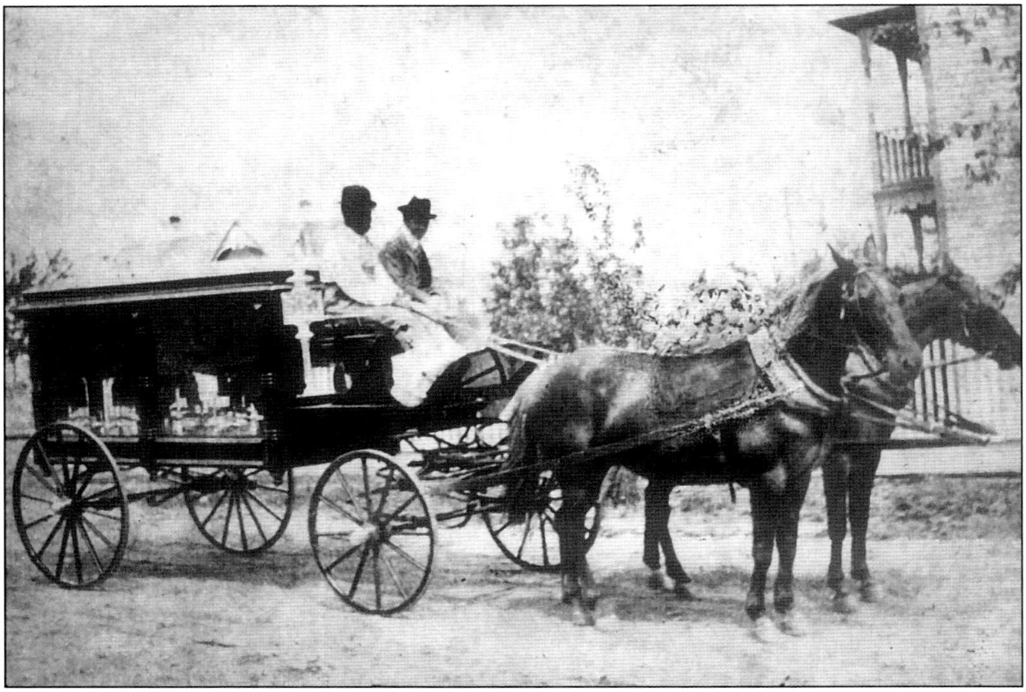

Harry S. Trice arrived in Paragould in 1885, at the age of 32, and he soon became a leading citizen. Trice, the first licensed embalmer in northeast Arkansas, is seen above in 1899, on the seat of his hearse, beside a man named "Boone." It was said that Boone simply showed up at Trice's home one day and stayed with the family from then on; he even took on the last name of Trice, according to some family members.

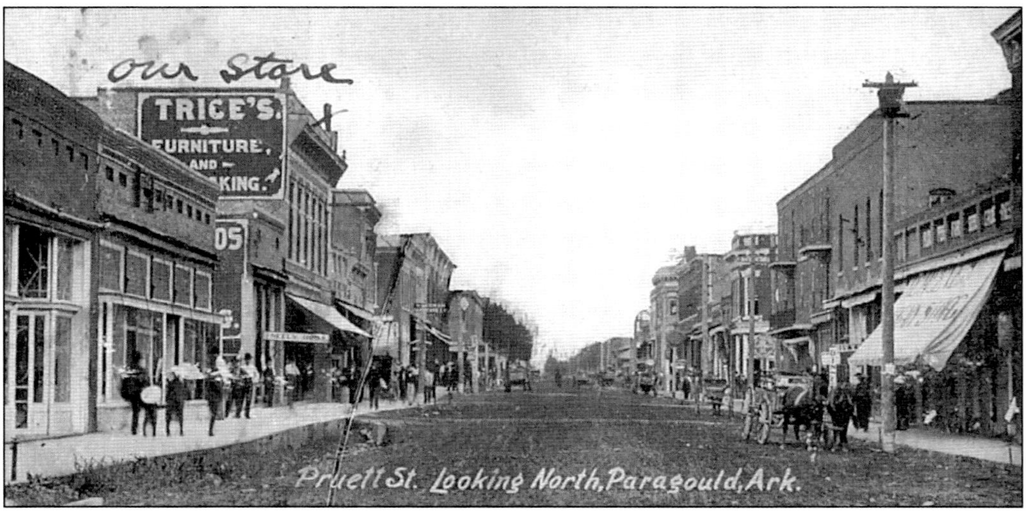

The 1909 card above was of the Pruett Street business district, home to Trice's store. By this time, H.S. Trice had combined his embalming and funeral (undertaking) business with a furniture business, not an uncommon practice in that day. The card was mailed to a young lady in Missouri, signed "You Know Who." It was sent perhaps by a member of the Trice family, for "Our Store" is penned above the landmark building on the left.

Harry Trice and his brother advertised aggressively in the local newspaper, as in this 1910 ad from the *Daily Press*. The selected product for this ad was "Cole's Hot Blast Steel Range—Made to Please the Housewife," with an "odorless and smokeless broiler and toaster" and "extra large ash pan.... A range is used in a home daily—three times each day—oftener than a sewing machine or any other article. It can be a source of pleasure to you." To entice further, the ad promised "EASY PAYMENTS."

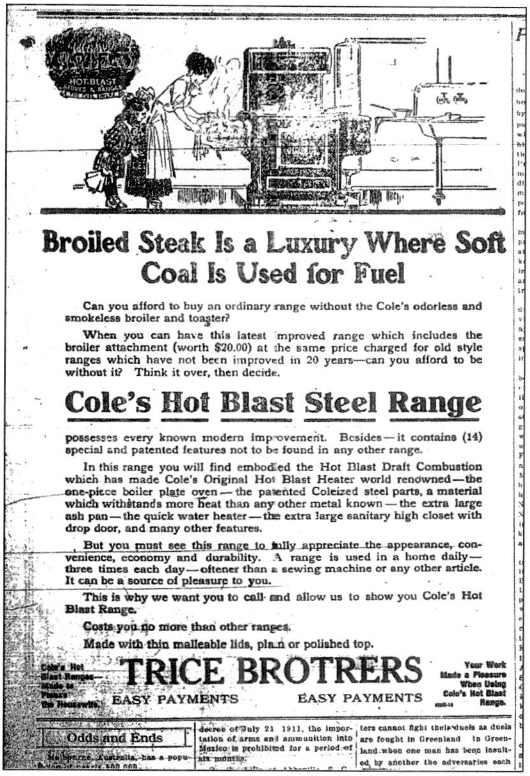

Broiled Steak Is a Luxury Where Soft Coal Is Used for Fuel

Can you afford to buy an ordinary range without the Cole's odorless and smokeless broiler and toaster?

When you can have this latest improved range which includes the broiler attachment (worth $20.00) at the same price charged for old style ranges which have not been improved in 20 years—can you afford to be without it? Think it over, then decide.

Cole's Hot Blast Steel Range

possesses every known modern improvement. Besides—it contains (14) special and patented features not to be found in any other range.

In this range you will find embodied the Hot Blast Draft Combustion which has made Cole's Original Hot Blast Heater world renowned—the one-piece boiler plate oven—the patented Coleized steel parts, a material which withstands more heat than any other metal known—the extra large ash pan—the quick water heater—the extra large sanitary high closet with drop door, and many other features.

But you must see this range to fully appreciate the appearance, convenience, economy and durability. A range is used in a home daily—three times each day—oftener than a sewing machine or any other article. It can be a source of pleasure to you.

This is why we want you to call and allow us to show you Cole's Hot Blast Range.

Costs you no more than other ranges.

Made with thin malleable lids, plain or polished top.

Cole's Hot Blast Ranges—Made to Please the Housewife.

TRICE BROTRERS

EASY PAYMENTS EASY PAYMENTS

Your Work Made a Pleasure When Using Cole's Hot Blast Range.

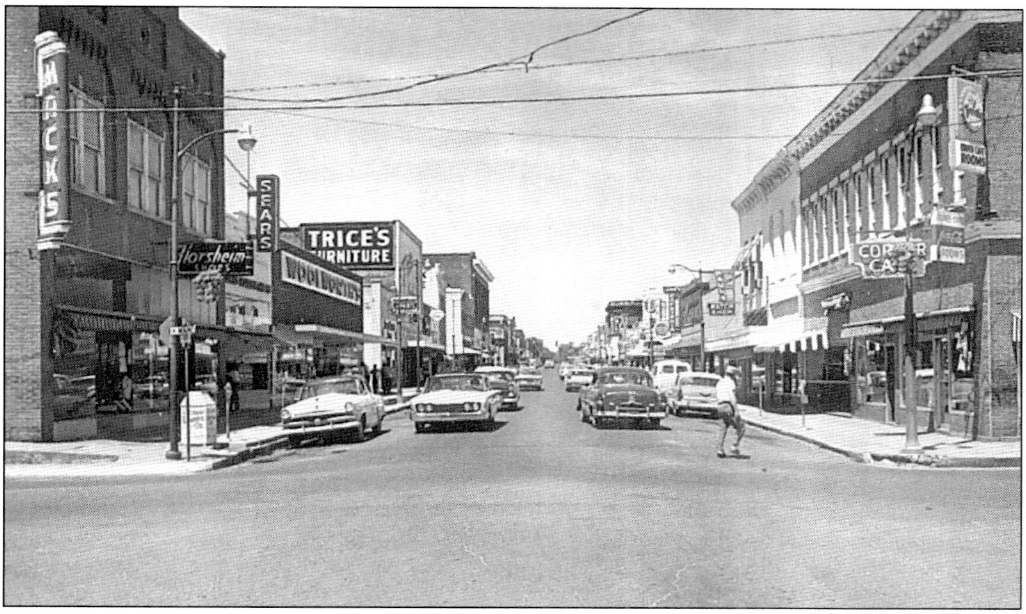

This card from the late 1950s shows the remarkable long-term success of the Trice Furniture Company; the business was still in the same location it was in almost 50 years before, as seen in the postcard above. Even the sign is in the same spot. The store did eventually close, after more than 50 years of furnishing Greene County homes.

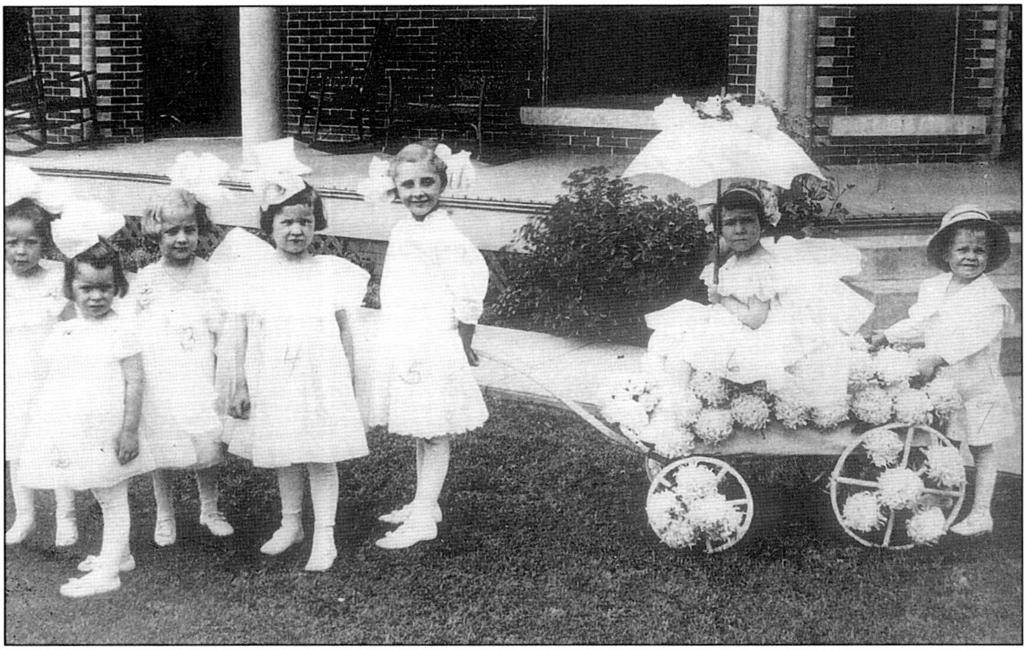

Some of Mr. Trice's profits from the funeral and furniture business went into his home on Court Street, the yard of which is seen here filled with children. The occasion that day was participation in the 1910 Parade of the City Beautiful Organization. Some of the children have been identified, including, from left to right, Elise Hardin, Bessie McAllister, Francis Wrape, and Hodges Wall.

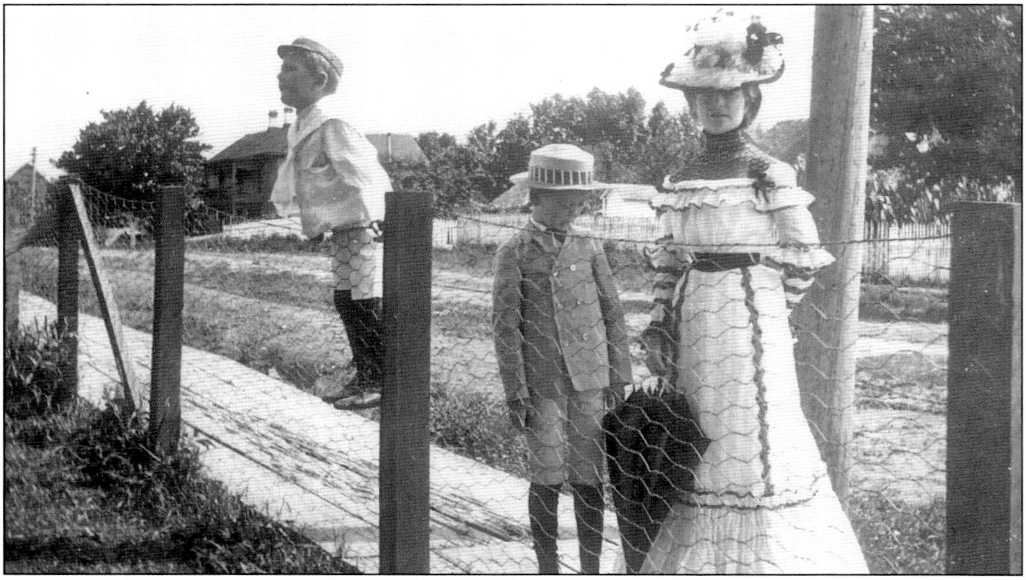

Photos of Greene County have left a legacy of the rich, the poor, and those in between, sometimes identified by name and sometimes not. This photo falls in the latter category, but most likely the well-dressed mother and sons were from one of Paragould's upper-class families, perhaps posed after church. What the boy on the fence was straining to get a view of is lost to history; perhaps he spied a passing train, horses, or any of the things that still make boys climb fences today.

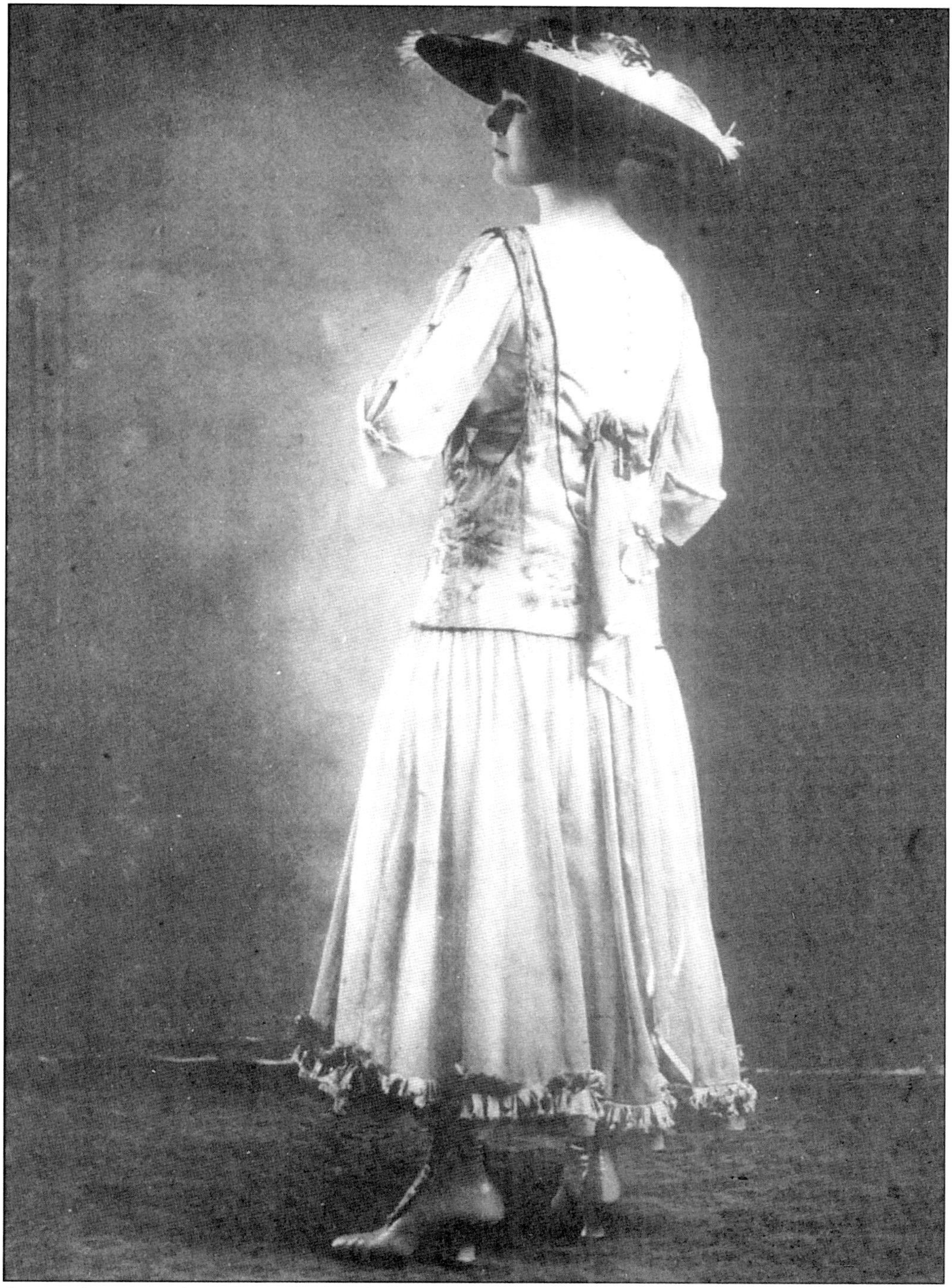

Certainly among the prominent people attending society affairs over the years at the Vandervoort Hotel was Mrs. Ora Yantis, seen here posed in 1921. Mrs. Yantis, wife of businessman Frank Yantis, was the daughter of J.W. McDonald who, among other civic works, had helped raise funds to build an opera house in Paragould in the 1890s.

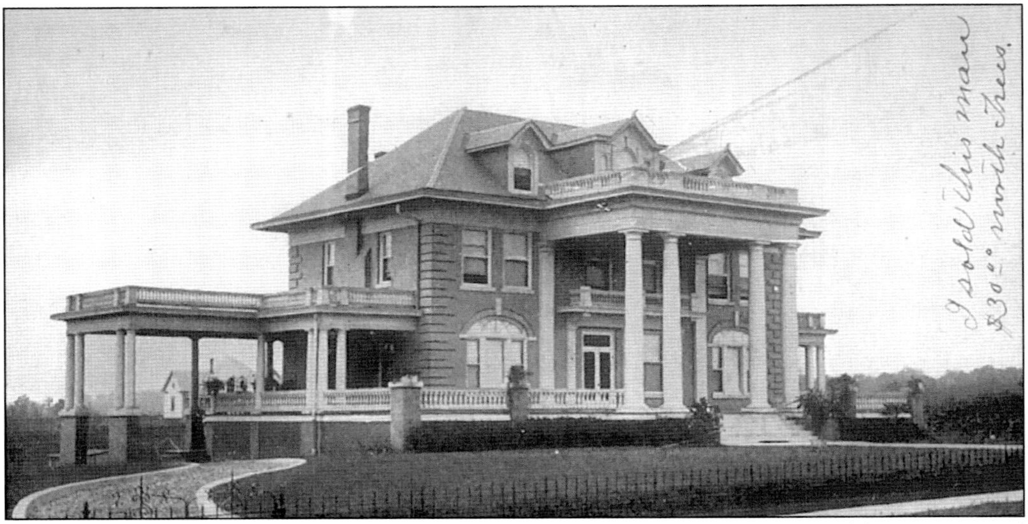

Likely a customer of Trice Furniture, J.D. Block was a successful Paragould attorney and banker who erected this mansion in 1904 at what is today 827 West Kingshighway. The estate, covering most of a block, was bounded by Vine, Eighth, and Ninth Streets. The 3-story, 14-room brick home had a slate roof, 12-foot ceilings, and several fireplaces. The second floor had five bathrooms, while the third floor consisted of a ballroom where grand parties were held. The curved driveway leading from the portico on the left opened onto Kingshighway and to the coach house at the rear. With the death of Block's daughter in 1964, the mansion was razed and replaced by a grocery store and parking lot. Penned on this 1905 card, when the home's new landscaping was being completed, are the words, "I sold this man $30 worth [of] trees."

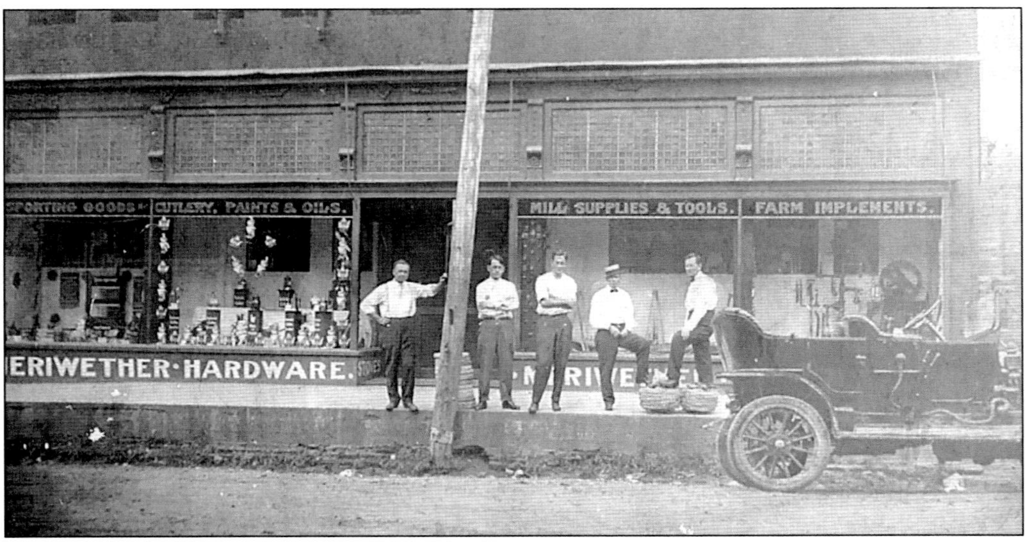

Among the enduring businesses of Greene County was R.W. Meriwether's hardware store, seen above *c.* 1910 with Mr. Meriwether and his son Ray beside the pole. First opened in 1883 by Civil War veteran C.W. Meriwether on Main Street, the store was soon destroyed by fire but quickly rebuilt and relocated to Pruett Street. In an era long before the rise of "mart" merchandising, stores such as Meriwether's Hardware carried a huge variety of goods. Advertised on the windows is a partial listing: "sporting goods, paints, oils, mill supplies & tools, farm implements."

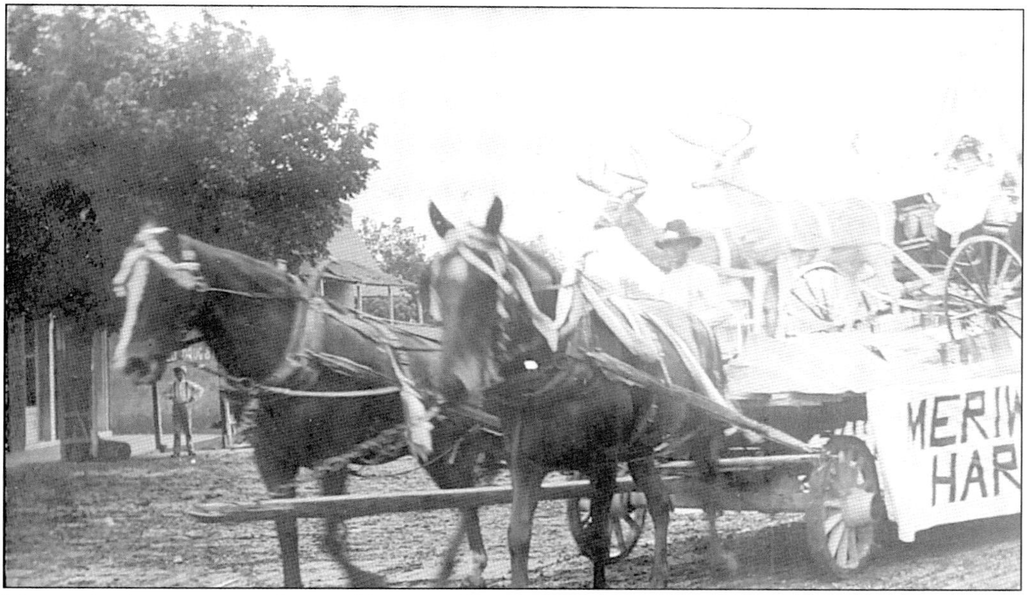

Meriwether's store was also well-known for its display of mounted wildlife of many types. Sometimes the mounted wildlife even left the store, as seen above c. 1910. The two mounted deer from the store posed on a parade float, seemingly pulling a covered wagon.

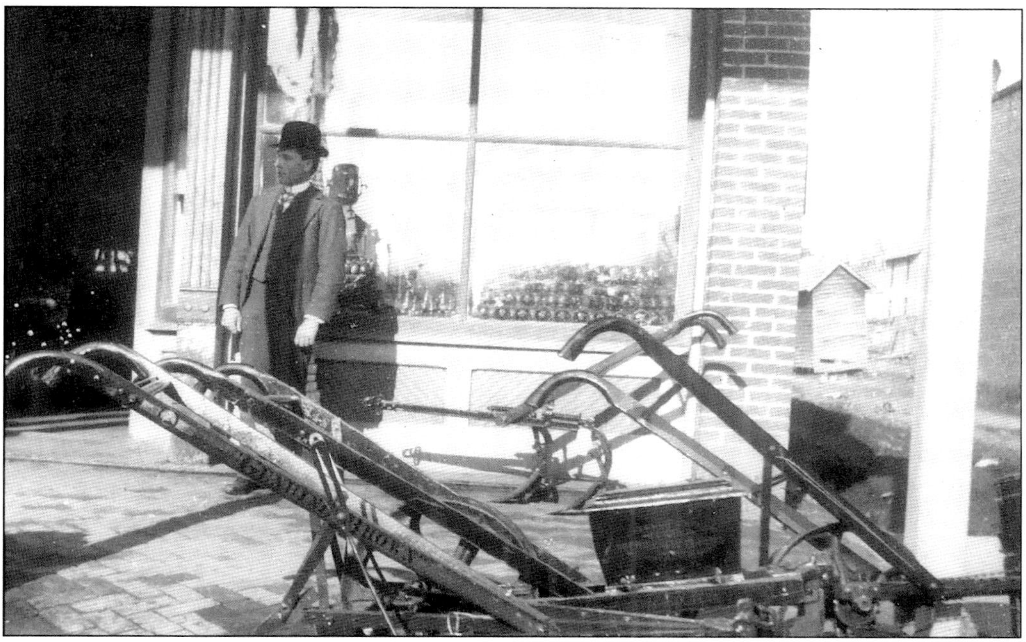

Meriwether's supplied many of the tools and supplies needed by area farmers, who worked long hours to produce food and income. Among the popular items stocked was always the newest model of plows, some of which are displayed here on the store's porch. As the forests of Greene County were cleared, implements like these—aided by the labor of men and beasts—gradually converted forestlands into farm fields. Operated by four generations of the Meriwether family, the store finally shut down in 1956, after more than 70 years.

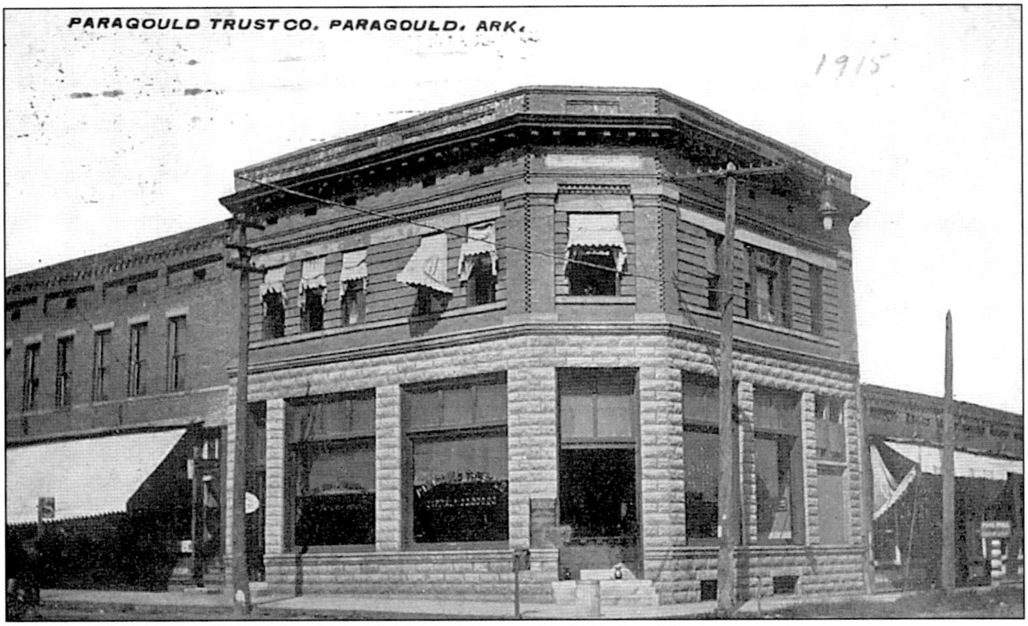

The economic growth from railroads, timber, and agriculture gave rise to the demand for competing banks in Paragould. The Paragould Trust Company, which was located at 101 North Pruett and is shown above in 1915, opened for business in 1905, with a capital of $100,000 with which to do business. The writer of the postcard below, of the First National Bank located at 115 North Pruett, might well have been in need of a loan to offset his misfortunes in 1908, as he wrote, "I suppose that you have heard of the fire Saturday night. We were burnt out good and proper."

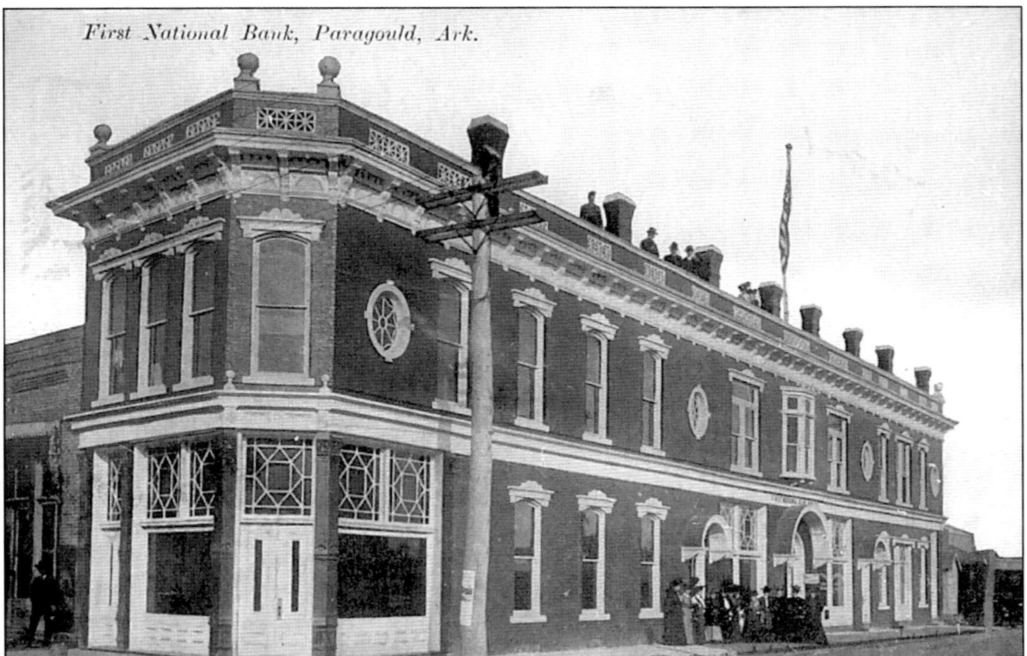

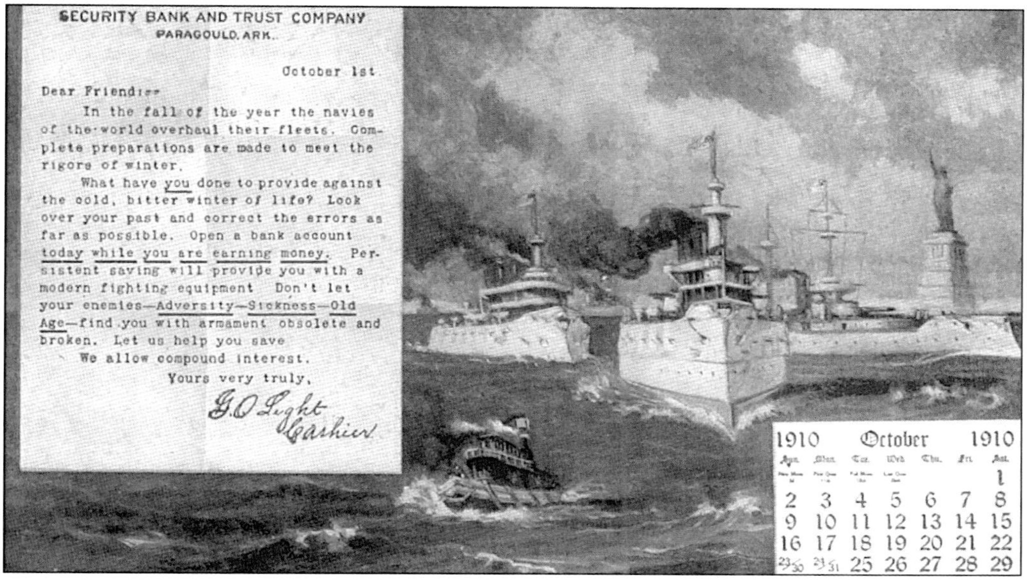

The Security Bank and Trust Company used monthly calendar postcards in 1910, to promote reasons to save money in an account at the bank. The postcard above reads in part, "In the fall of the year the navies of the world overhaul their fleets. Complete preparations are made to meet the rigors of winter. What have you done to provide against the cold, bitter winter of life? Don't let your enemies—Adversity—Sickness—Old Age—find you with armament obsolete and broken. Let us help you save." Below, the bank's July card took a patriotic theme, pointing out the population of the U.S. was 100 million people and challenging people to open a savings account, "...When to fully enjoy Liberty, Equality and Fraternity they must have that sordid handle to this triple combination—Money. Start a bank account today and celebrate your Declaration of Independence from the errors of the past and the limitations of the future." Both cards carried the printed signature of G.O. Light, the cashier.

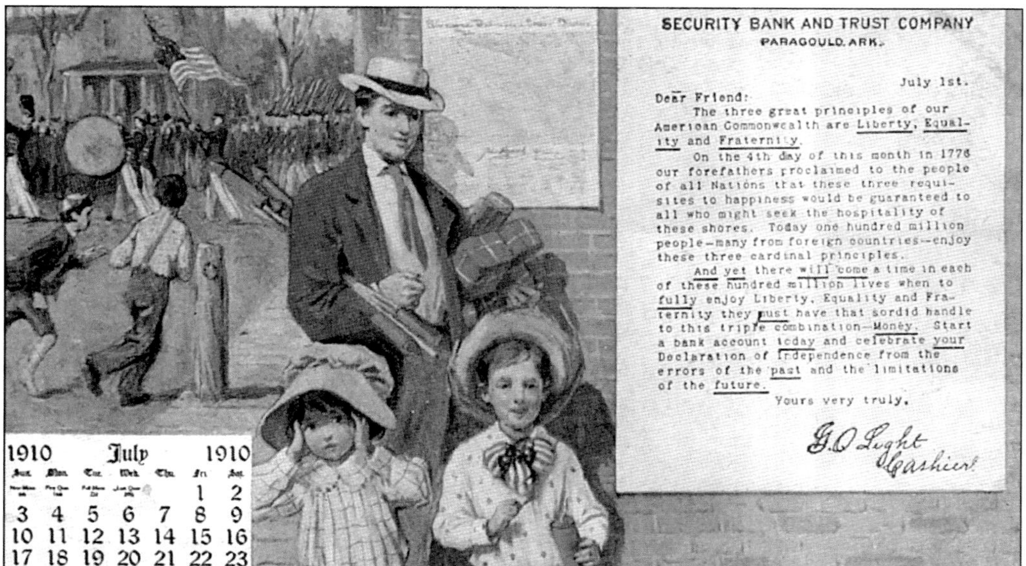

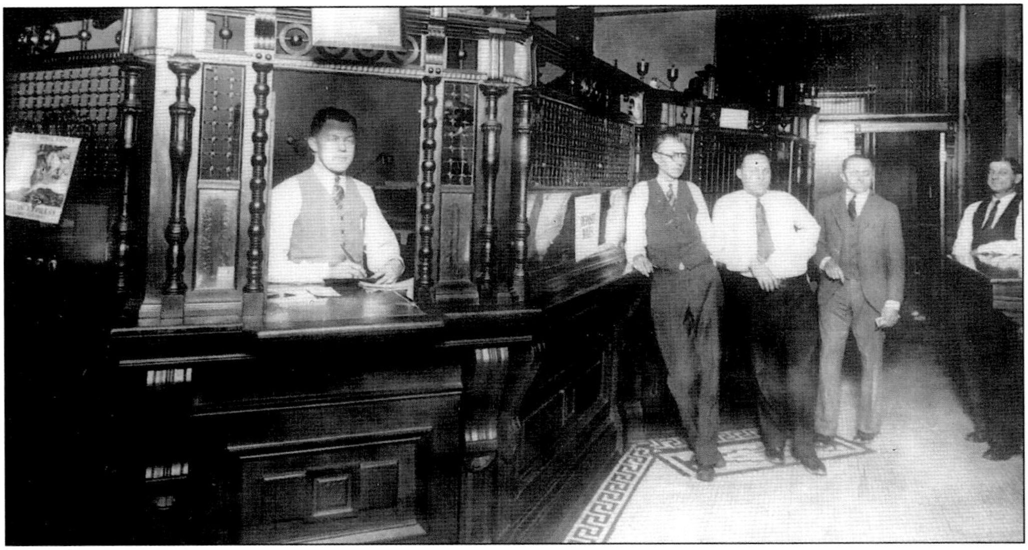

This *c.* 1915 photo depicts a teller window at one of the banks on Pruett Street, most likely First National, and offers an excellent look at how much more compact the lobbies were then, compared to today. One feature not found in modern banks is the spittoon seen in the lower center of the photo. The wall-mounted desk to the far right was equipped with deposit tickets, in order for customers to complete their preparations before seeing the teller.

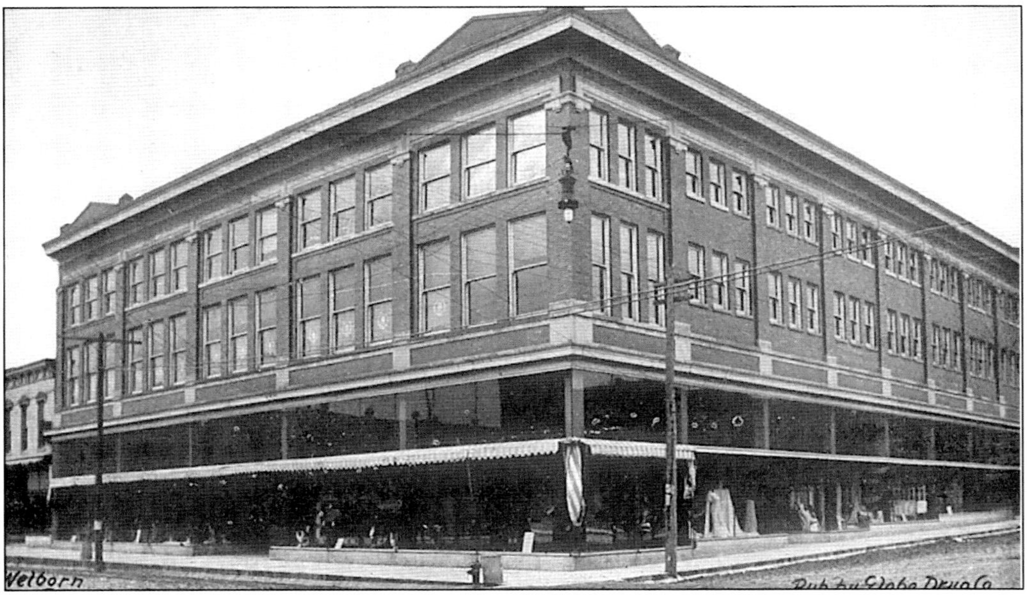

What Meriwether's of Paragould was for hardware, the Bertig Brothers' huge department store on south Pruett Street was for just about everything else, especially clothing. Adolph and Sol Bertig arrived in Paragould in 1881, as penniless young Jewish orphans. Over the next few decades they became wealthy in real estate, cotton, and their landmark department store. The brothers first opened their store in 1909, though it was quickly damaged by fire. They rebuilt it in even grander fashion, with elevators and fine rugs among the touches that set it apart from other retailers. The store closed in the mid-1930s, and the entire block was destroyed by fire around 1990.

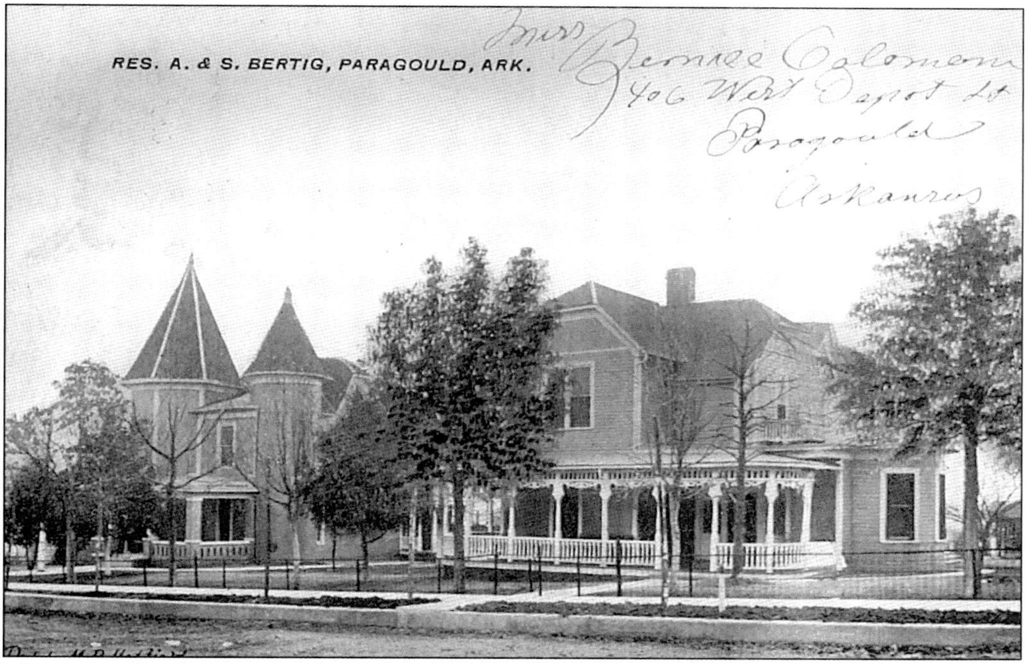

The Bertig brothers invested part of their store's profits in fine homes, located adjacent to each other on Main Street. To the left at 506 West Main was the home of Adolph and Mary Bertig, which still stands today. To the right is seen the home of Sol and Rae Bertig, which was unfortunately destroyed by fire years ago. As noted by the sender of this card in 1912, "This is Bertig Bros. dwellings, they have the best store in town."

The Bertig brothers promoted their store as the finest in the area, promising a unique look to enhance a man's chance of success in his endeavors. This ad from a 1910 edition of the *Daily Press* promoted the store as a place for a man to get a fine suit. A "distinctiveness of cut and pattern" was assured so that "Just two or three suits of a pattern insure you from meeting your double at every corner." Stetson Hats were also advertised along with Manhattan Shirts—all with a money-back guarantee. Another ad read, "Bertig's Mammoth Department store is in reality a collection of small stores, all under one roof, with individual heads for each, but with one directing spirit pervading the whole—the spirit of fair dealings with the public."

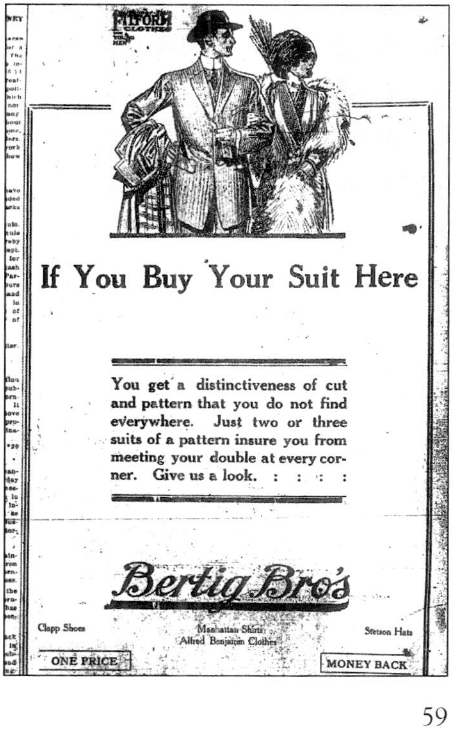

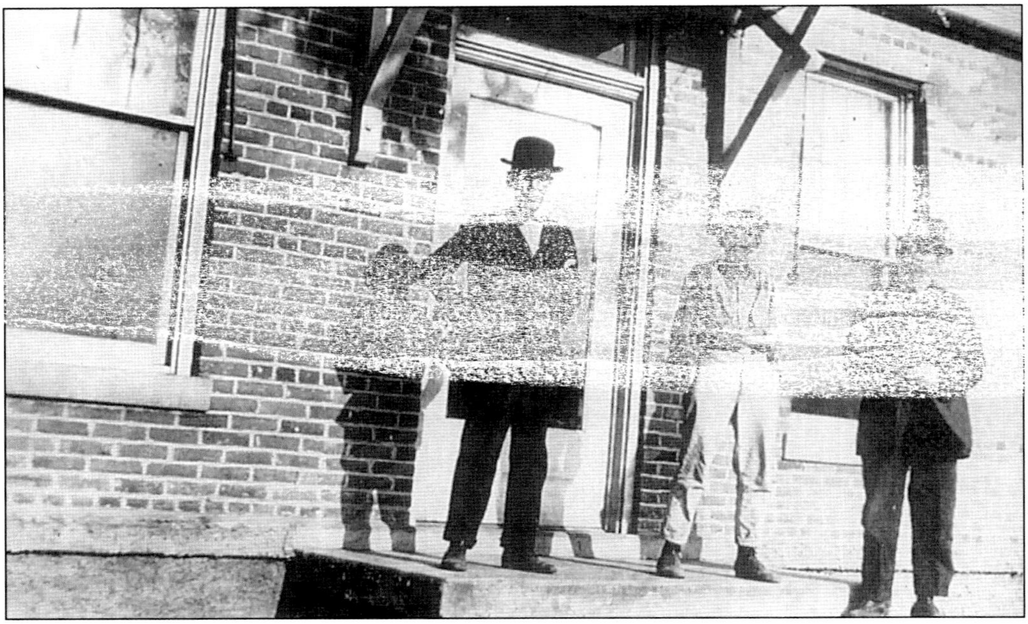

W.C. Hasty, seen above to the left outside of his mill, numbered among the successful men migrating to Paragould to leave their mark on the community. Hasty moved to Greene County from Michigan in 1888, went into the lumber business, and served as president of the Paragould Southeast Railroad. Seen below, Mr. Hasty's family home reflected some of the extra features money provided, such as a backyard greenhouse along with the family name and a Masonic symbol outlined in whitewashed stones on the lawn. The railroad-style water tower in the yard likely came from one of Hasty's railroad projects.

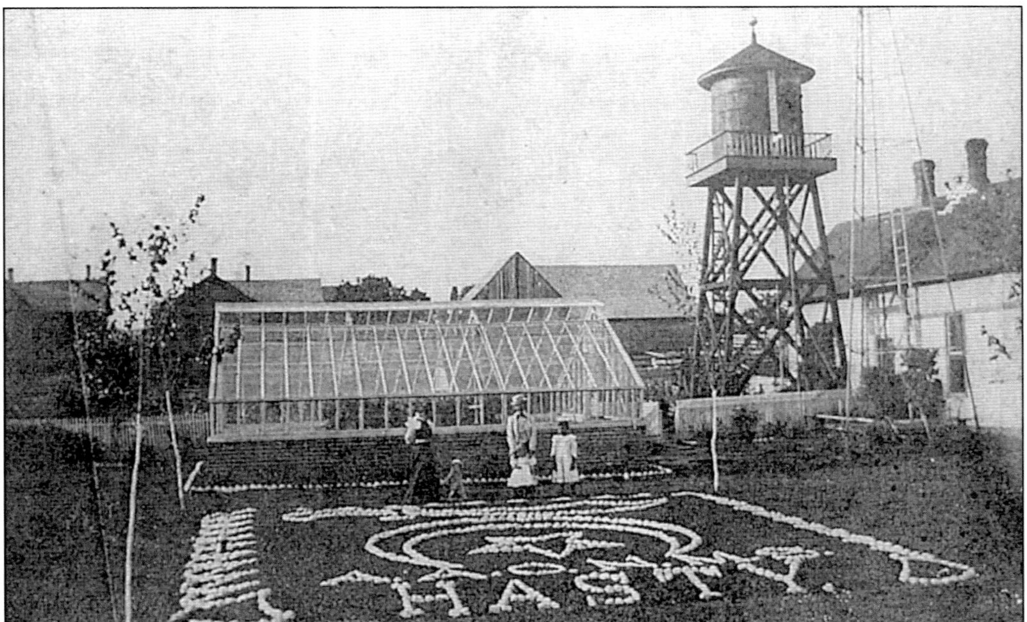

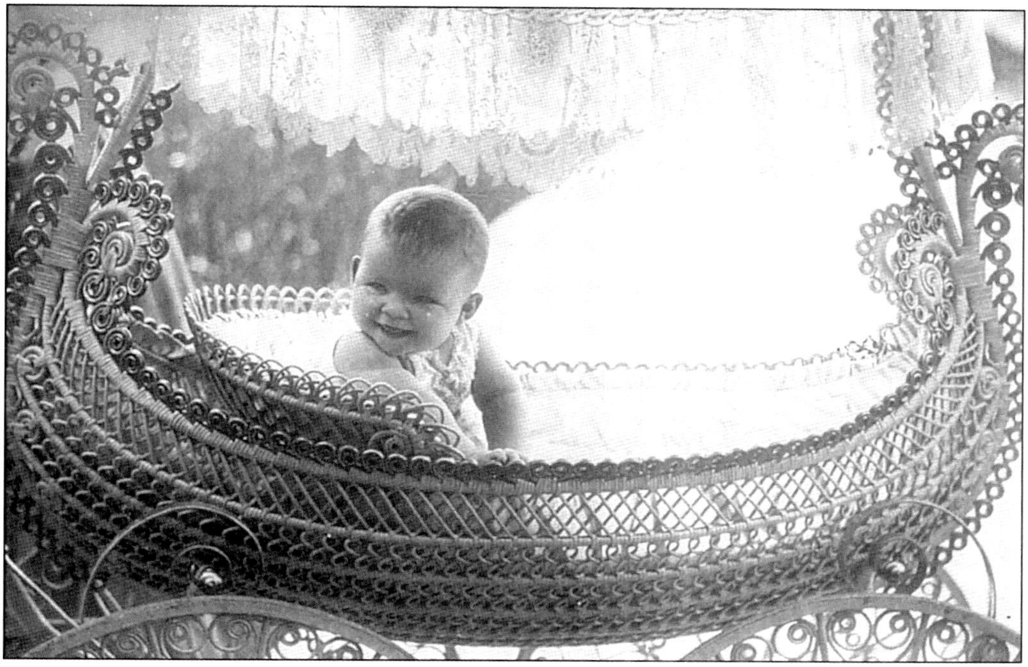

W.C. Hasty left more than his business legacy, as evidenced by this 1895 photo of his infant daughter Harriet, seen in an intricate Victorian-era cradle.

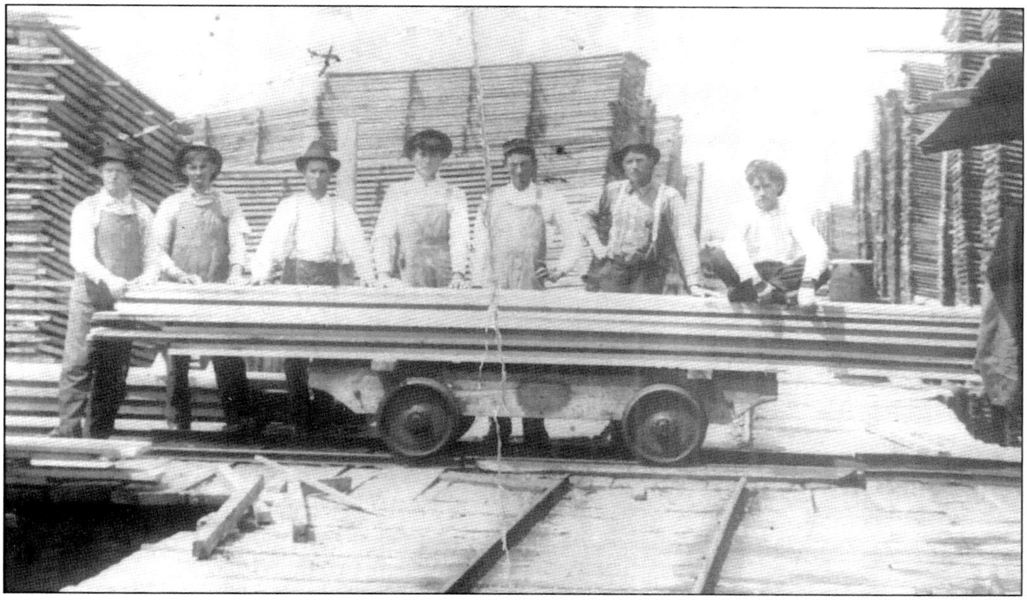

In the early 1900s, W.C. Hasty acquired the Wrape Stave factory, one of Paragould's larger employers. Established in the 1880s by Irish-American Henry Wrape, the plant turned the area's hardwood lumber into barrel staves and other wood products. In the 1900 photo above, a drying yard is seen, with workers posed behind a rail cart loaded with planks from the mill. The John Hooker Mill near the Clay County line had a capacity for 10,000 board feet per day around the time of this photo.

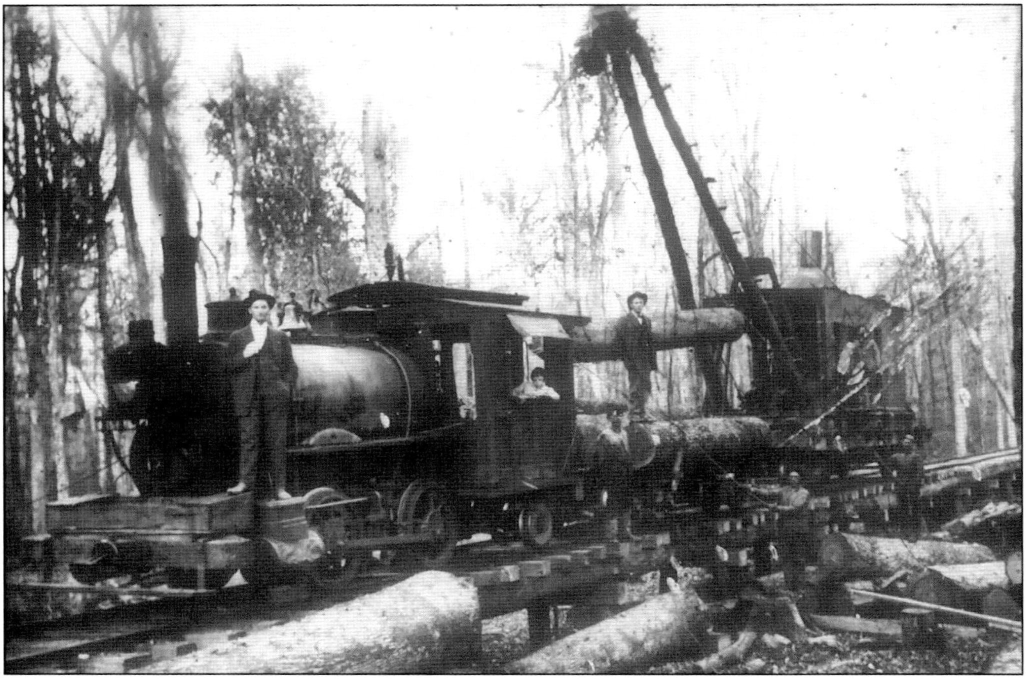

The Wrape Stave Mill was only one of many timber-related enterprises that sprang up to profit from the vast hardwood forests of Greene County after the railroads came in the 1880s. In 1889 alone there were 34 steam-powered sawmills, 6 stave factories, a shingle mill, and 2 planing mills in the county. Spur rail lines like the one seen above were equipped with steam-powered equipment that moved into the dense forest and swampy bottoms to bring out the timber. Once the land was cut over, it often was sold for taxes and converted to farmland. Another industry, the local concrete and tile plant that put out a variety of concrete pipe and related products, is seen below in this 1915 postcard. The adjacent rail line would have brought in shipments of cement and shipped out finished products.

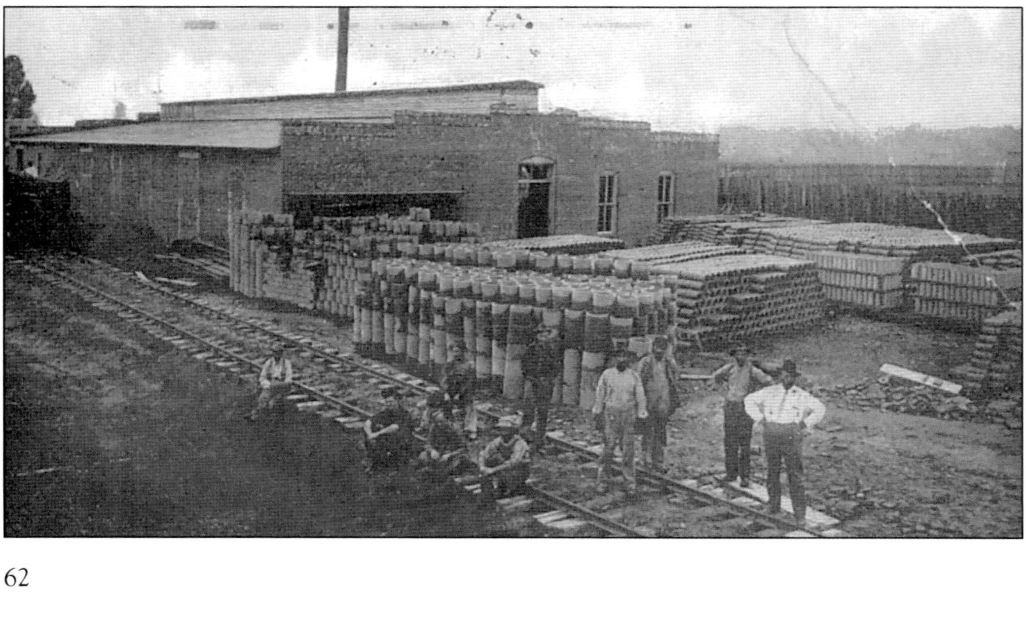

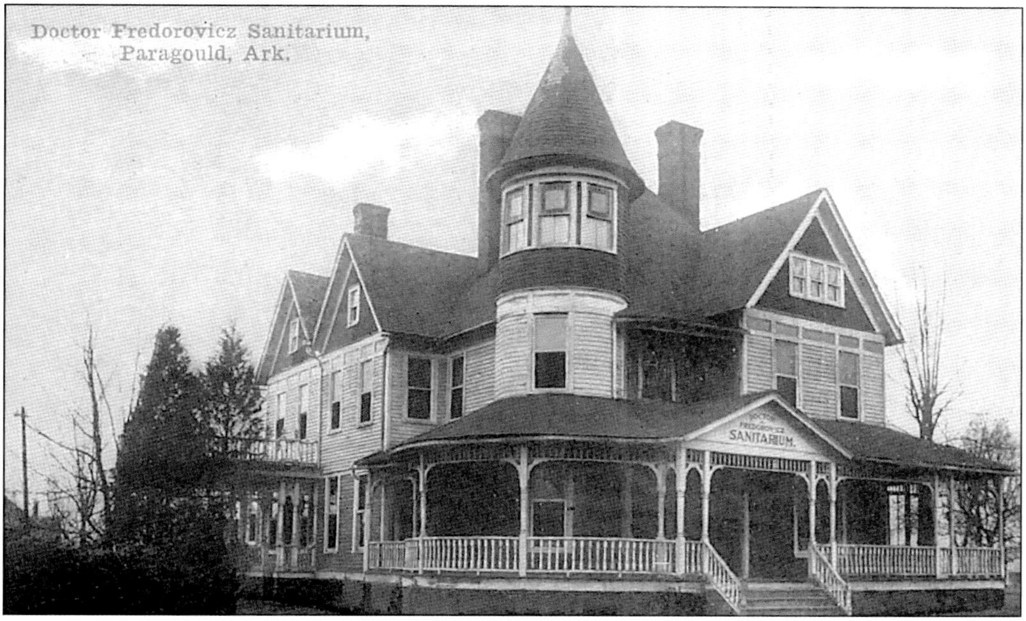

Paragould's growth seemed assured by the 1890s with the impact of the railroads and burgeoning industries, but the development of medical facilities was lacking for some time. While the Benedictine sisters in 1900 had opened a hospital at Jonesboro, some 25 miles away, Paragould was still in need. For a time, the house above on East Hunt housed the sanitarium of Doctor Fredorovicz, whose medical credentials and services may have been lacking.

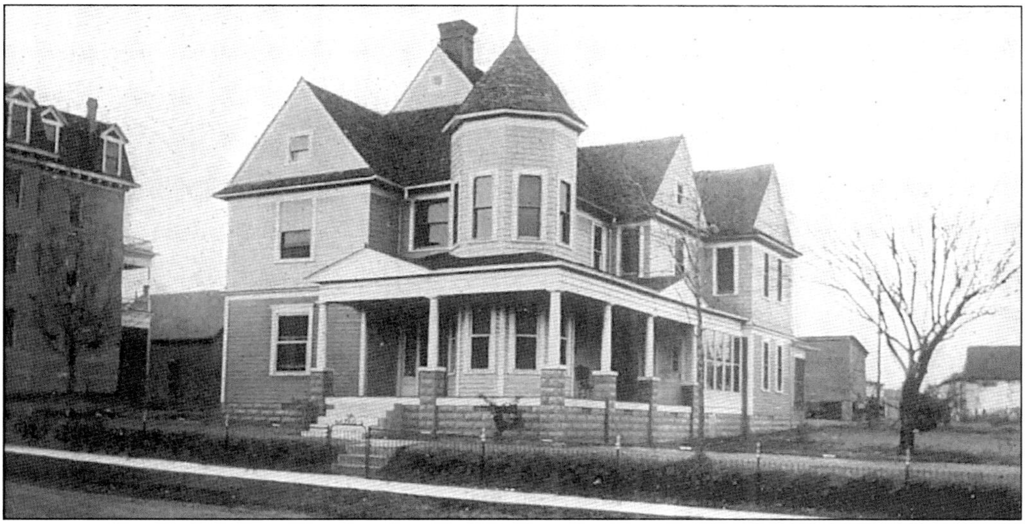

The hospital situation in Paragould would significantly improve through the efforts of the owner of this home at 209 West Court Street, which no longer stands today. Mrs. Letha Dillman, apparently a woman of some means, was the sister of Dr. A.G. Dickson, a native of Paragould who got his medical training at Vanderbilt University. Dr. Dickson had opened an office at 112 North Pruett Street in 1890, and opened the City Drug Store in 1895. His sister, Mrs. Dillman, funded the construction of the town's first hospital for him in 1905; a corner of the hospital can be seen to the left of the Dillman house.

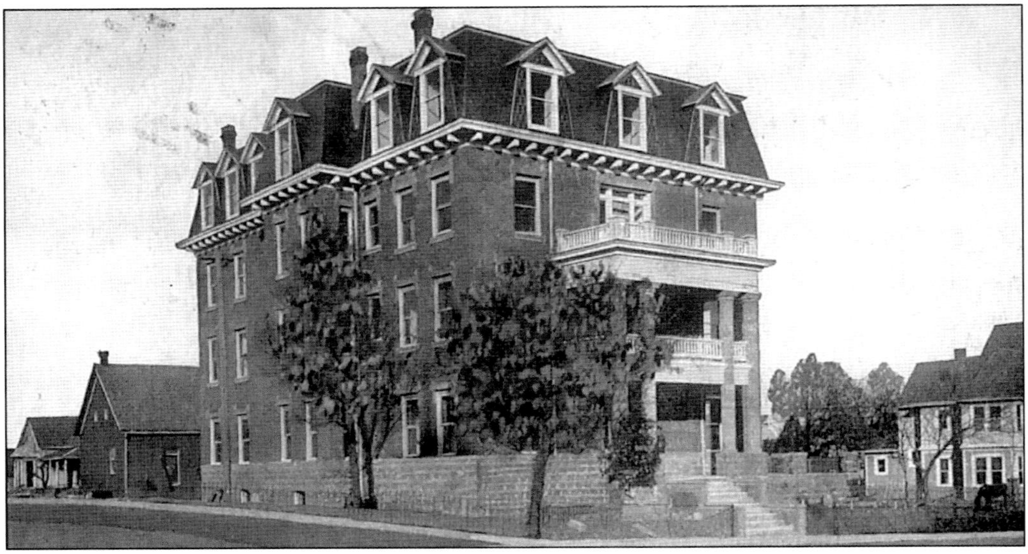

Dr. Dickson's hospital was built on his home site; the house was moved out of the way, according to newspaper accounts. Dr. Dickson himself designed the structure, hiring Tol Ware of Paragould to build it. Per newspaper accounts, it was, "with massive concrete basement, five stories high and covered with a Mansard roof. Thirty-three rooms in the sanitarium [as hospitals of the day were often called]. The building is heated by a furnace, lighted by electricity, and equipped with phones and electric call systems for patients." At a final cost of $30,000, the facility opened February 1, 1907; sadly, Dr. Dickson died in 1909, reportedly of pneumonia contracted while making house calls in the dead of winter. The Paragould Sanitarium Company was quickly formed, selling stock for $25 a share to keep the hospital operating. The name changed to Dickson Memorial Hospital in 1920; it operated until the 1940s, when it was replaced by a larger modern hospital on West Kingshighway, near today's location of the very modern Methodist Hospital of Arkansas. Dr. Dickson's old hospital, minus the top two floors, later served as City Hall. Seen below in a 2001 photo, its fate hangs in the balance between restoration and razing for a parking lot.

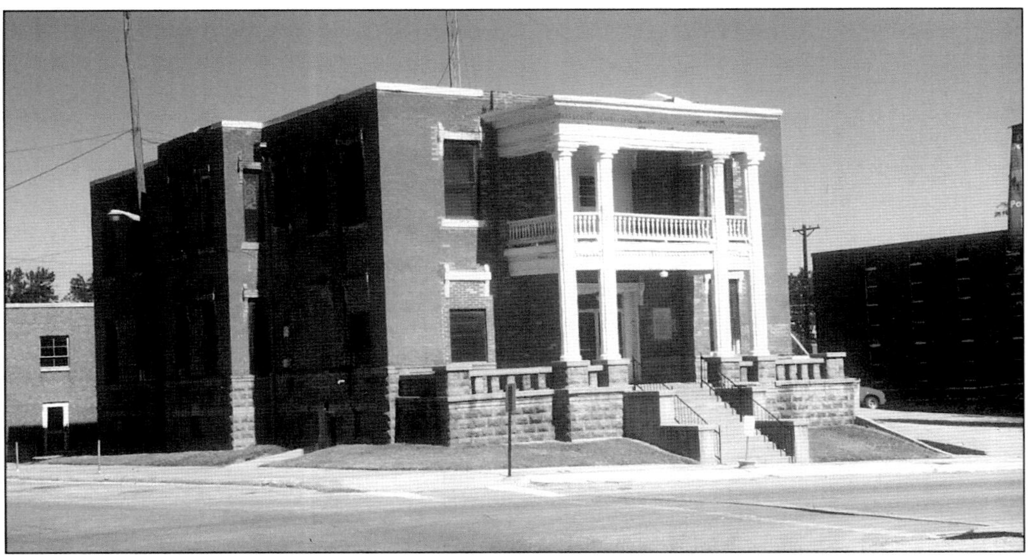

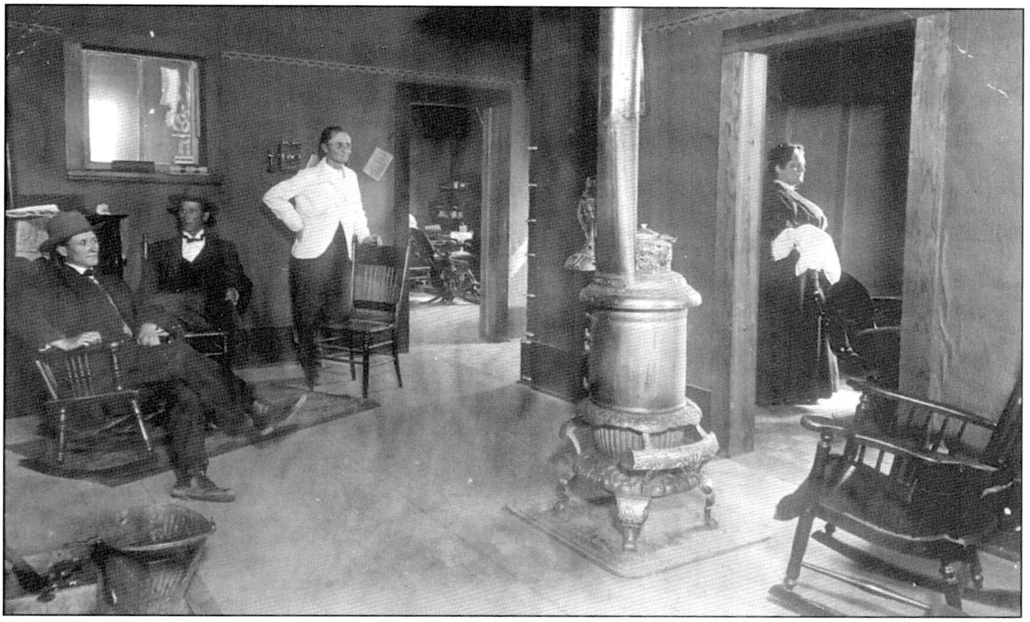

Paragould residents with a toothache often climbed the stairs at 211 1/2 Pruett Street to the offices of dentist Dr. F.C. Johnson. They would have sat in the waiting room above, perhaps warming by the stove, and perhaps dreading their turn in the room seen in the far center of the photo. Below, an unidentified patient is seen taking his turn in the chair, while a boy watches Dr. Johnson work. Today the building houses the Child Art Studio, showcasing the work of photographer and history buff John Kennte.

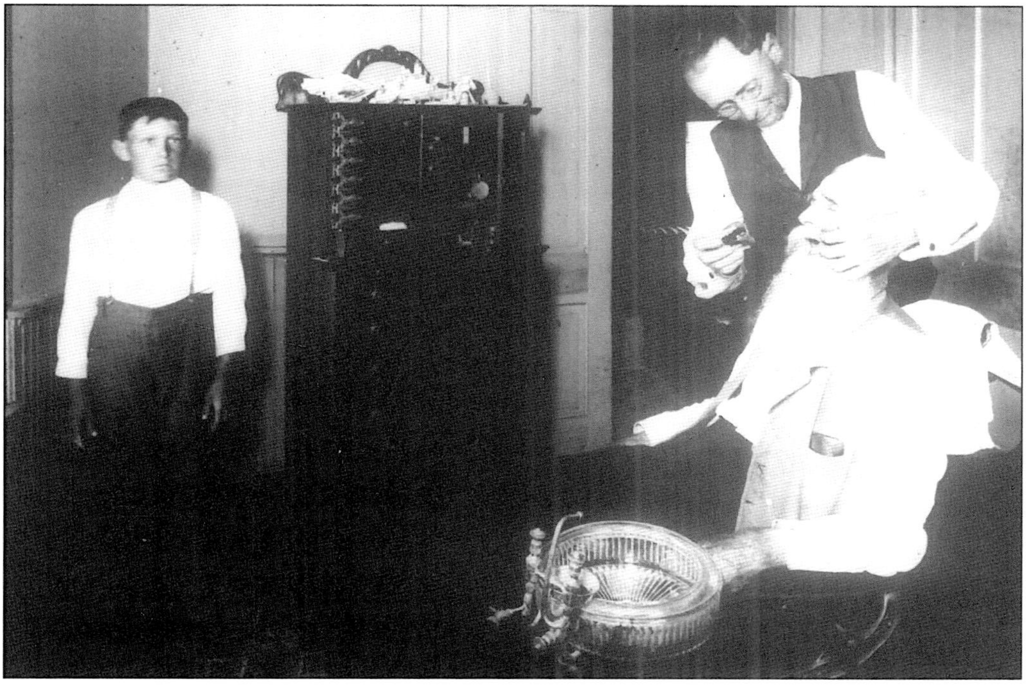

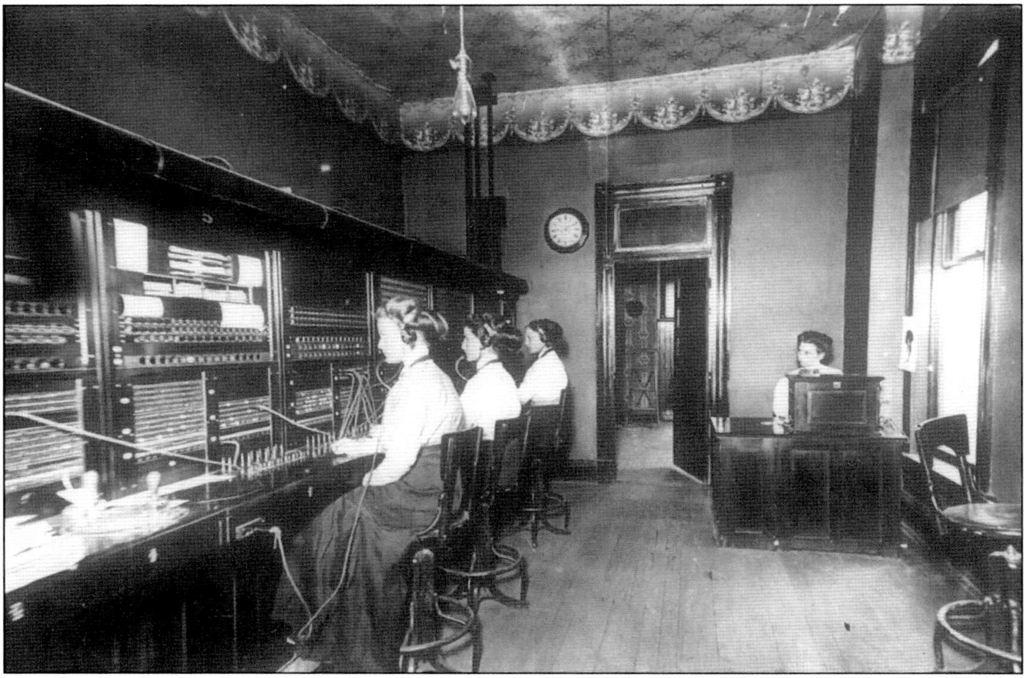

By 1910, the growing number of Paragould residents with telephones might have spoken to one of these operators while placing a call to Dickson Hospital or seeking the services of the dentist, Dr. Johnson. The first telephone system in the state had opened in Little Rock in 1879. By the turn of the century, growing communities like Paragould were also seeing telephone poles going up among the local stately homes, connecting prominent citizens and businesses through switch boards such as these located at 106 West Emerson.

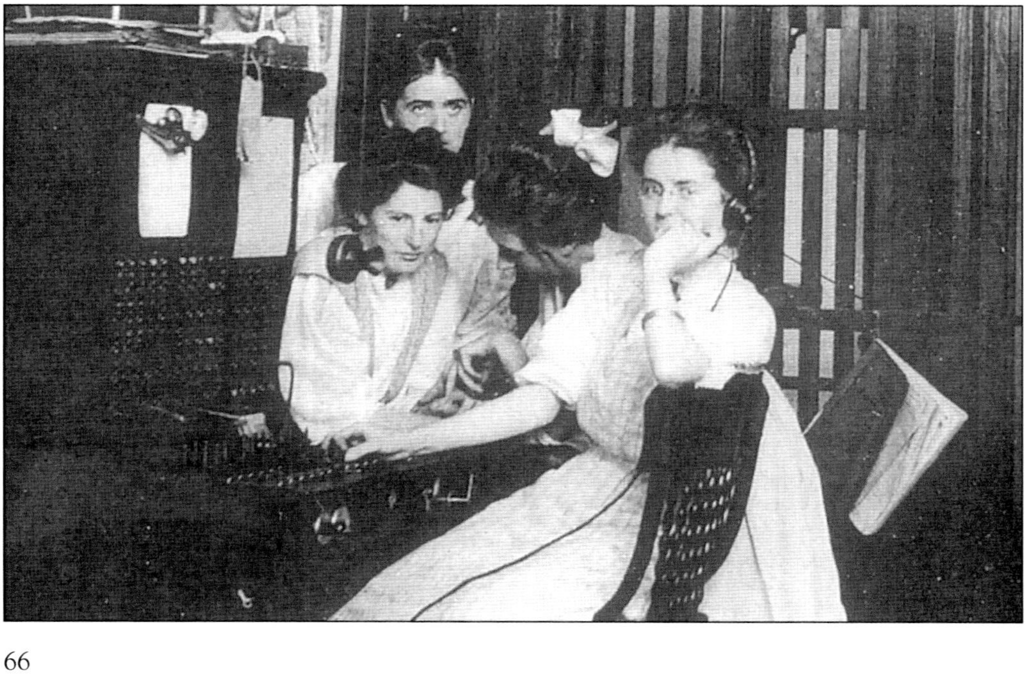

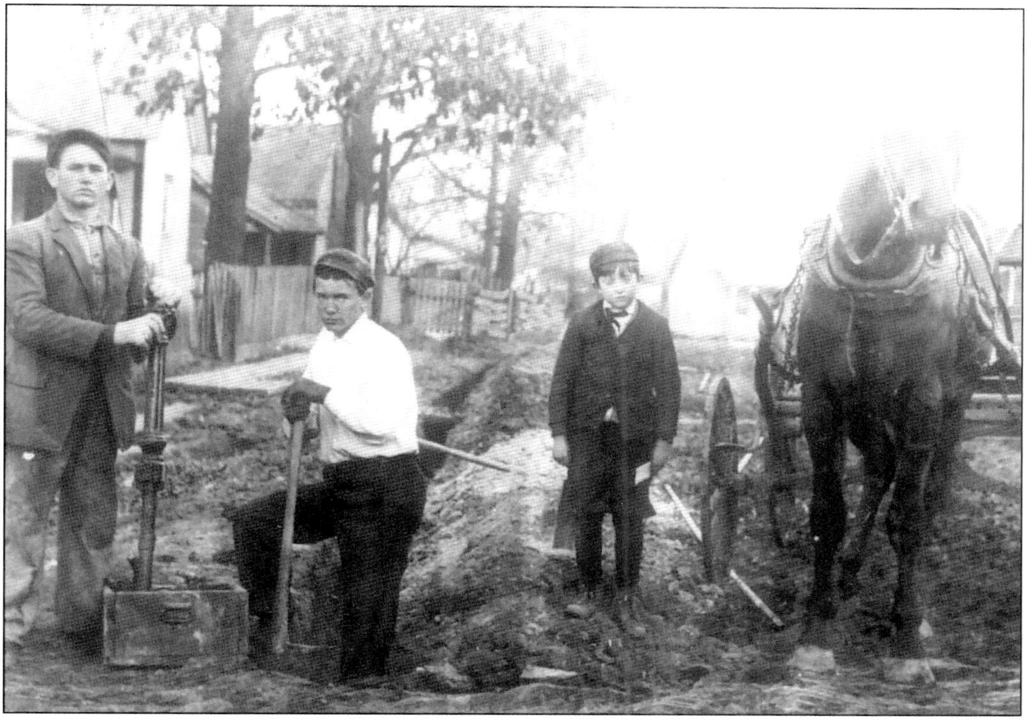

Paragould, like most Arkansas cities, was a town of dirt streets and a lagging infrastructure of city services. Change was coming to the Greene County seat by the time these photos were made, for water lines were being laid by the backbreaking work of these young men along a residential street in 1905. Their labor made possible the services of the City Plumbing Company, the wagon for which is seen below, parked outside a portrait studio off Fruett Street that same year, with a dog peeking from beside a new bathtub and toilet.

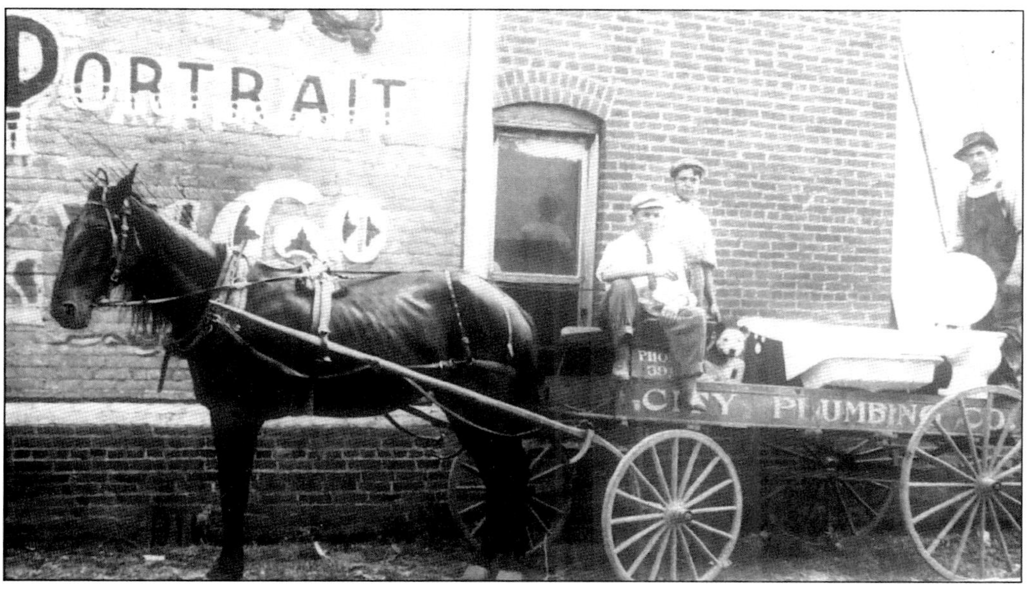

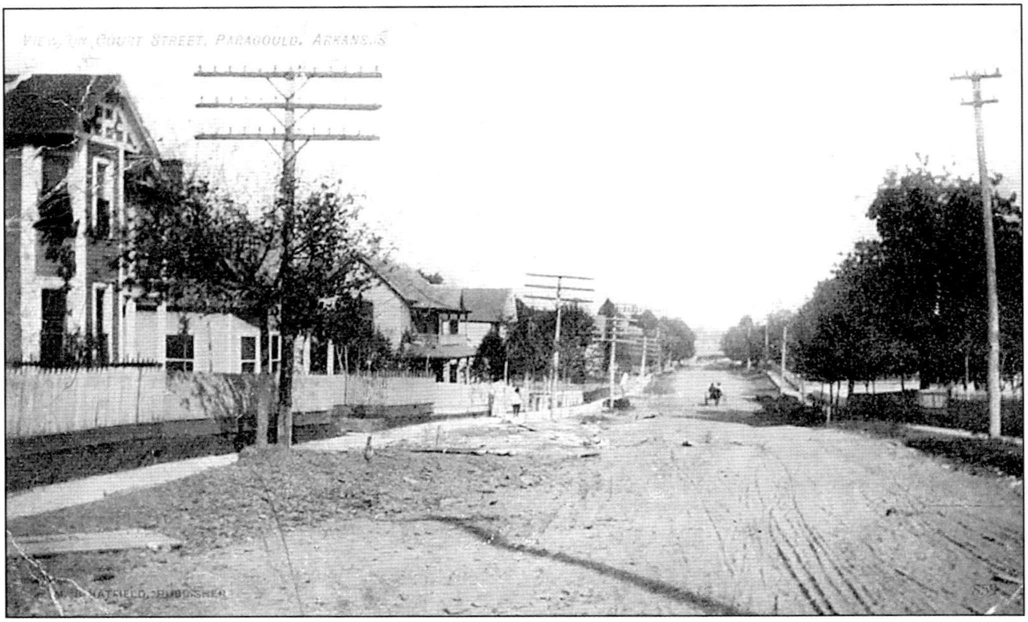

After Pruett Street, almost certainly Paragould's next main thoroughfare was Court Street, seen here *c.* 1908. At the time, the street passed large homes, its rutted tracks dusty in the summer and often a muddy hazard in winter. Yet sidewalks were present, and Paragould was meeting the young 20th century with many improvements on its business and civic agendas.

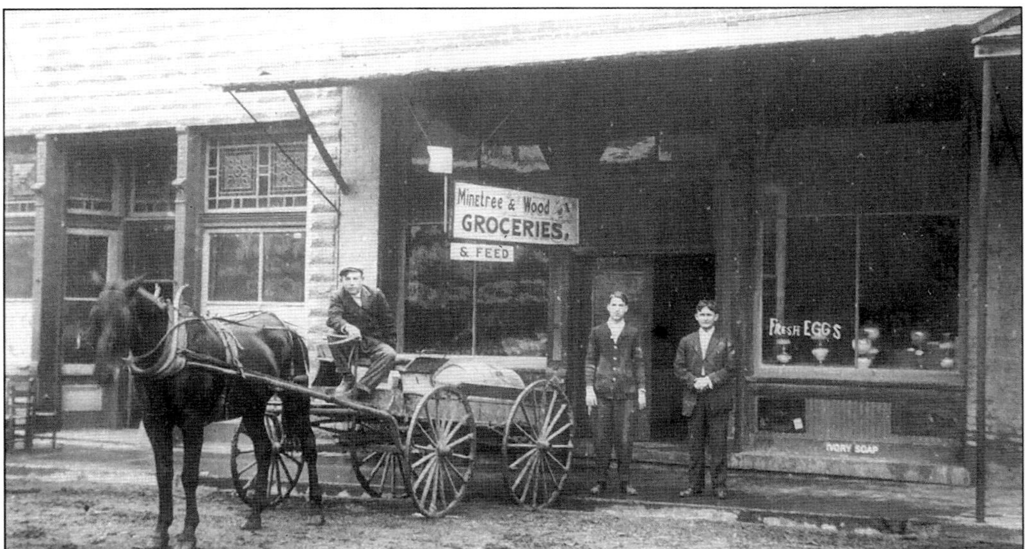

Among the many wagons traversing the rough dirt streets of 1905 Paragould was the delivery wagon of Minetree & Wood Groceries & Feed located at 702 West Junction. Typical of small town grocery stores, before the rise of supermarkets by the time of World War II, the store bought its fresh eggs (advertised in the window) from local farmers. A small sign below the window says "Ivory Soap," a hint of the name brands that would still be found a century later in the huge supermarkets of today.

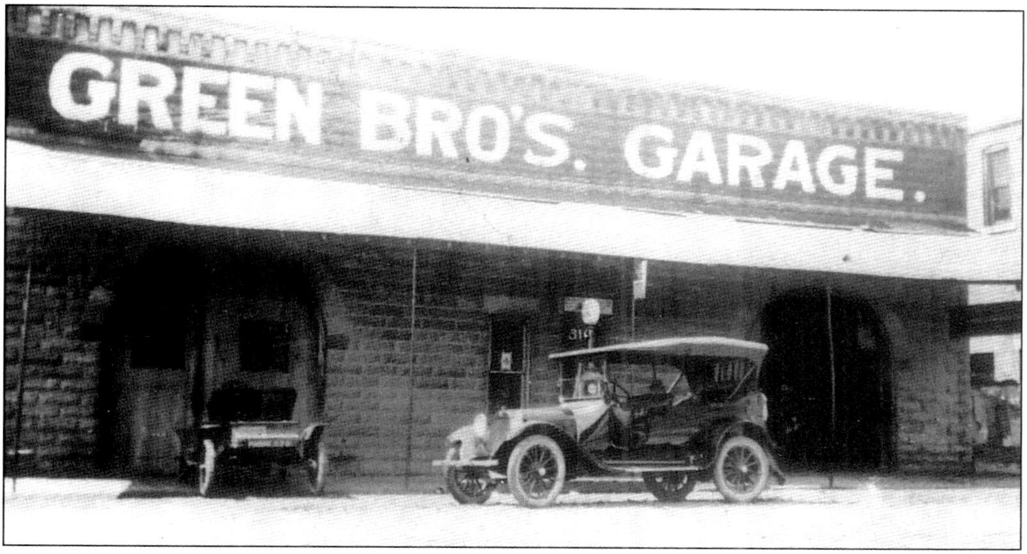

Though all the county roads were still unpaved—as were many of the streets of Paragould—by around 1910, the age of the automobile was closing in upon that of the horse and buggy. The years leading up to World War I saw the Green Brothers open both a garage and a "gas station," reportedly on the lower end of Pruett Street. The lone gravity-fed pump sat on the sidewalk outside the garage, where automobiles could pull up on the dirt street and fill up for perhaps 10¢ a gallon. The globe atop the pump read "Filtered Gasoline," while the sign above it advised that the garage was a "Sales & Service Depot for the United States Tire Co." On either side of the gas pump was an arched "service bay" door.

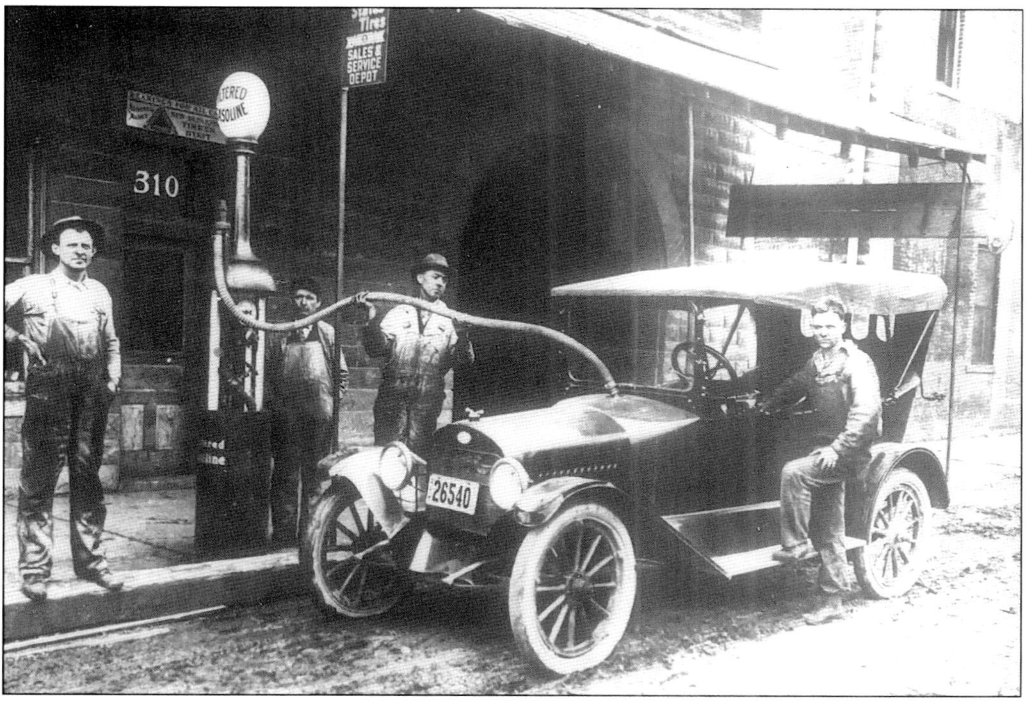

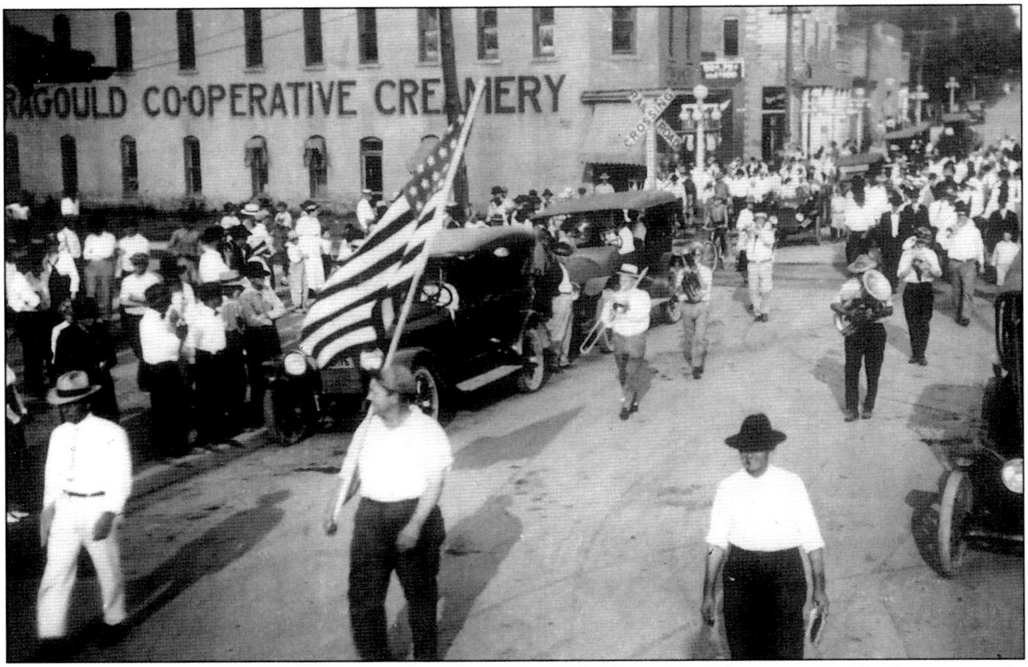

By 1916, a long line of automobiles had crowded out the horse and buggies that had once made up the Labor Day parade, seen here passing the Paragould Cooperative Creamery. By this time Pruett Street had been paved, a fact surely appreciated by the marching band members on what would have almost surely been a hot first Monday of September.

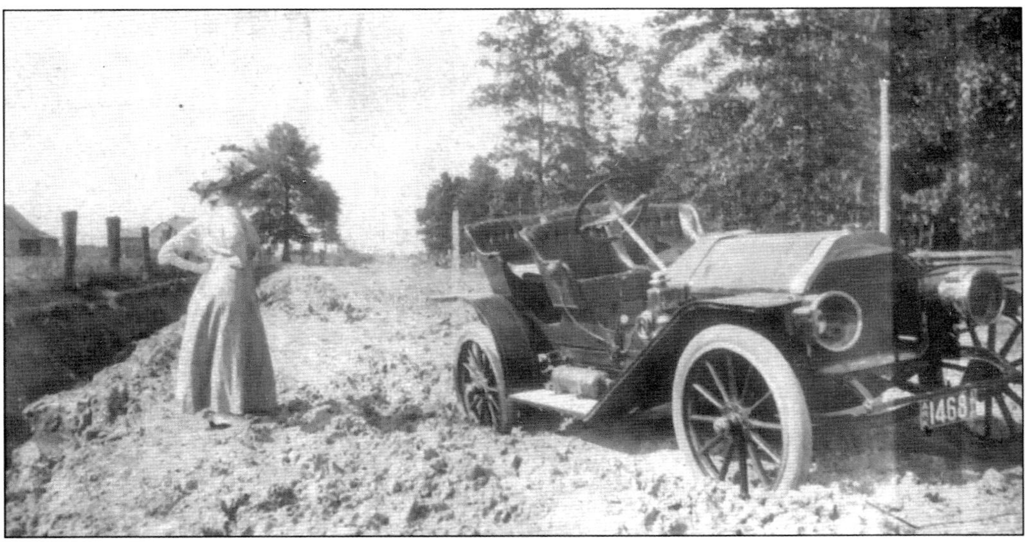

While pavement and sidewalks were starting to spread out through the city of Paragould, the roads leading to and from the town were slower to improve. This photo was made on the Jonesboro highway outside of Paragould c. 1912. The lady, exasperated with hands on hips, likely had been the passenger in the car with license plate #1468. The driver taking the picture was perhaps also standing in the deep mud. In such cases, it often took a local farmer's mules to extract the "horseless carriages" from the mire of Arkansas roads of the era.

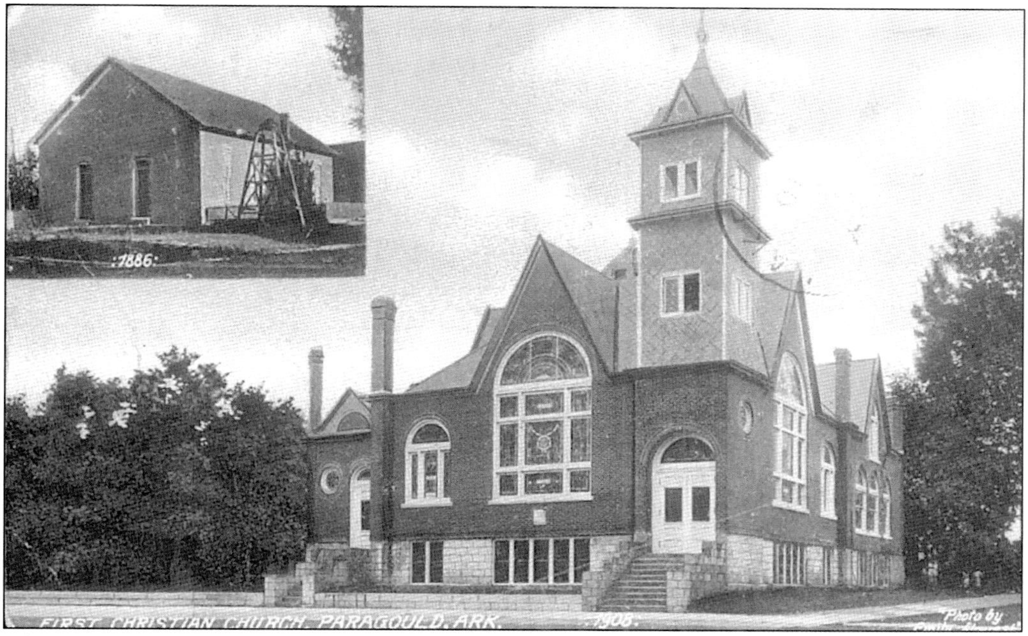

Like many emerging towns in early 20th century Arkansas, much pride was taken in area churches and schools as community landmarks. The progress made by the congregation of the First Christian Church is evident in the above 1910 card. The inset photo shows the small, original 1886 church, with a large bell in the yard, contrasted to the new, much more imposing structure opened in 1908 at a cost of $15,000 at the corner of Court and Third Streets. The congregation split over the question of having a piano in the new church, as some opposed any musical instruments. The building was torn down in the 1940s. The card's message read, "Mother is not expected to live and I am getting up every night, don't have time to write."

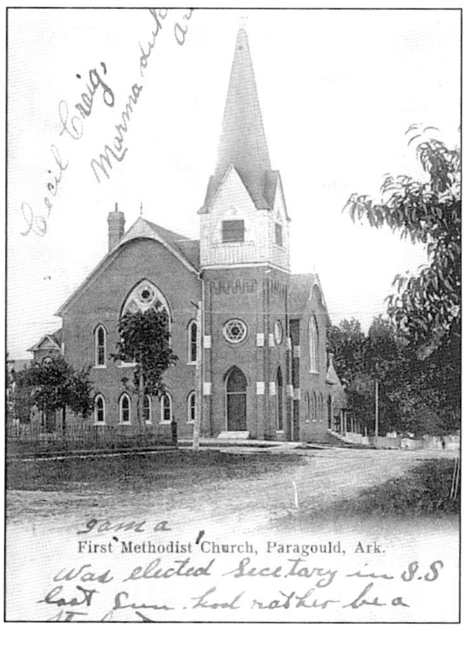

The Methodists laid claim to holding the first church services in Paragould, meeting on a chilly, February Sunday in 1882, with thirteen people in an unfinished store building on West Main. The service had been arranged by Jonesboro circuit preacher Reverend F.E. Taylor; the congregation sat on rough plank benches, with the cold room lit by lanterns. In 1884, those humble beginnings gave birth to this handsome building at the corner of Emerson and Third. The card's 1908 message to Massachusetts read, "Was elected Secretary in the S.S. [Sunday School] last Sunday but rather be a student. Please send me a postcard of Bunker Hill Monument." The growing congregation worshipped in the building until moving to a larger one in 1926, at West Main and Fourth streets.

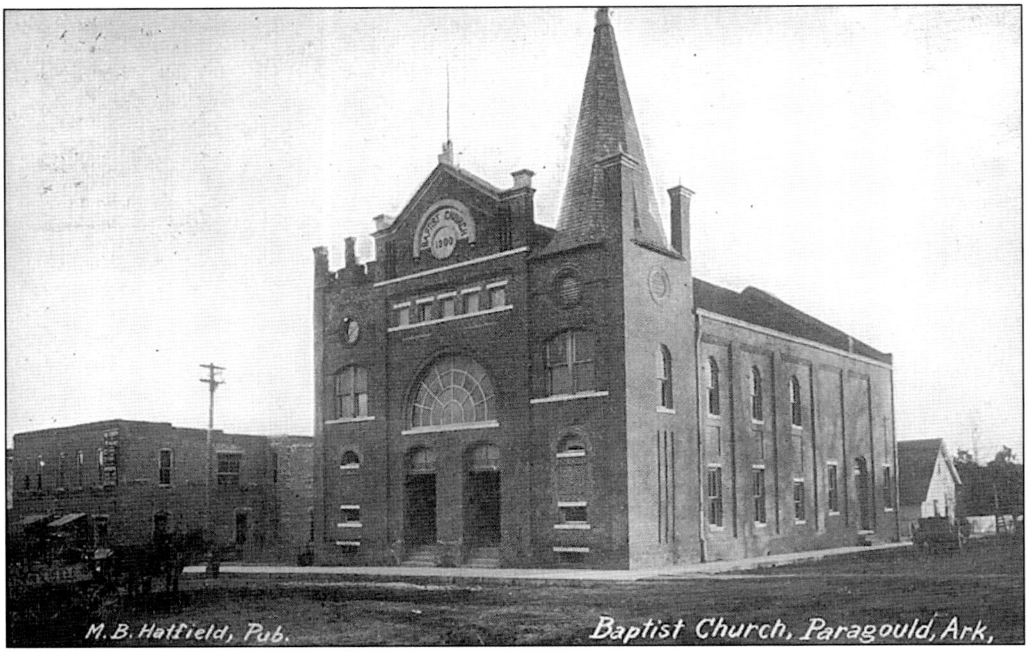

Paragould's First Baptist Church claims a very interesting history of structures. Formed in 1885, and initially known as Beulah Baptist, the congregation erected a one-room building. In 1900, they purchased the Opera House at the corner of Court and Second Streets, which had opened in 1893, with a large stage and many opulent appointments. It proved too large and elegant to be profitable in a small town, but with the construction of a steeple, as seen above, little else was needed to convert the theater to a house of worship. The building is gone today. The congregation outgrew the opera house by 1924, and built the new building, seen below, which still stands today.

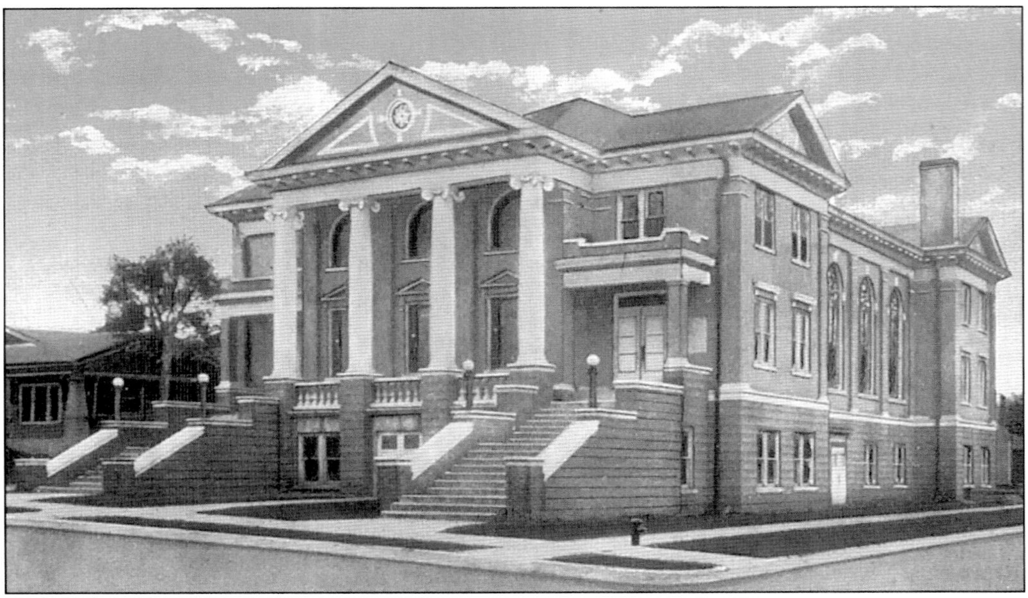

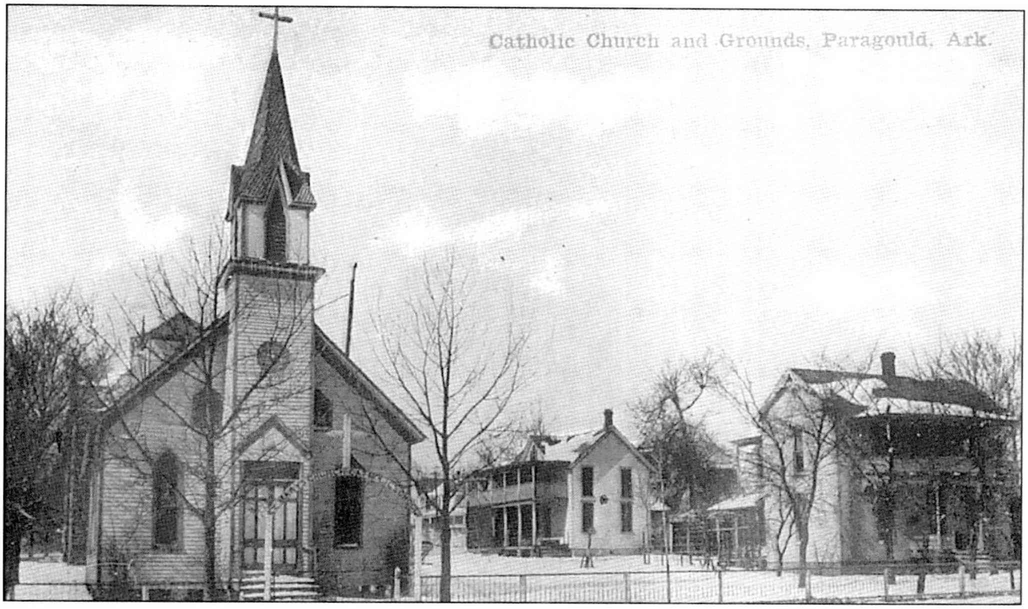

The first Catholic Mass held in Paragould was offered in December of 1883, in the Commercial Hotel, by Monsignor John Weibel of Jonesboro. Msgr. Weibel, a native of Switzerland, devoted himself to the growing flock in northeast Arkansas and, by 1889, found enough Catholic families to support a church building in Paragould. Initially, the structure seen above was built for another denomination, which had found it unacceptable upon completion. The Catholics of the city bought it for $625 and moved it to a lot purchased for $300 at West Highland and Second streets. For another $380 a steeple and three bells were added in 1895. Today a modern church serves the Catholic families of the area at the same site.

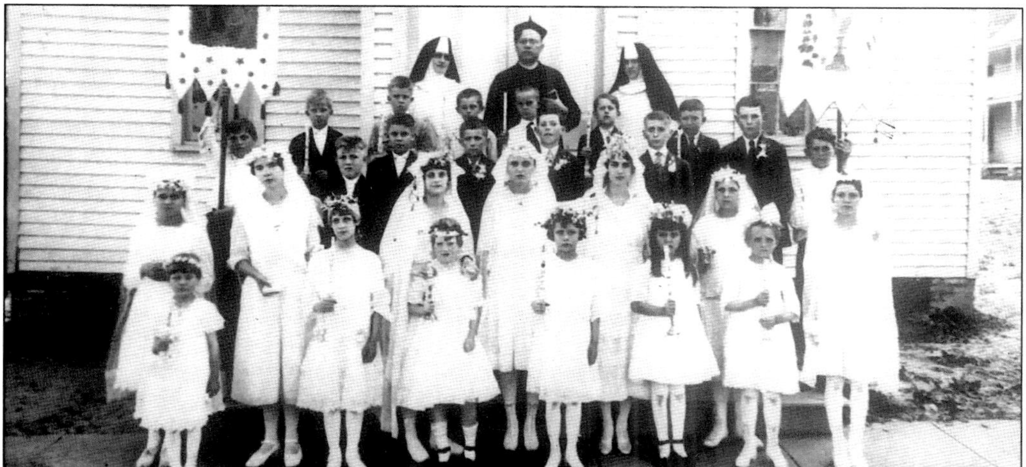

St. Mary's humble frame church was the annual backdrop for a portrait of the first Holy Communion class, like this one seen *c.* 1905 with the pastor and nuns who taught them. Each child holds a white candle, and wears outfits still traditional today for this sacrament—dark suits for the boys, white dresses and veils or flowers for the girls. Scuffed knees are evident on the girls' white stockings, perhaps from the wooden kneelers in the church. Many of the children would have been students at the adjacent school operated by the sisters.

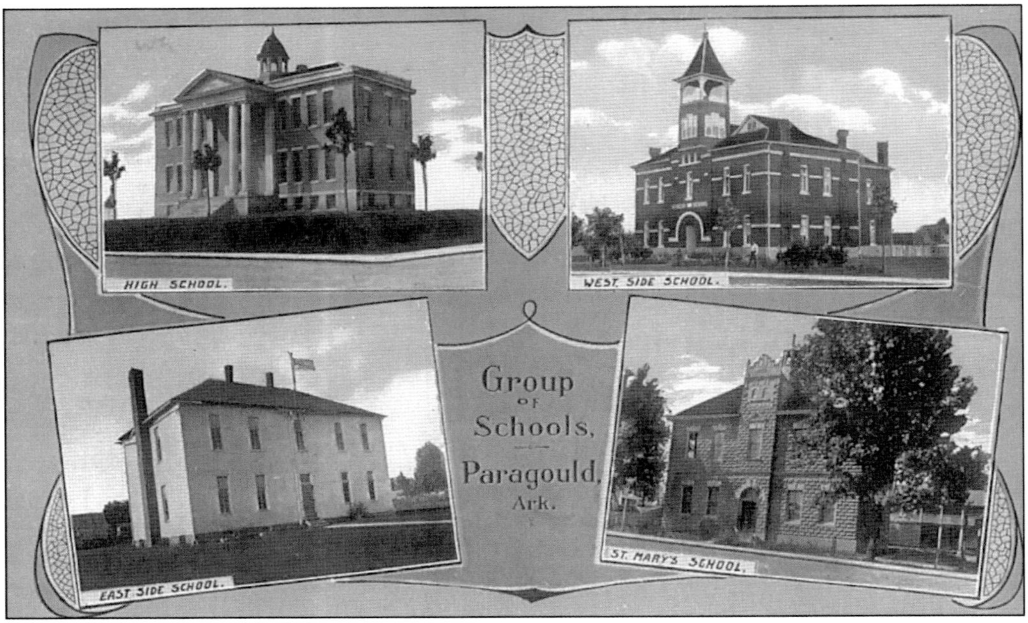

The first school in Paragould opened in 1883, in a one-room building on West Main Street, which was shared with the Methodists who worshipped there on Sundays. By the time this card was mailed in 1916, the city proudly showcased from bottom left, clockwise, East Side School, the new high school, West Side School, and St. Mary's Catholic School. If the teachers in the three public schools met the statewide average, they would have earned less than $400 for teaching a school year of approximately 120 days.

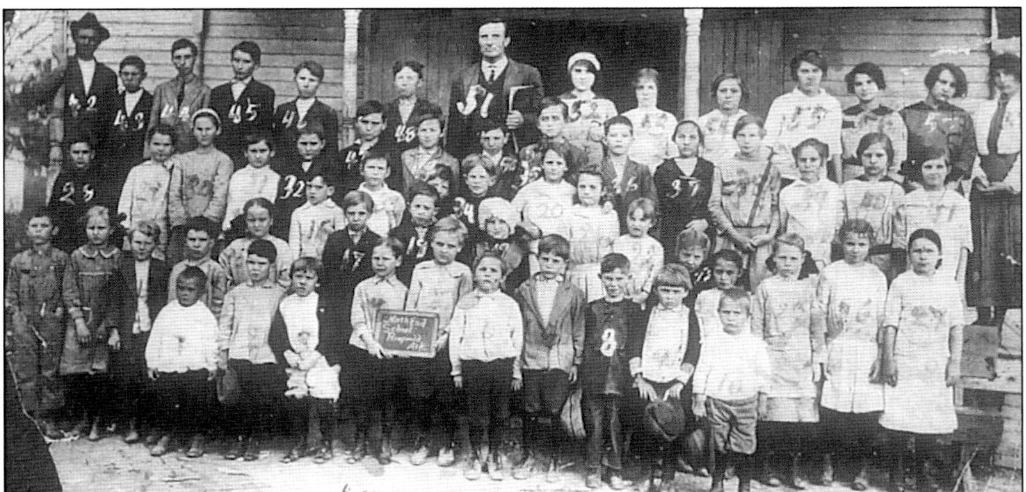

At least once a year, all the students and teachers from each school would pose for a group photograph on the steps of their school, much like the class photos made today. Such was the case in 1914, with the children of Paragould's North End School, who posed with their teacher, Mr. G.F. Bond, standing in the center. It is likely that the children were in grades one through eight, at a time when the average Arkansas school year was around 110 days. The school was located on what is now Royal Street; it closed in the early 1950s.

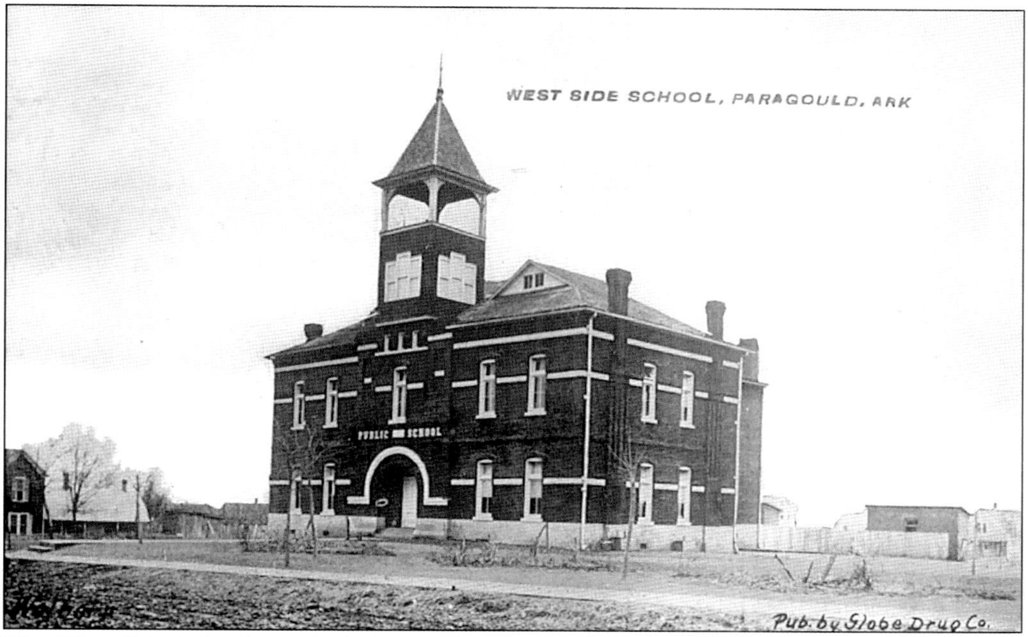

The West Side School was built during the 1890s, originally housing all grades one through ten, before the city had a high school. A student living nearby later wrote that she went home during recess to bring back a bucket of drinking water from the family's well, as the city lacked a water system at the time. The school, seen also on page 42, burned in 1918.

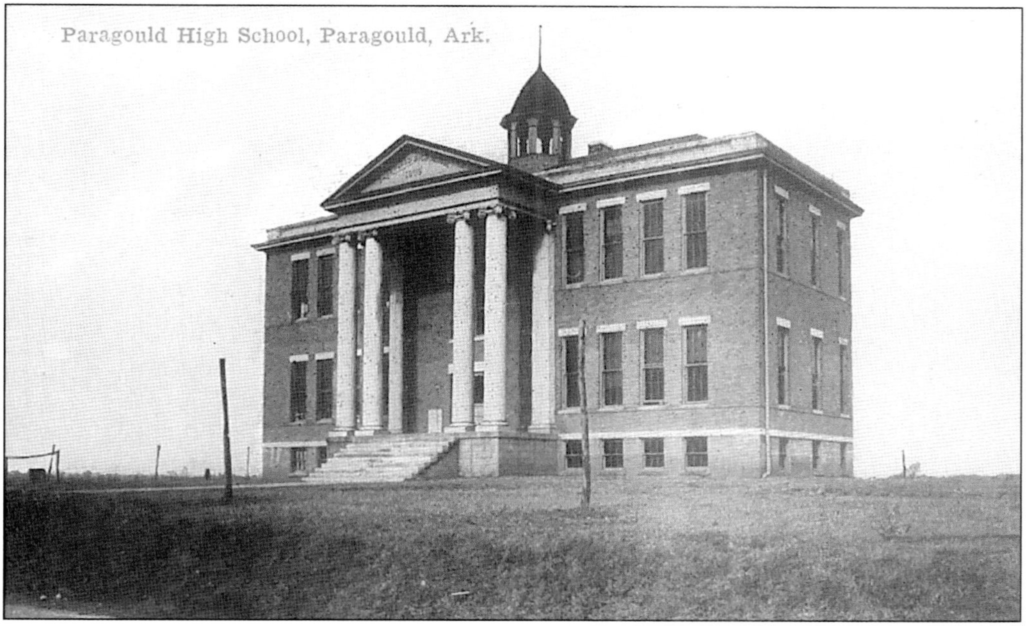

Paragould's first high school opened in 1909, at Main and Ninth Streets, and offered classes not previously available, such as art and music. The high school relocated in 1926, to a large new building at Court and Seventh Streets. The columned former high school served younger grades for years before being demolished in 1954.

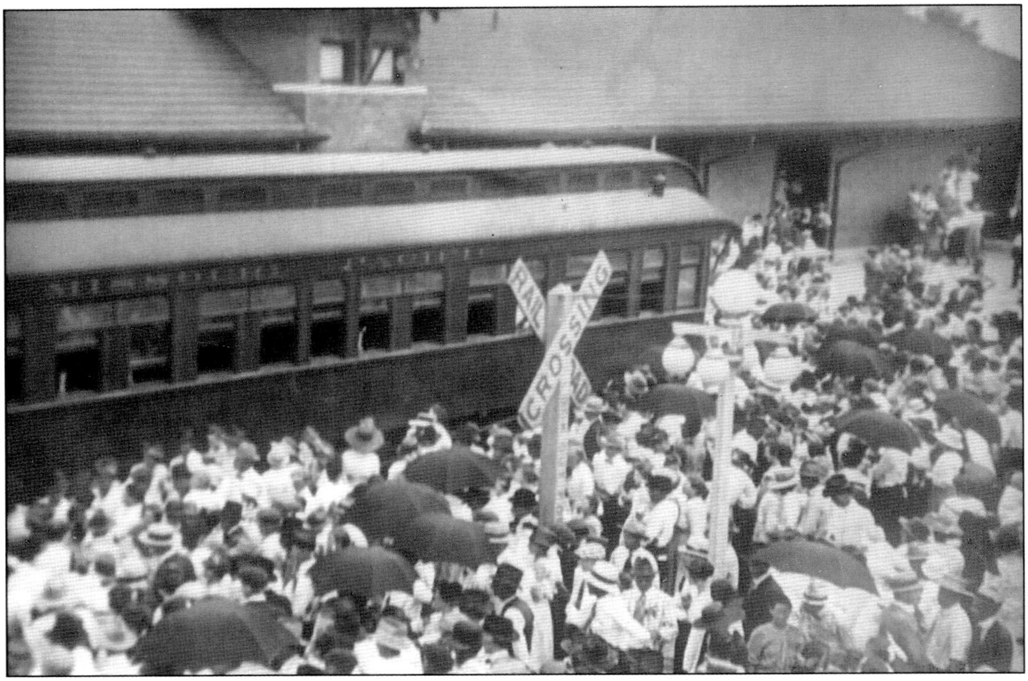

"120 BOYS LEAVE FOR CAMP PIKE" read the front page story in Paragould, for the young men of Greene County had heeded President Woodrow Wilson's call and shipped out for Army training on June 24, 1918. The entire group met first at the Greene County Courthouse, where Reverend A.C. Cloyes presented each with Bibles; they then marched to the train depot, with cheering crowds following. Not all would return home, sadly; Greene County lost some 40 young men in World War I.

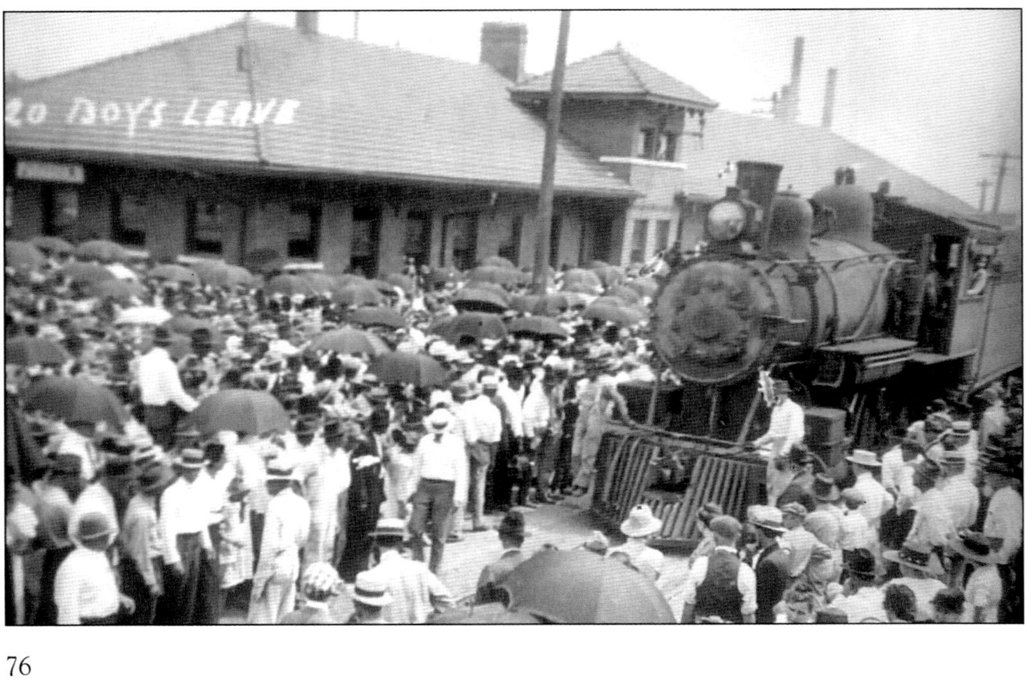

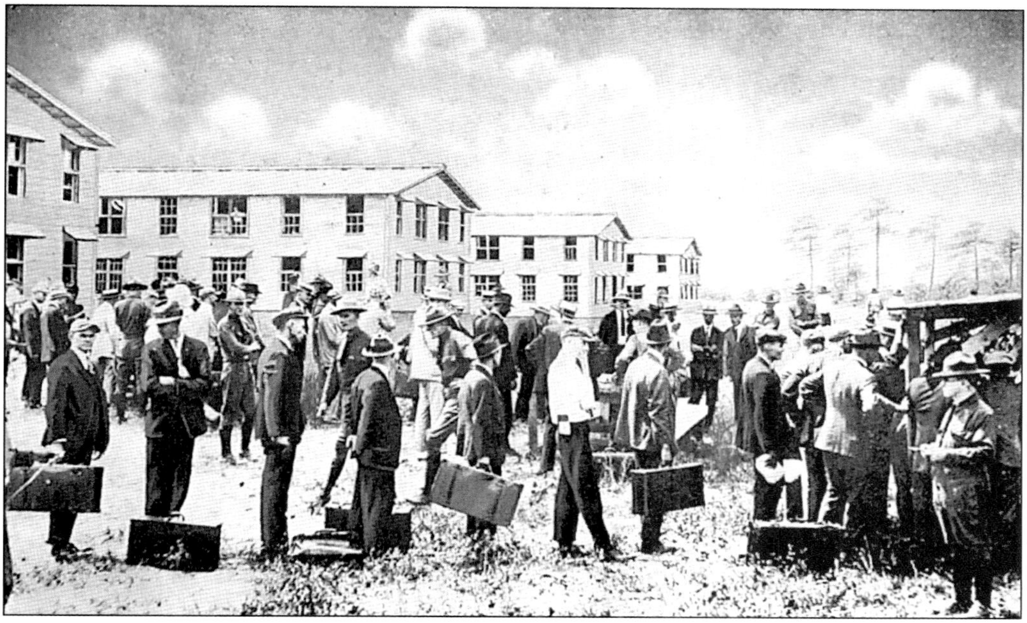

The 120-man contingent that shipped out of Paragould on the trains of June 24, 1918, were bound for the U.S. Army training post located near Little Rock, ready for basic training just as was the unidentified group seen above. The massive camp, consisting of some 2,000 buildings, sprang up in the winter of 1917–1918, in what had been only forests and farms. Camp Pike had its own train station to receive the men, mostly eager to train for the conflict raging in France. After the war, the camp was deactivated, but it was put into service again, under the new name of Camp Robinson, with the coming of World War II.

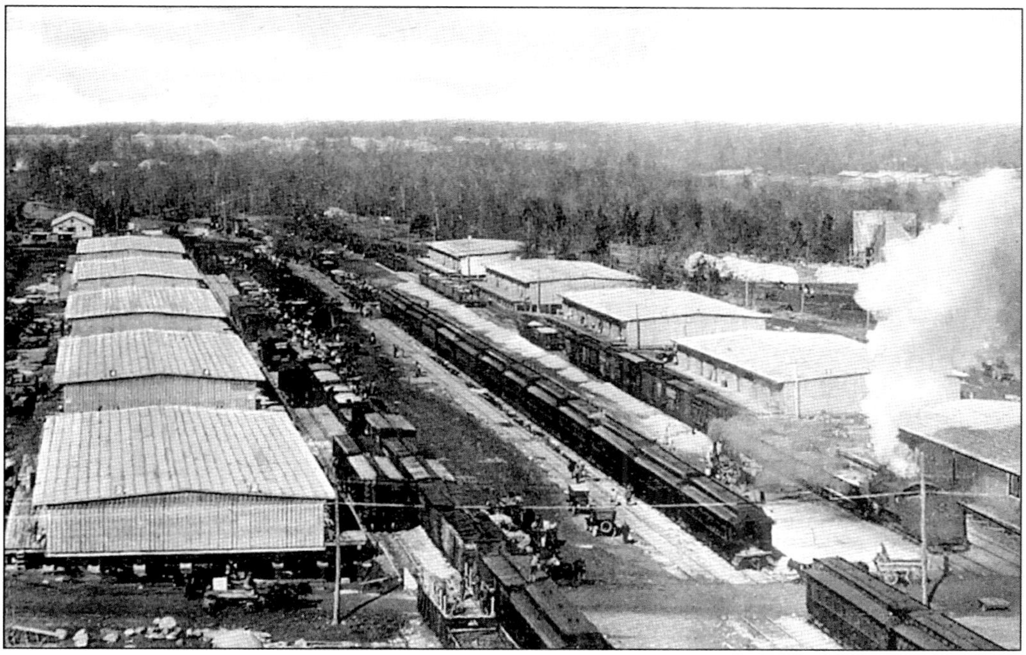

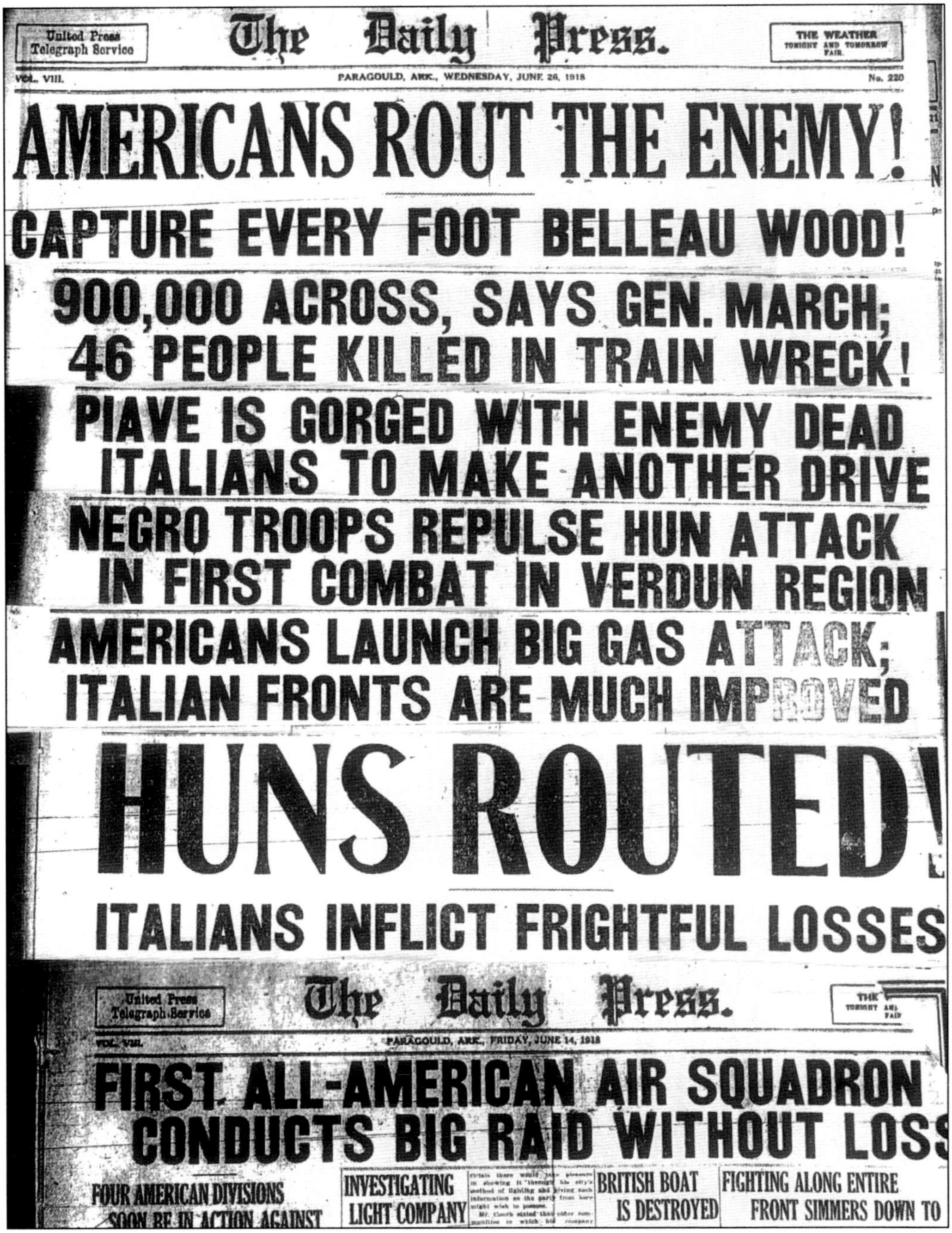

United Press Telegraph Service

The Daily Press.

THE WEATHER TONIGHT AND TOMORROW FAIR.

VOL. VIII. PARAGOULD, ARK., WEDNESDAY, JUNE 26, 1918 No. 220

AMERICANS ROUT THE ENEMY!

CAPTURE EVERY FOOT BELLEAU WOOD!

900,000 ACROSS, SAYS GEN. MARCH; 46 PEOPLE KILLED IN TRAIN WRECK!

PIAVE IS GORGED WITH ENEMY DEAD ITALIANS TO MAKE ANOTHER DRIVE

NEGRO TROOPS REPULSE HUN ATTACK IN FIRST COMBAT IN VERDUN REGION

AMERICANS LAUNCH BIG GAS ATTACK; ITALIAN FRONTS ARE MUCH IMPROVED

HUNS ROUTED!

ITALIANS INFLICT FRIGHTFUL LOSSES

United Press Telegraph Service

The Daily Press.

VOL. VIII. PARAGOULD, ARK., FRIDAY, JUNE 14, 1918

FIRST ALL-AMERICAN AIR SQUADRON CONDUCTS BIG RAID WITHOUT LOSS

FOUR AMERICAN DIVISIONS SOON BE IN ACTION AGAINST

INVESTIGATING LIGHT COMPANY

BRITISH BOAT IS DESTROYED

FIGHTING ALONG ENTIRE FRONT SIMMERS DOWN TO

During the summer of 1918, the front-page headlines of Paragould's *Daily Press* screamed reports from the trenches of France, where raged the greatest war in history up to that time. This composite of headlines reflects only a sample of seven days during the summer of 1918. The paper proclaimed "900,000 across," along with the glories won by "Negro troops" on the battlefield and the bold victories in the sky from a war in which fighter planes were introduced as a military tool for the first time.

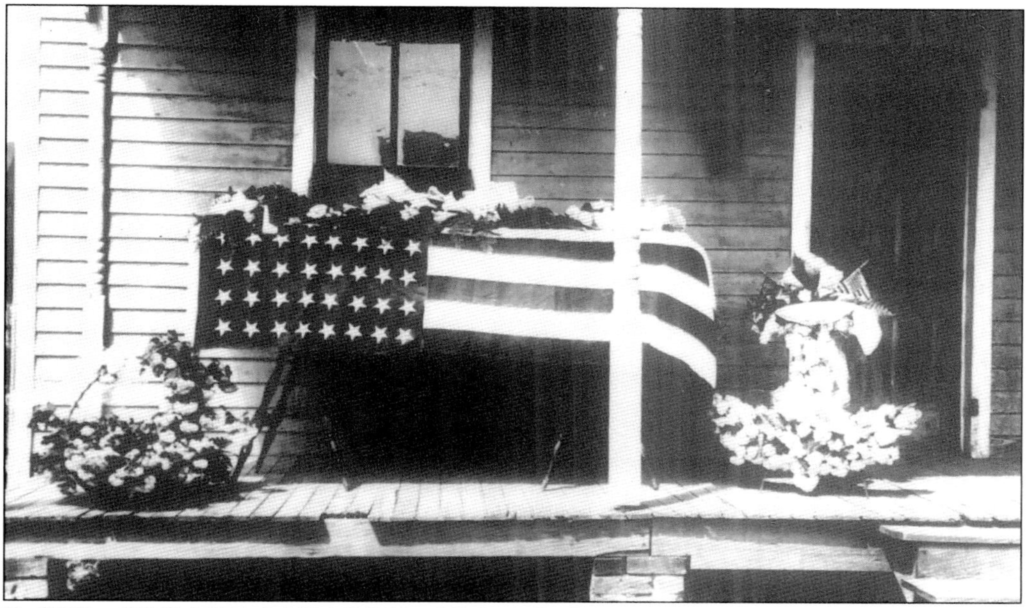

"I WILL GIVE THE LAST DROP OF MY BLOOD FOR MY COUNTRY," were the remembered words of 23-year-old Ranzie Adams, as he had prepared to leave for the Army in the summer of 1917. On April 22, 1918, Ranzie shipped out for France, telling his mother, Mrs. Emma Mayo of the Greene County community of Bethel, "I willingly give my last drop of blood, gladly, before I would see those Huns overrun our land and deal with you and sister as they have with women in Belgium and France." Sadly, Private Adams would live little more than a month after arriving in Europe.

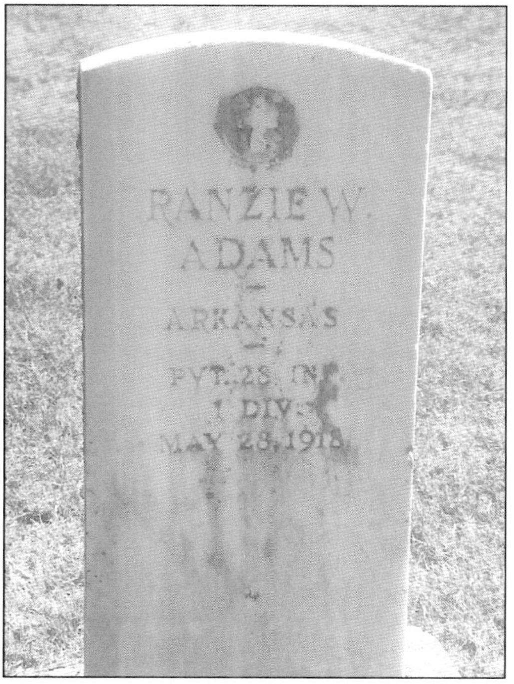

"Spirit of Ranzie Adams Wafted Into Eternity Through the Sacred Folds of Old Glory," read the June 27, 1918 newspaper account telling Paragould that Private Ranzie Adams had been killed in action fighting the Germans on the Western Front of France on May 28. His flag-decorated casket was taken to his mother's home in the Bethel community, where she said, "It nearly breaks my heart to lose my boy. To have died so far from us and his home, but I am glad to give him for his country. Glad that he had the strong heart, courage and honor to volunteer." The earthly remains of Private Adams, buried with full military honors, rest today in the cemetery of Browns Chapel Cemetery, outside Paragould.

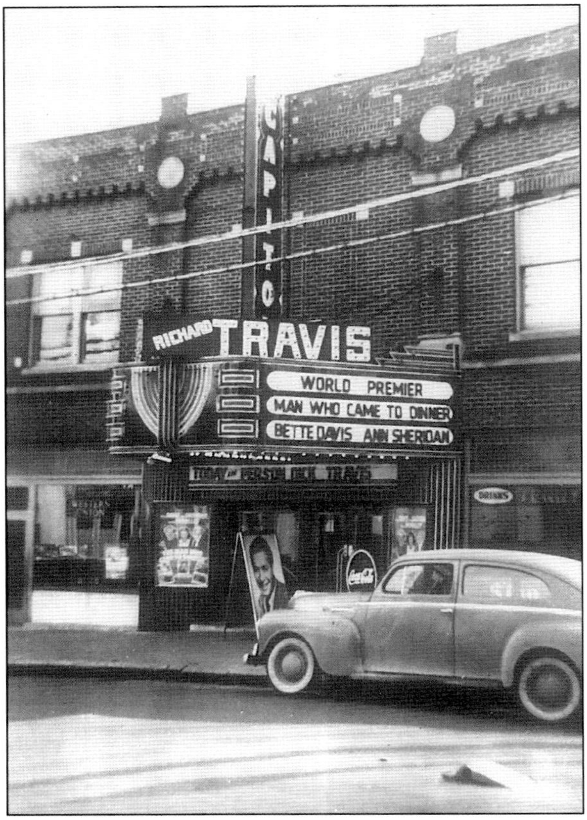

As the 20th century rolled on, the "show" that is life rolled with it in Greene County, through good times and bad. Gone are the community leaders—like Trice, Hasty, and Meriwether—who built the town, and war heroes like Ranzie Adams. Gone are such historic structures as the Vandervoort Hotel and Bertigs' Department Store. Movies no longer screen at the Capitol Theater as they did in this c. 1940 photo, nor do Diggs' Ice Cream wagons still come down the tree-shaded blocks to delight children with nickels clutched in their hands. However, much of the past remains, in the county's heritage and its hardworking people, and in the delightful slice of middle America found in Paragould and Greene County, Arkansas, as the 21st century opens.

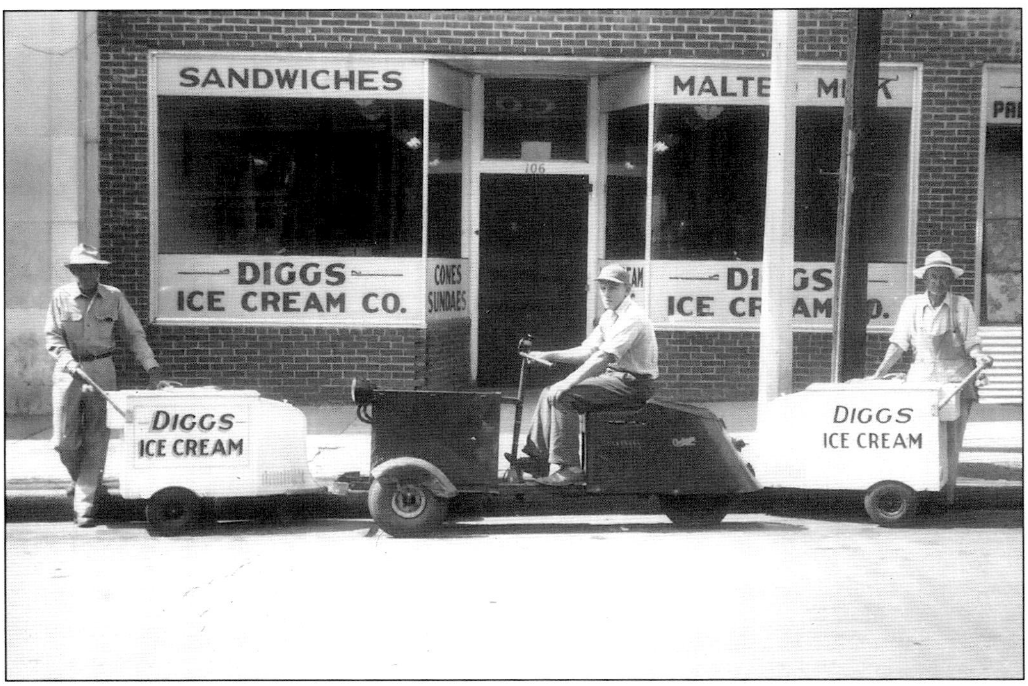

Three

JONESBORO AND CRAIGHEAD COUNTY

Craighead County, Arkansas, was formed as the nation was nearing the brink of civil war in 1859. The Arkansas Senate, taking note of the expanding population, pushed through a measure to carve the new county out of the then very large Greene, Mississippi, and Poinsett Counties. The measure passed over the vocal opposition of State Senator Thomas Craighead, who objected to downsizing Mississippi County, which he represented. In a gesture of goodwill, Senator William Jones of St. Francis and Poinsett Counties, who was the victor on the issue, moved to name the new county after Senator Craighead.

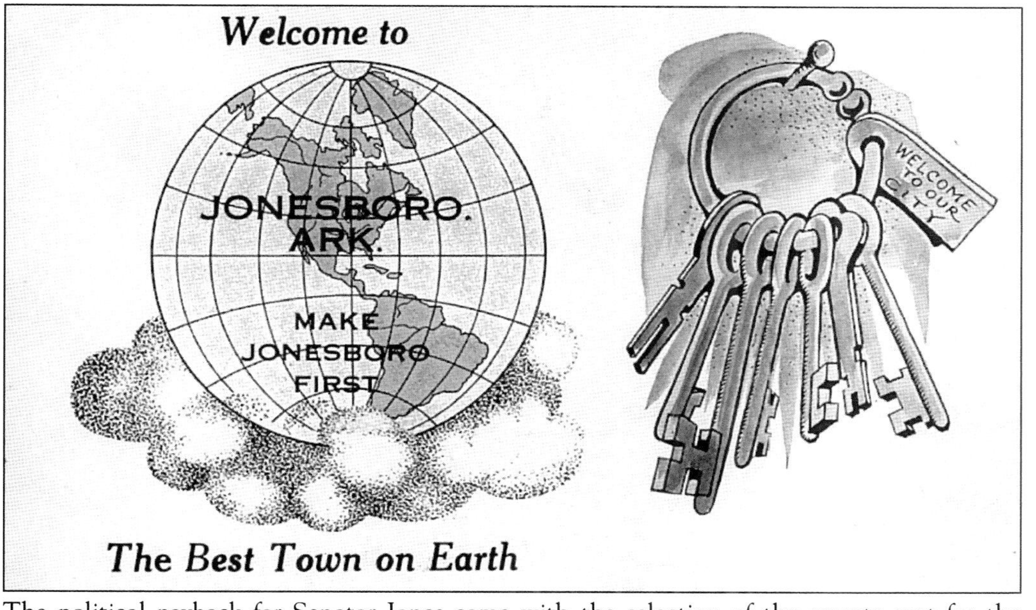

The political payback for Senator Jones came with the selection of the county seat for the newly created Craighead County, after four horsemen set out to find the highest point of land on which to begin a new town and seat of government. Thus was born the city of Jonesboro, named for the Senator. From an initial recorded population of 50 souls in 1860, the town today has more than 50,000 people and is the economic center of northeastern Arkansas. In the intervening 140 years, much history has transpired. Part of the pride of the city was shown on this 1915 postcard, proclaiming it "The Best Town on Earth."

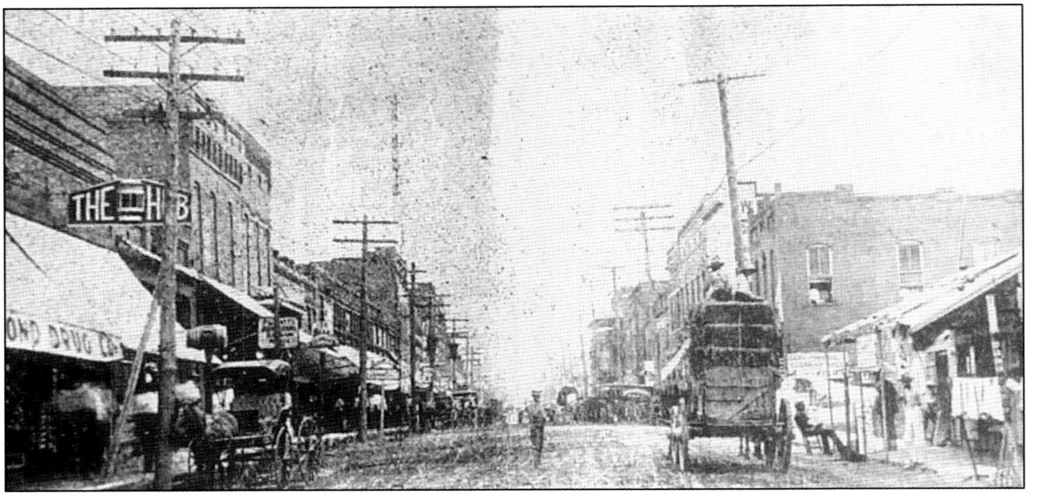

By the 1880s, Jonesboro was gaining population, hotels, churches, and industry; it counted a population nearing 1,000 in the city and some 8,000 in Craighead County, almost all of whom were farmers. Around 1885, when this photo of Main Street was made, businesses like the Hub clothing store and Diamond Drug, both seen on the left, stretched out for blocks. The frontier feel was still there with the muddy street full of wagons and horses, but the city was on the move.

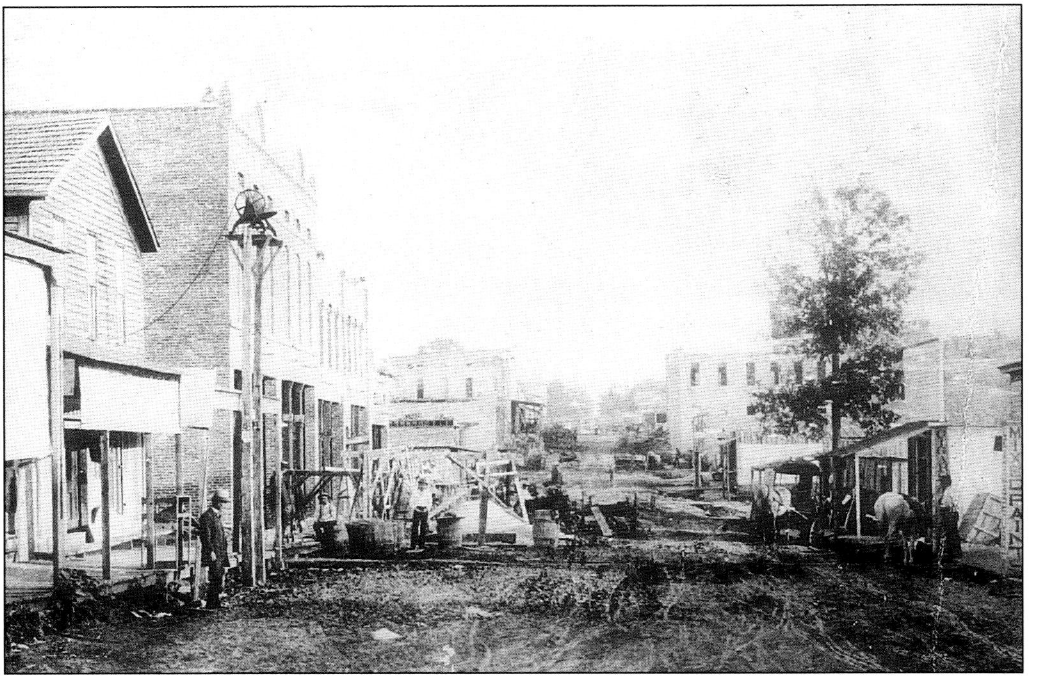

By 1890, Jonesboro's population had surged to 2,065—an eightfold increase from the 1880 census. This view, looking south on Main from Huntington Avenue, shows the scaffolding and construction that occurred as brick buildings were replacing more of the frame structures sitting along the muddy, rutted street. A great fire in 1889, which began in Marcus Berger's Saloon, had wiped out many of the frame buildings in the town. City fathers determined that the future of Jonesboro must be in brick buildings.

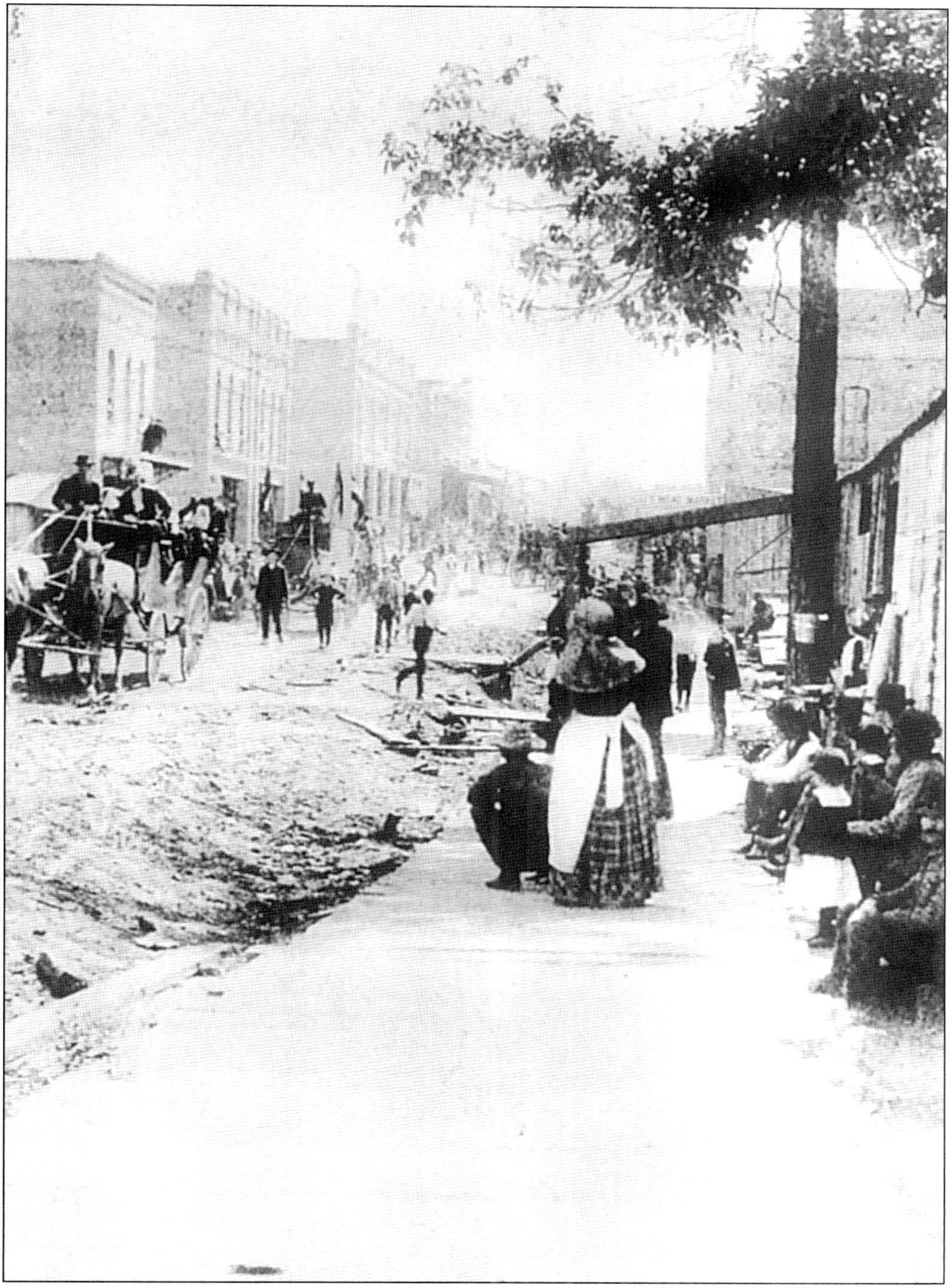

By 1890—on what was likely a Saturday—much of Jonesboro's population crowded the streets, apparently watching a parade. The women in long dresses kept to the relative safety of the plank sidewalks as the wagons, marching band, and other parade participants came down the rough dirt track that was Main Street.

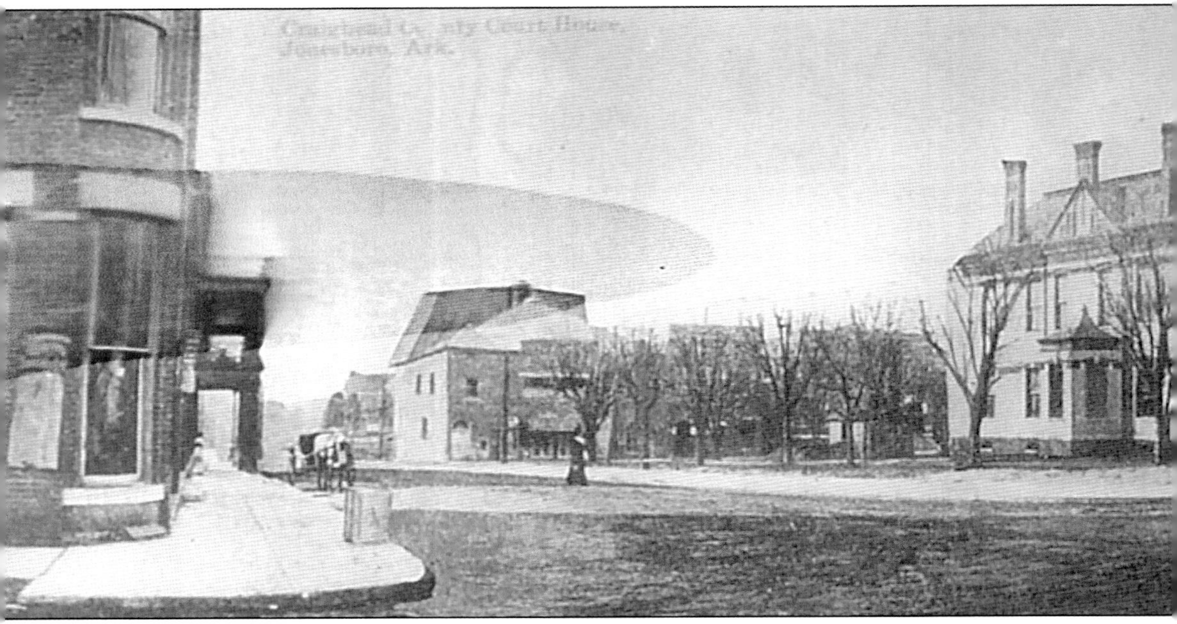

Craighead County has had a series of misfortunes with its courthouses. The first was erected in 1869, but burned later the same year. A rented store building used as a replacement burned in 1876; a man named Marion Sanders was sentenced to two years in prison for setting the fire. The replacement was built on the same site, but—alas—it burned in 1878. The three fires

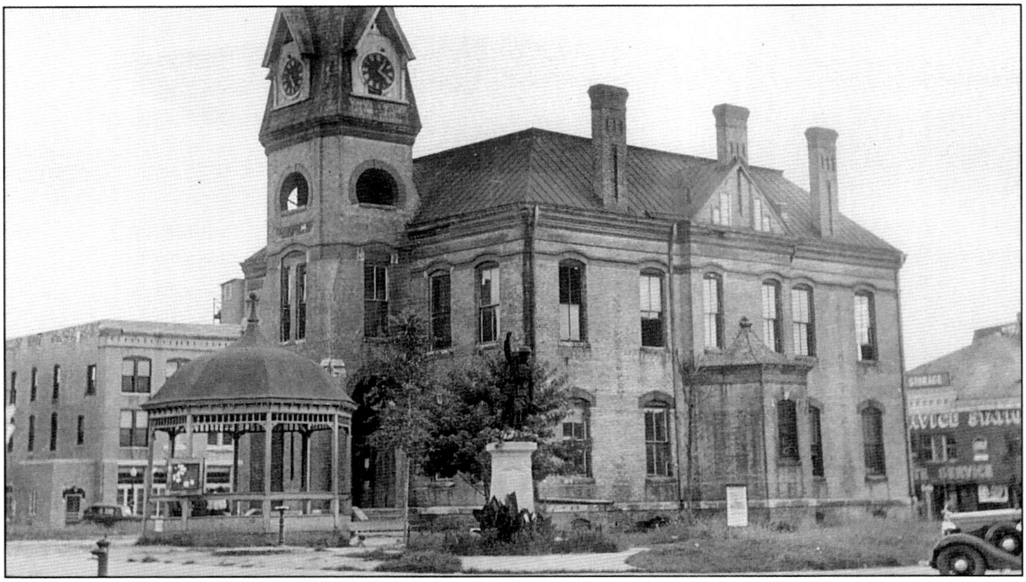

The 1886 Craighead County Courthouse fared much better than its three predecessors, surviving and serving into the early 1930s. The eastern side of Craighead County was served by a smaller, 1883 wooden frame courthouse, which is still standing and has been placed on the National Register in the small farming community of Lake City. However, the main courthouse in Jonesboro was aging and crowded, and it was razed c. 1933, sharing the fate of many of the courthouses erected in the late 1800s in Arkansas.

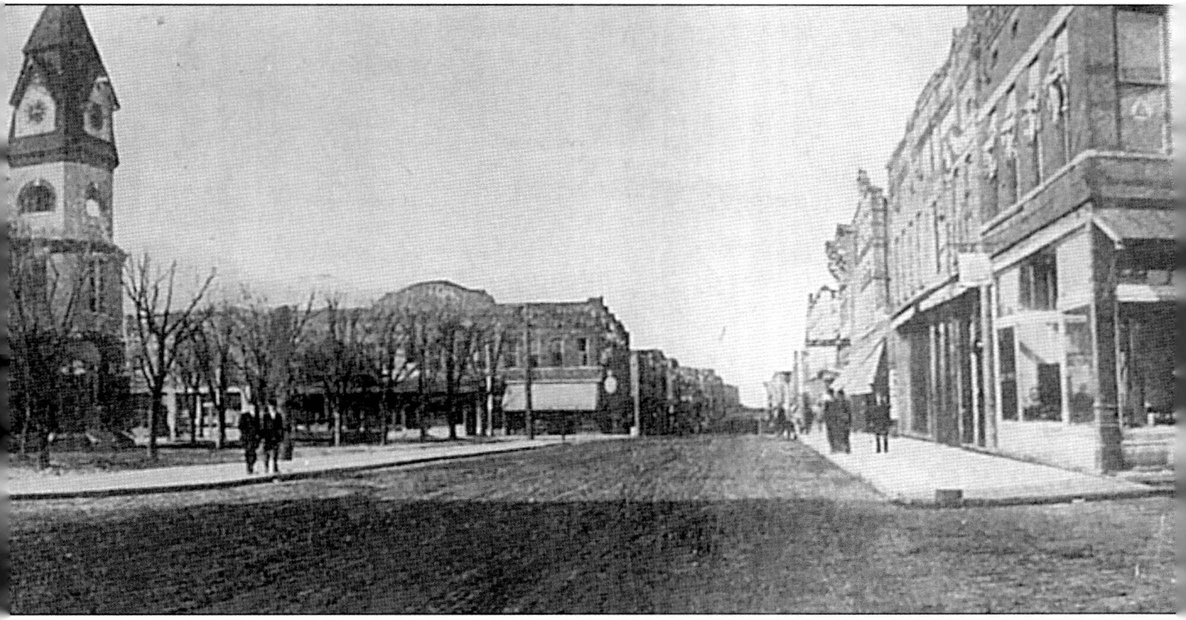

cost much more than the structures; all the county's early records were lost in the flames. After more years in a converted store building, the affairs of county government finally moved in 1886, into a handsome new $16,000 courthouse, seen above, in the center of the city.

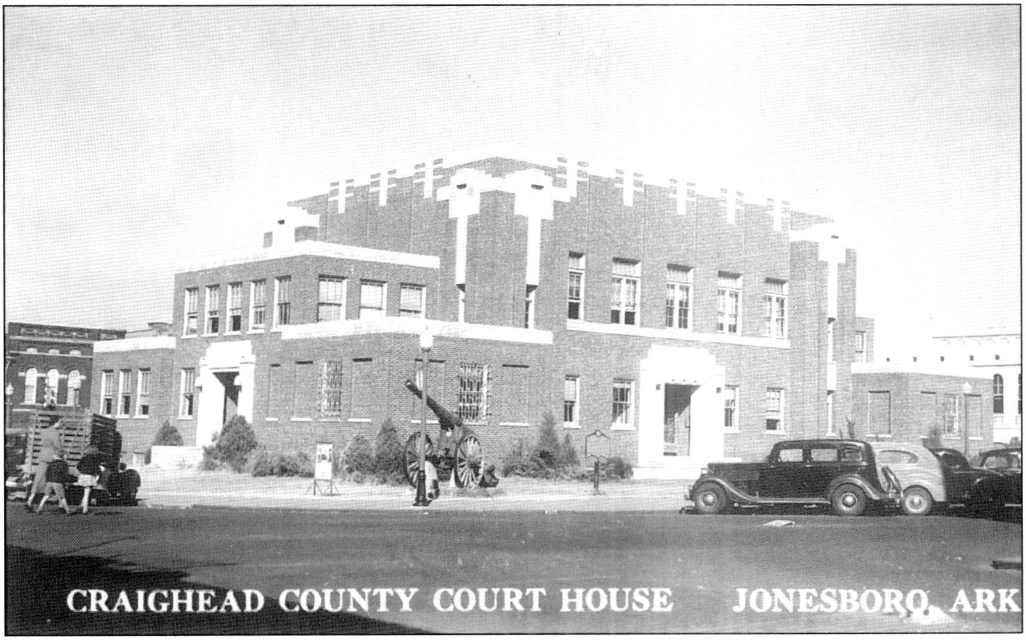

Seen here on a 1940 postcard, the art-deco style Craighead County courthouse had been erected in 1934, and still serves today. The card's message to California reads, "It's been over 100 degrees the last seven days. I attended the 'Tomato Festival' last week and they're wilder than I thought possible—it's said that there is a bounty on democrats."

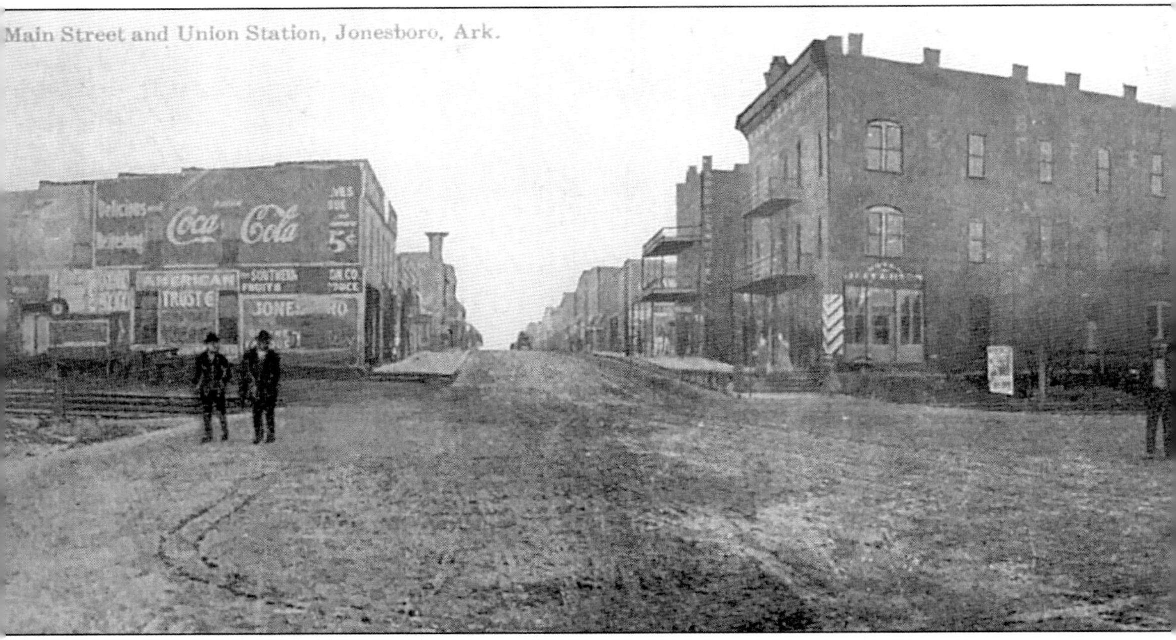

The first rail service to reach Jonesboro came in 1882; the Texas and St. Louis was a narrow-gauge railroad that eventually succumbed to financial problems. The Cotton Belt Route was formed in 1891, and would serve the area into the 1960s. At the turn of the century the railroad erected the Union Station at the end of Main Street; one end was used by the Cotton Belt and the other by the Frisco Railroad. The two railroads ran their tracks only a block apart in Jonesboro. Passengers alighting from the several passenger trains that stopped at the station each day had only a short walk to the stores and hotels of the city, still pictured with dirt streets

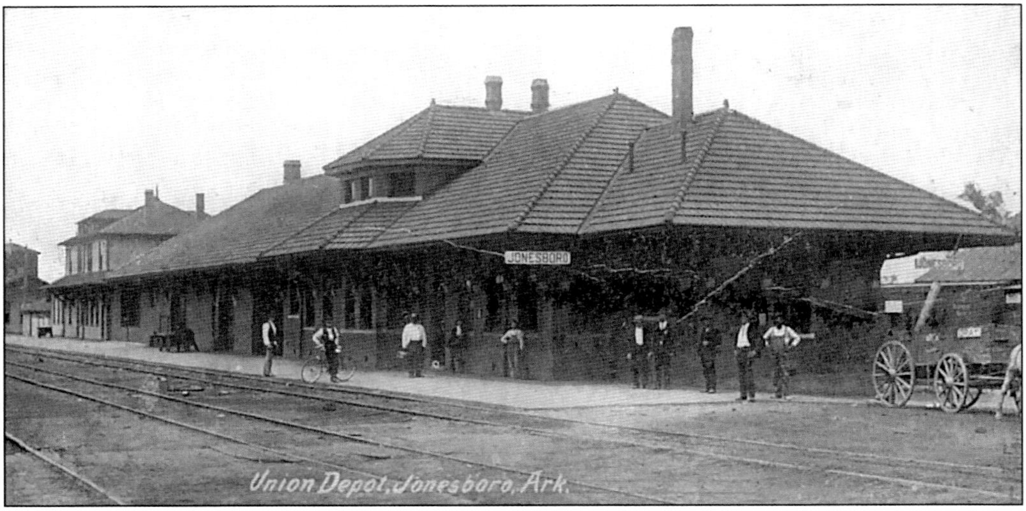

The Cotton Belt Railroad's tracks came out of southeastern Missouri, through Paragould to Jonesboro, then diagonally across the state and into Texas. The rail line brought freight, such as goods to stock the local stores, much of which could have been transported from the depot in the horse-drawn wagon to the right; the sign "dray" designates the local delivery wagons. The depot was razed in the 1980s; on the site today is a highway overpass spanning the tracks.

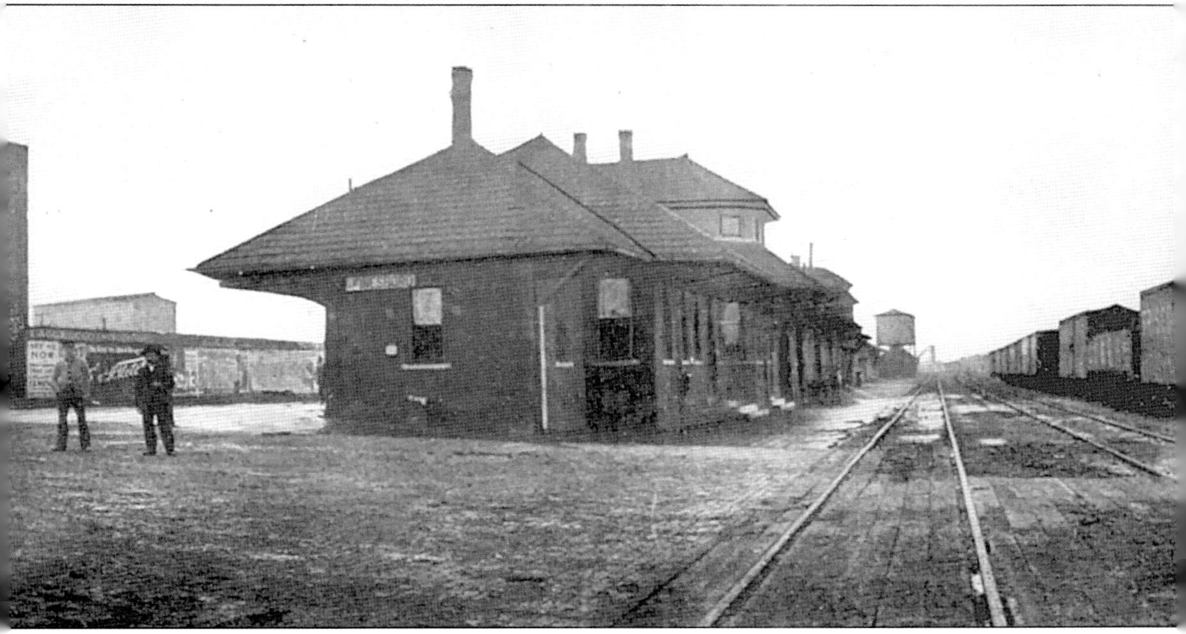

on this rare 1911 double postcard. The sender of the card wrote of a lonely Christmas: "Here is our Union Station, would be glad to go down there to meet any of you folks. We ate Christmas dinner all alone for the first time in my life here. Received several nice presents, my brother from KC sent me a fine pair of spectacles in a plush case, Willie got some fancy hankerchiefs. Your Uncle Charley gave ma a pretty broach and I received a postcard from most all of the relatives," wrote Aunt Sarah Smith to a niece in Kansas.

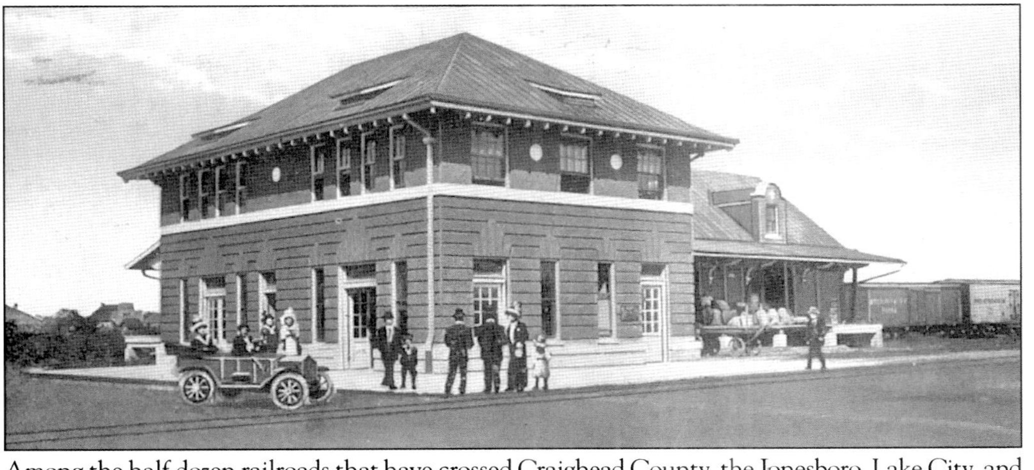

Among the half-dozen railroads that have crossed Craighead County, the Jonesboro, Lake City, and Eastern Railroad lays claim to having been formed locally. In 1898, investors funded the difficult construction of a line through the swamps and dense hardwood forests of the "sunken" lands, still impacted by the 1811 New Madrid earthquake. In 1902, the J.L.C. & E. hauled 65,817 passengers and 11,447 cars of freight. The handsome brick depot was erected in 1911, at the corner of Main & Johnson Streets, at a cost of $10,000. "Through Arkansas today, will reach Waco Sunday night," were the words of a traveler who stopped off at the Jonesboro depot of the J.L.C. & E. in 1917. The line was bought by the Frisco Railroad in 1925, and the depot is gone today.

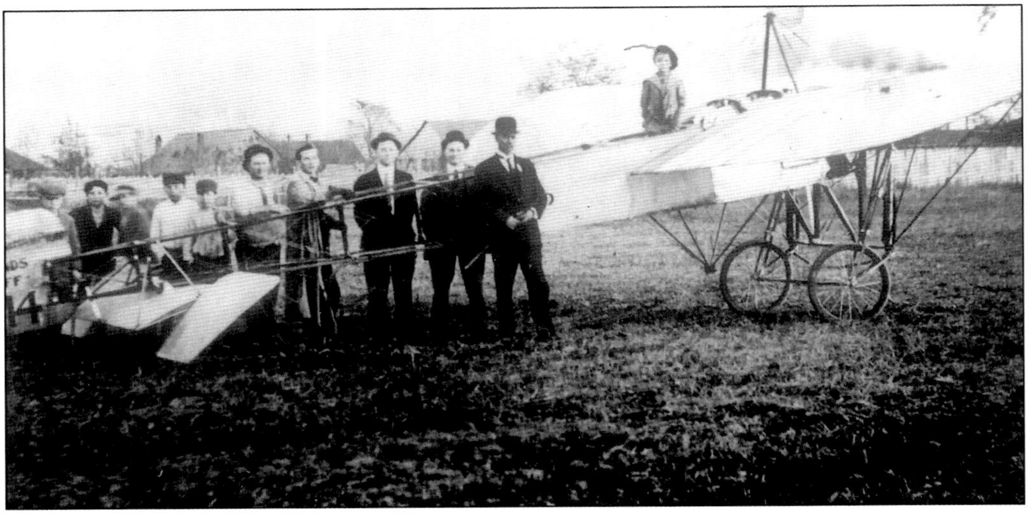

As the 20th century advanced through its first decade, trains were not the only mode of transport seen in Craighead County. In 1912, Jonesboro was host to this aviation tournament, at which aviator Frank Champion showed off his plane. Such events were becoming common, drawing crowds away from school and work to watch often daredevil flyers put on shows. Newspaper accounts said, "1,500 enthusiastic spectators burst forth with one grand ovation to the skillful bird man, Frank Champion, as he handled the wonderful machine of the air, guiding it as successfully as a driver would handle a family horse and with the same ease and agility as a genuine feathered bird of the woods." Seen below in 1913 is race driver William Vogel and his mechanic after winning a $100 prize at the Craighead County Fair in Jonesboro. The Ford Runabout—with gasoline powered headlamps—reportedly clocked a time of 6 minutes, 10 seconds over a 5-mile course.

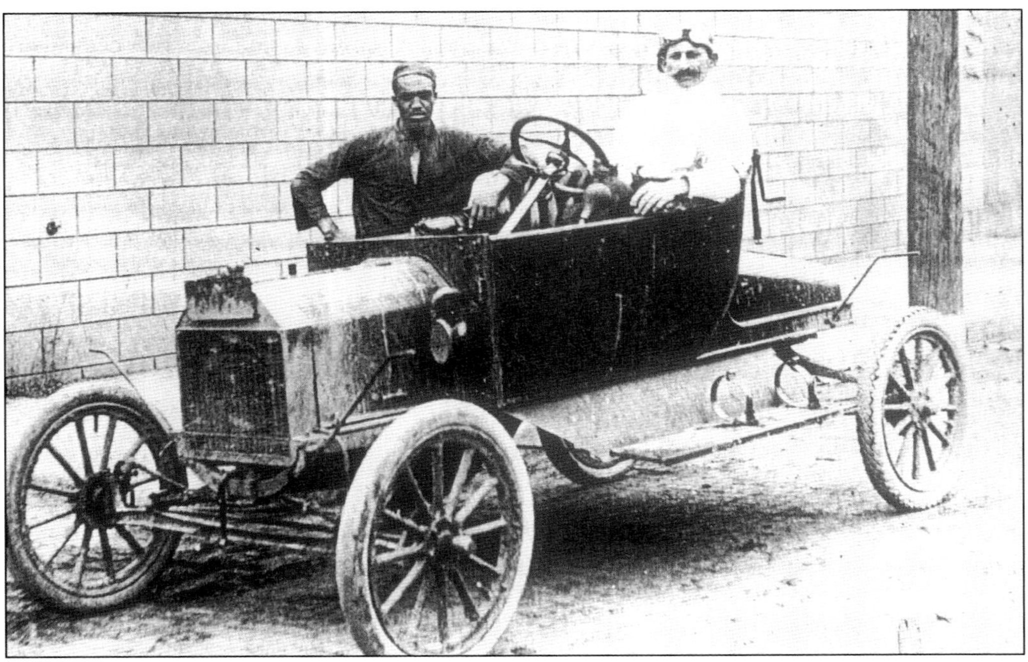

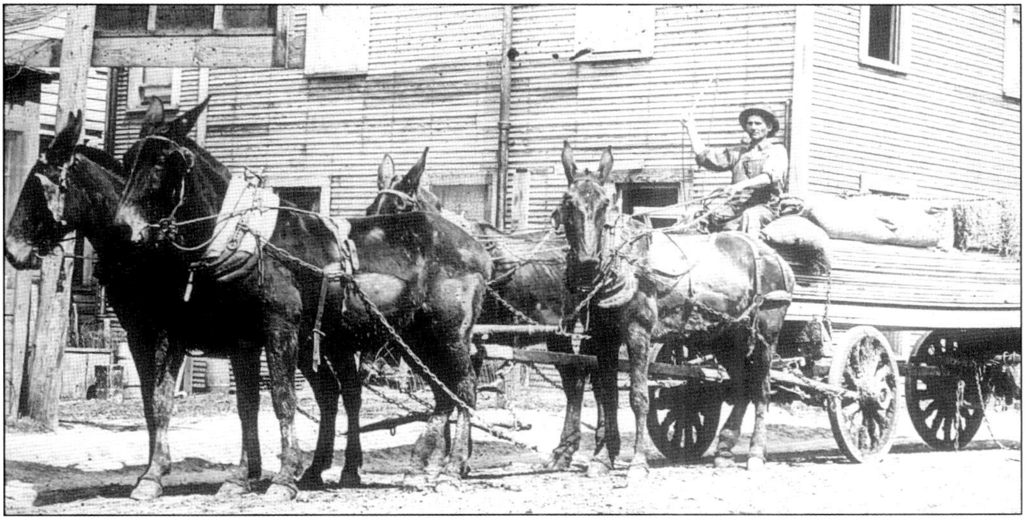

Despite the arrival of trains, planes, and automobiles in Jonesboro, largely horse-drawn conveyances still moved heavy loads on the dirt streets of the city. Seen above c. 1905 is a driver posed to whip his four mules forward, pulling a wagon loaded with lumber, feed, and hay bales. Below, in 1908, T.E. Osment—an employee of the Chicago Mill & Lumber Company—was driving a massive, ancient oak log on his wagon. The 23-year-old logger would work for the company for more than 20 years, overseeing the clearing of vast tracts of virgin timber. Here, Osment had paused in front of Z.T. Matthews mercantile store. Matthews was perhaps the largest property owner in the city, having interests in farming, a cotton gin, banking, and numerous other aspects of life in Jonesboro.

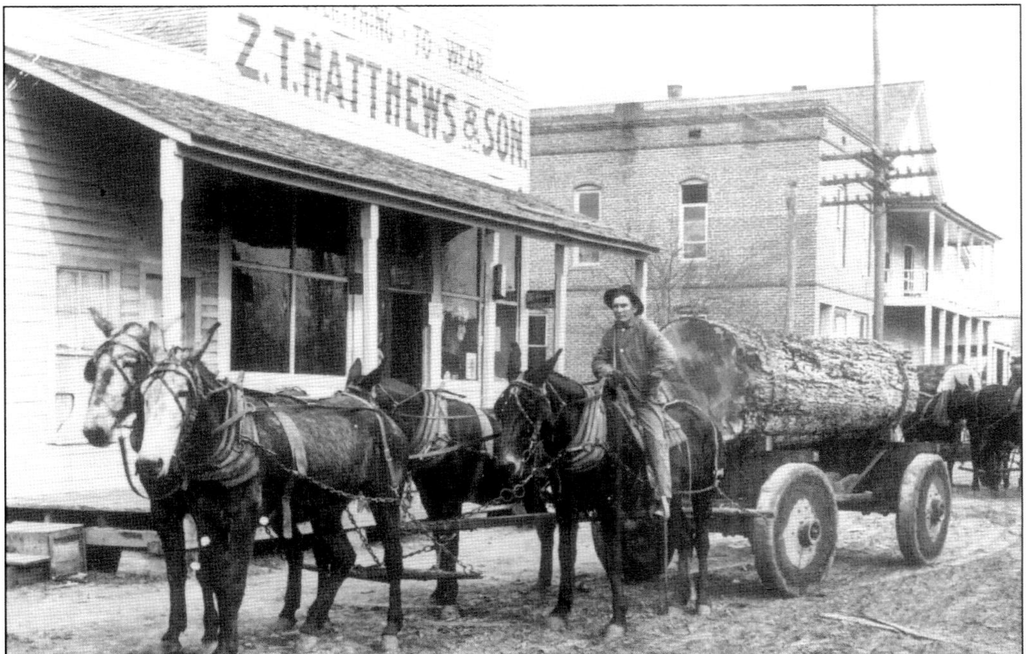

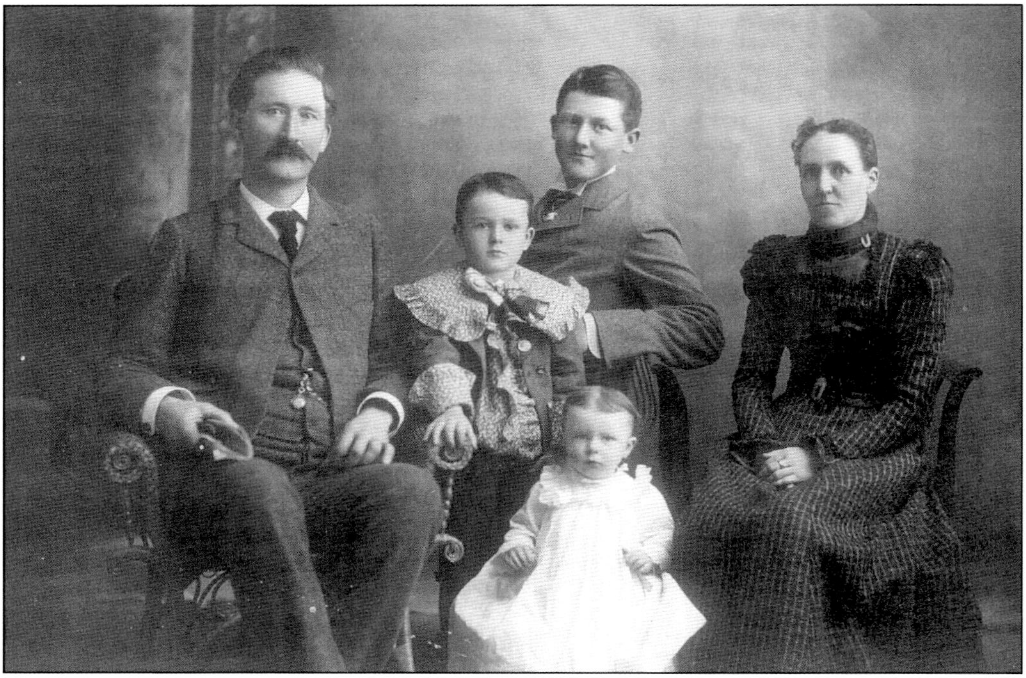

Perhaps no family better represents the pioneer heritage that built Craighead County than that of the Puryears. William Puryear arrived in the area in 1840, married, and fathered 15 children; he opened what may have been the first store in what later became Craighead County. One of the 15 children born to William was George Puryear, seen above with family in 1856. Following in his father's footsteps, George became an even more successful merchant; among other things, this enabled him to build the fine home—seen below—in 1882, located at 819 Parr Street. Puryear became one of Jonesboro's leading citizens, serving as the President of the Bank of Jonesboro and of the Jonesboro Roller Mill (flour); in 1909, he organized the Puryear-Jones Grocery Company.

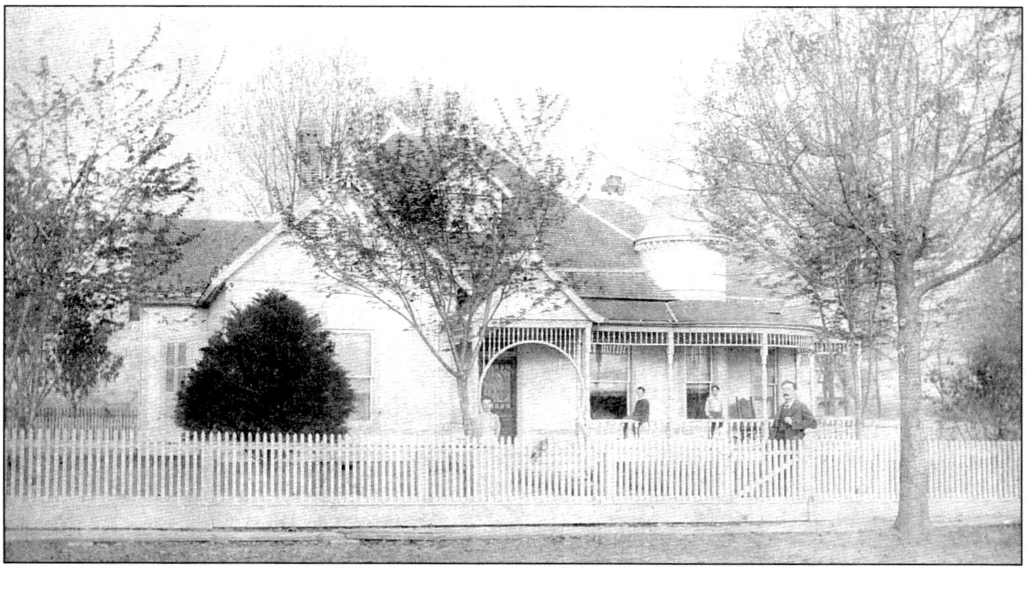

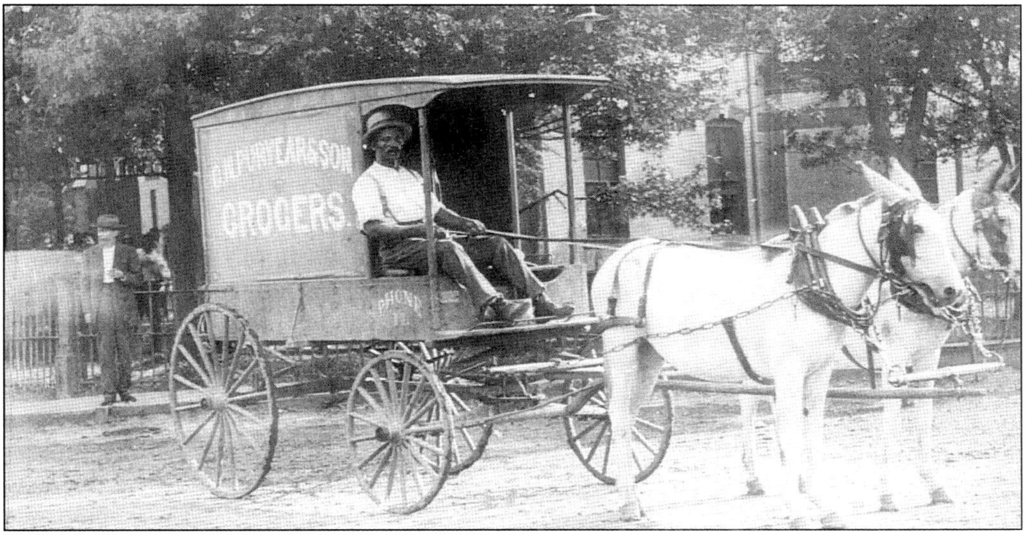

George Washington Puryear's grocery business delivered to the customer's door using the wagon seen here *c.* 1910. To place an order, one could have called phone #17, painted on the wagon below the driver. From the wealth that flowed from the grocery business, Mr. Puryear gave much back to the community. He served as the president of the Board of Sewer Commissioners when the city laid its first sewer line and as a prominent Baptist held offices on the boards of the Baptist State Convention, three Arkansas colleges, and the Baptist Orphans' Home. Mr. Puryear died in 1954, at the age of 98, having witnessed both the Civil War and World War II during his lifetime.

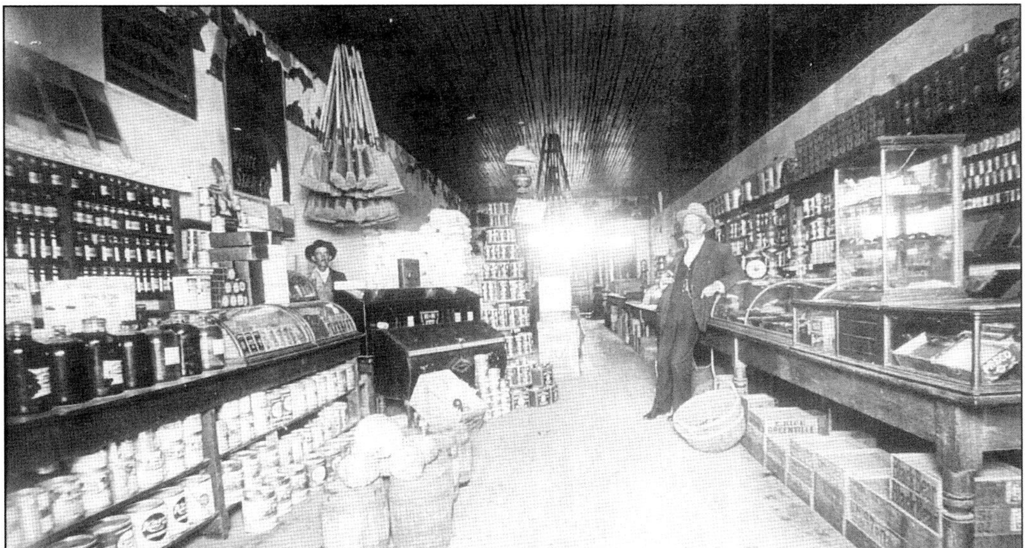

One of G.W. Puryear's brothers, J.T. Puryear, also went into the grocery business with this store north of Jonesboro near what are today Fisher Street and Highway 351. As seen here *c.* 1900, Puryear's store was typical of the era with small shelves lined with cans, glass display cases of candy and tobacco, and oaken barrels on the floor holding produce. Reportedly, J.T. did not meet with great success like his brother George, and little has been recorded of his life.

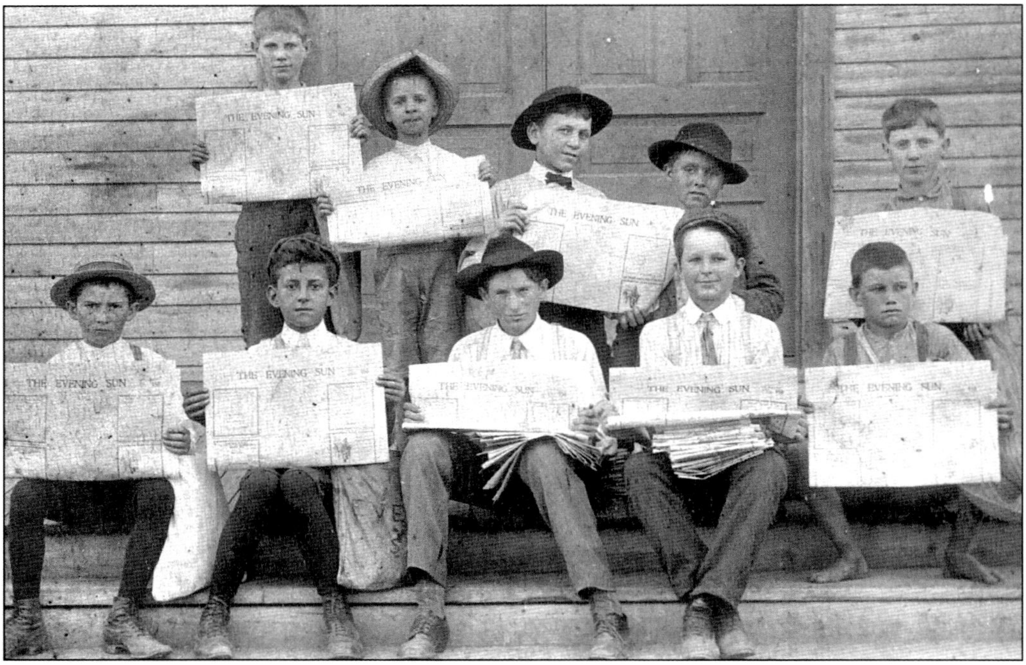

As did other merchants in the era before radio and television, Puryear's grocery stores advertised heavily in the newspaper, with ads often appearing on the front page. These boys, posed around 1900, delivered the *Jonesboro Evening Sun* at a time when afternoon newspapers were common. The boys were photographed while folding their papers in preparation to set out on their assigned routes of homes and businesses. Today the dominant paper in the area is the *Jonesboro Sun*, a morning paper.

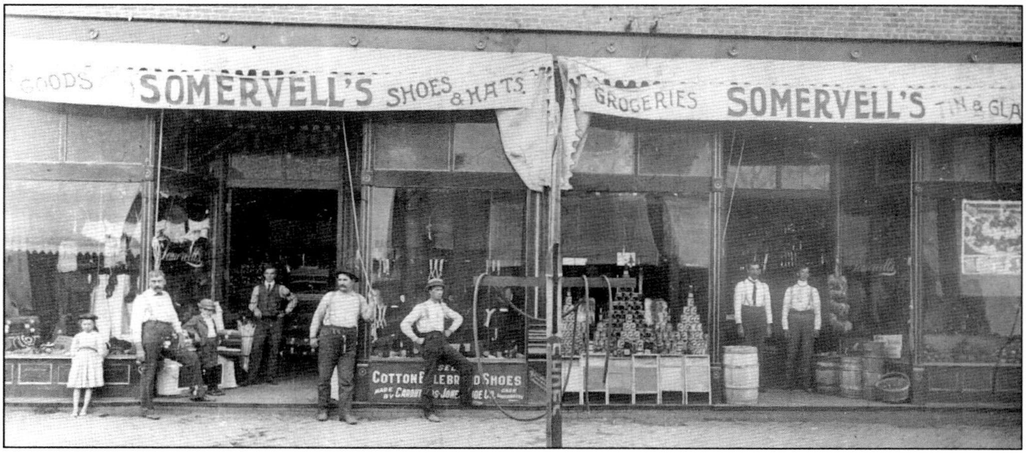

One competitor for the Jonesboro grocery trade was Somervell's at 206 Main Street. Opened by W.A. Somervell in 1897, the store boldly advertised, "There is nothing in the way of groceries, dry goods, shoes, notions and novelties that are not to be found in this store." Said the *Jonesboro Enterprise* in 1903, "Mr. Somervell is one of those old-time gentlemen who believe in strictly honest dealings, who will not misrepresent or resort to intrigue to make money." Among the offerings on this day *c.* 1900 was a selection of wash boards, near the casks and canned goods by the door. Today the building houses the Harris Furniture Company.

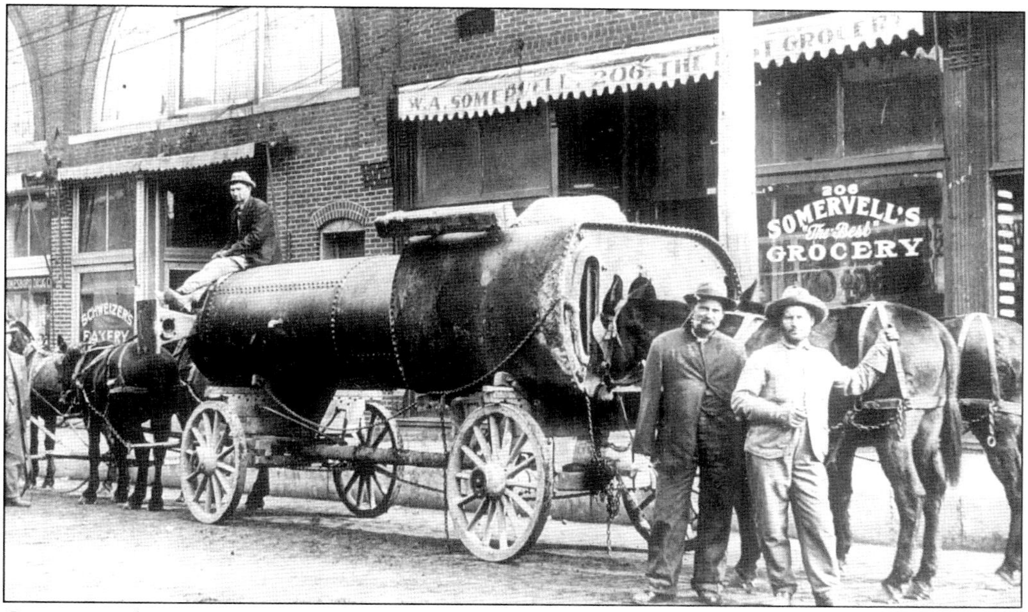

Customers shopping Somervell's on this day in 1913 would have paused to look at this large boiler, which likely had arrived by train earlier in the day. The mule-drawn wagon was delivering the boiler to its intended location, probably a sawmill or rice mill. The wagon has mules hitched both front and rear; the rear pair could be moved up front in the event extra traction was required on a muddy road. Visible businesses in this view also include the Jonesboro Drug Company and Schweizer's Bakery to the left of the driver.

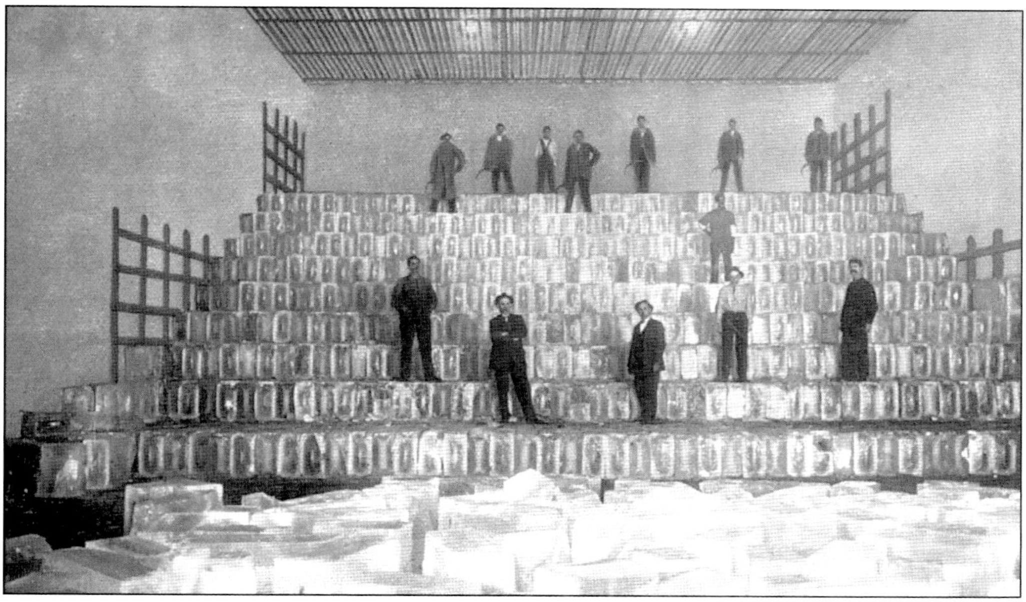

In an era before home refrigeration and freezers, the ice-making business was a part of every Arkansas city of size. Jonesboro's first ice plant opened in 1890, and by the time of this 1910 postcard was called the Jonesboro Ice Company. The storeroom here had a capacity of 3,000 tons, serving not only local citizens but also railroad refrigeration cars stopping in the city.

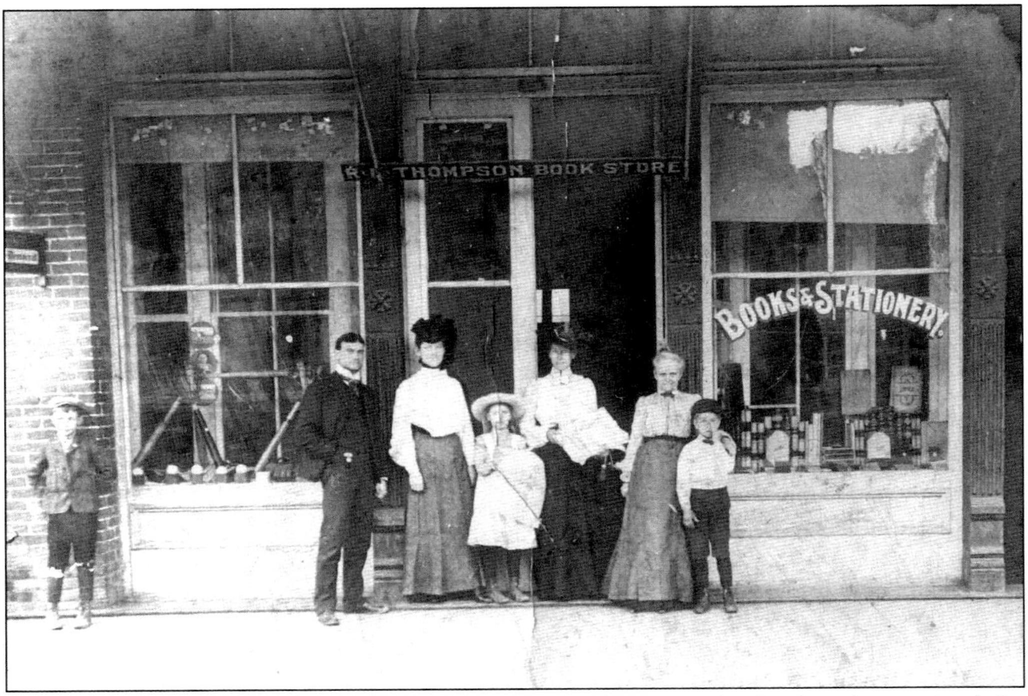

One sign of a progressive city of the era was its citizens' access to books; Jonesboro gained the Thompson Book Store around the time of this c. 1890 photo. In addition to books, postcards, and stationery—for those not inclined to reading or writing material—it apparently also carried baseball equipment. A display of bats, balls, and gloves is visible in the window to the left.

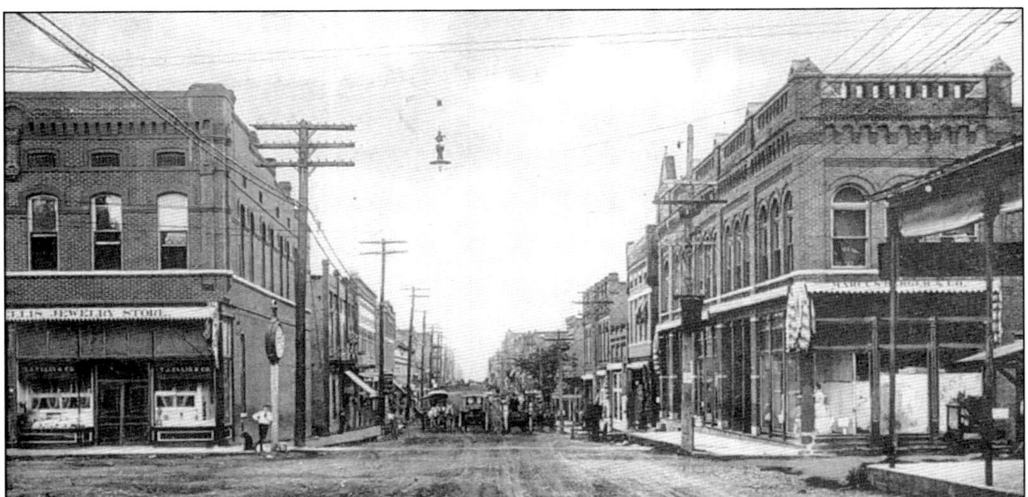

This 1907 postcard looked south down Main Street from the intersection with Washington Ave. The sturdy brick buildings had replaced the frame structures destroyed in the fire of 1889. The Ellis Jewelry Store is to the left, with Marcus Berger & Company Dry Goods to the right. Berger was a native of Hungary who began business in Jonesboro in 1882, becoming one of the most successful merchants in northeast Arkansas. In 1903, the store had advertised its ladies' hats as manufactured on-site and were sold for prices ranging from $1 to $30. The buildings are gone today.

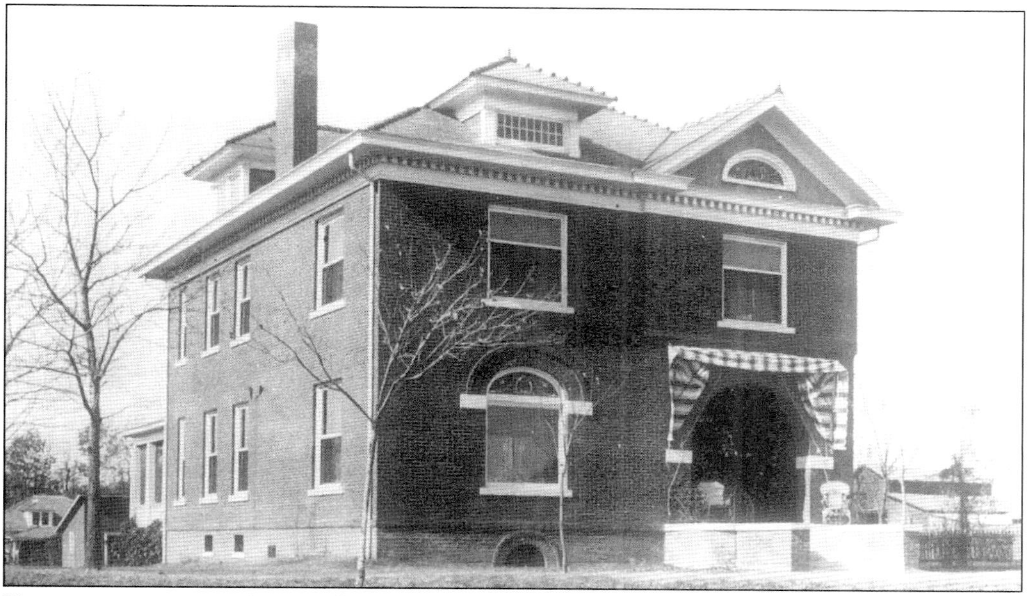

Hungarian immigrant Marcus Berger prospered with his Jonesboro store, and it showed in the wedding gift he bestowed on his son Joseph—this home built as a wedding present in 1904. The home, at 1327 South Main, was sold to Mr. and Mrs. Henry Graham in 1909; they would call it home for 30 years. The Romanesque and Classical Revival home has been restored and is today on the National Register of Historic Places.

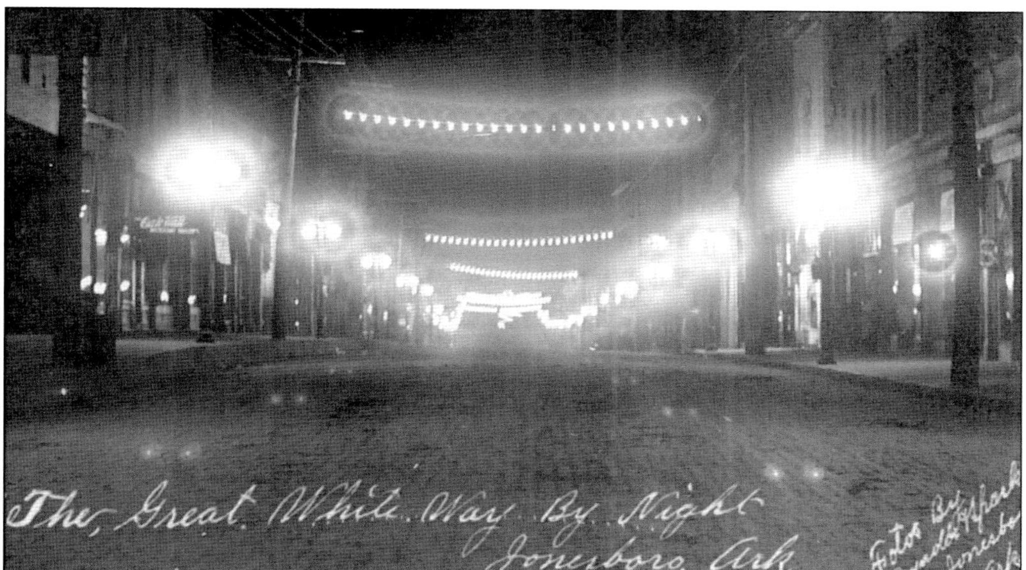

Most postcards and photos of turn-of-the-century Jonesboro were taken by day, but the few nighttime views offer a look at one of the town's bragging points, its "Great White Way." With stores open until 10 p.m. on Saturday nights, complaints from businessmen about the poorly-lit streets led to the installation of new lamp posts and overhead lights, giving a boost to stores' evening shopping. The enlarged city power plant and illuminated street became a promotional draw capitalized upon by the city fathers.

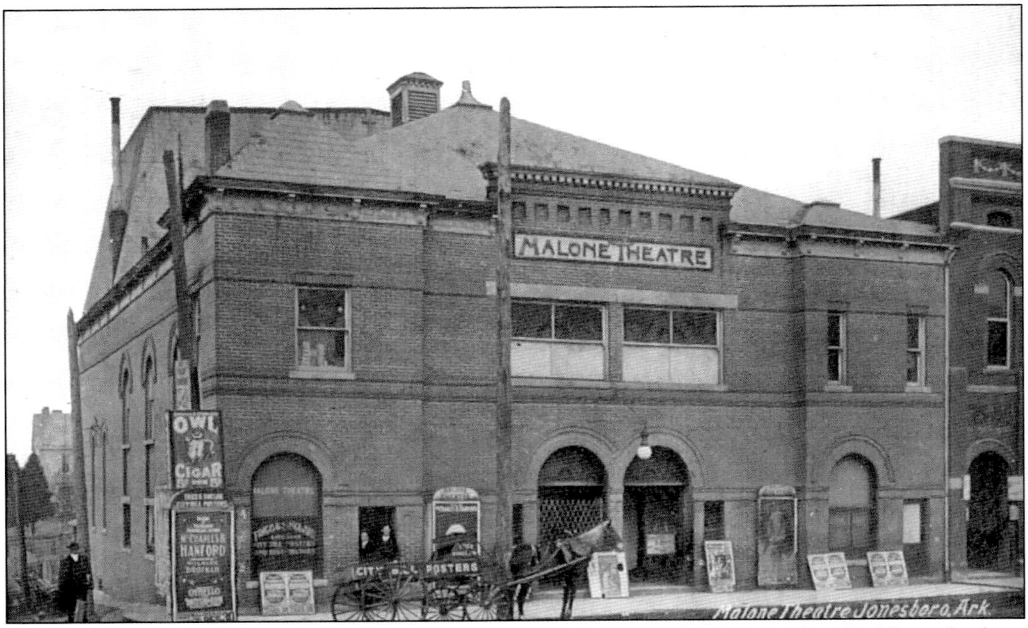

Jonesboro residents often traversed their well-lit streets to go to the theater that had been built in 1898 by Will T. Malone, on the northwest corner of Union and Jackson. In 1908, the theater put on a "talking" picture, to the delight of audiences; as the silent film ran, a band of actors stood behind the movie screen, loudly speaking the parts. The Malone later became the Empire Theater, screening films during World War I and for many years hosting graduation ceremonies for the Jonesboro High School. As seen in this 1910 postcard, the office of the City Bill Posters Company is owned by Trice and Sinclair, perhaps transplants from Paragould. Today the theater is gone.

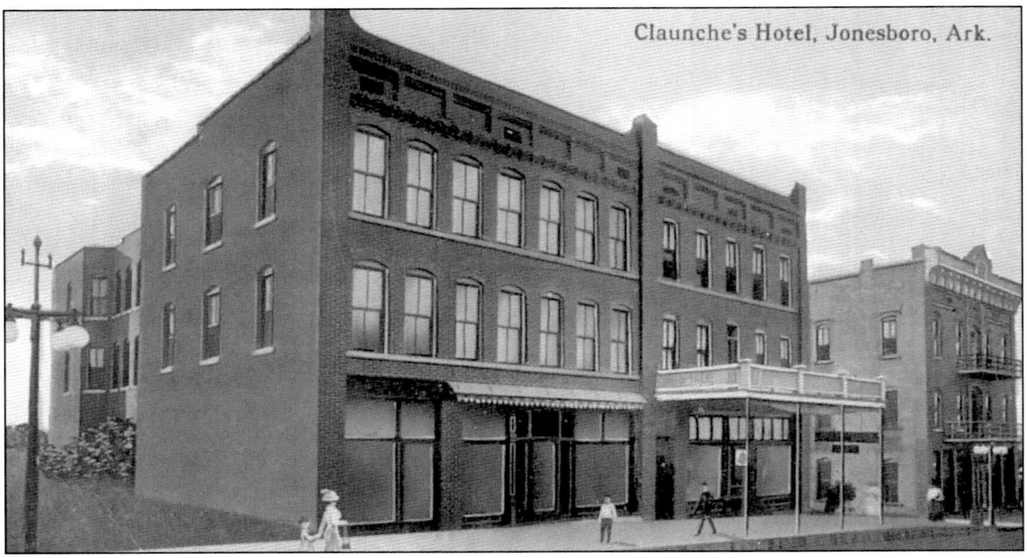

Out-of-town visitors to Jonesboro, perhaps to take in a show at the Malone Theater, could have lodged in one of several modest hotels. Charles and Agnes Claunch operated their hotel for a number of years at 109-111 South Main, near the train tracks. Built around 1910, the hotel stood until the 1980s, when it was razed to make way for an overpass spanning the railroad tracks.

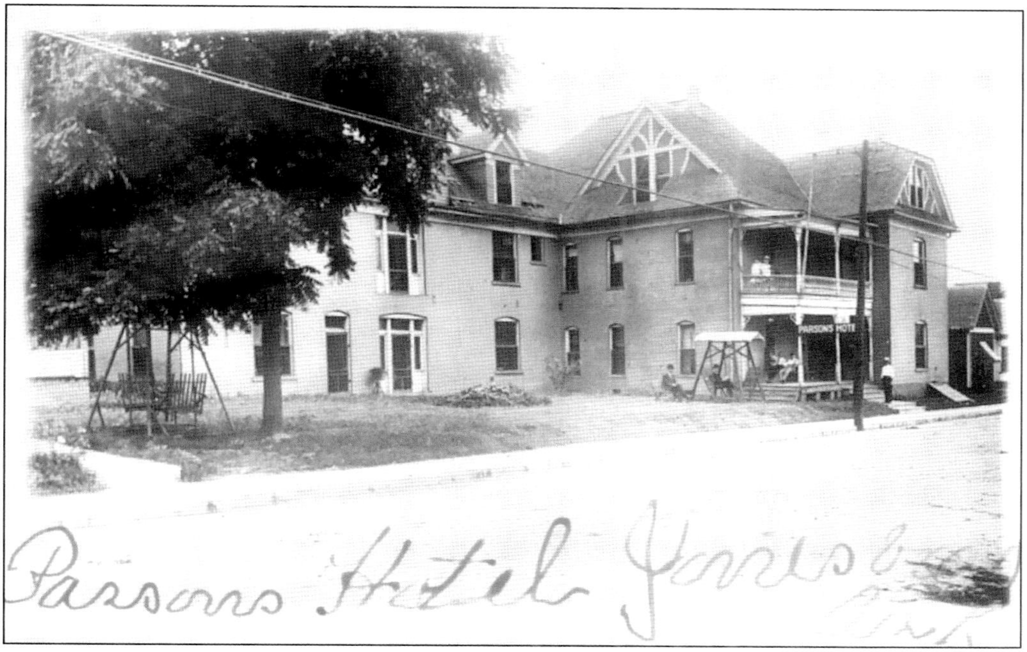

Visitors looking for a more home-like setting, perhaps with meals included, might have lodged at Parson's Hotel at 312 South Church Street. Originally the Hughes Hotel when it opened around 1905, it was taken over and renamed by J.S. Parsons c. 1911. Guests would have had their choice of yard swings or a seat on one of the two porches, watching the horse-drawn traffic that would have traveled the dirt street at the time of this c. 1915 postcard. The site is today a parking lot.

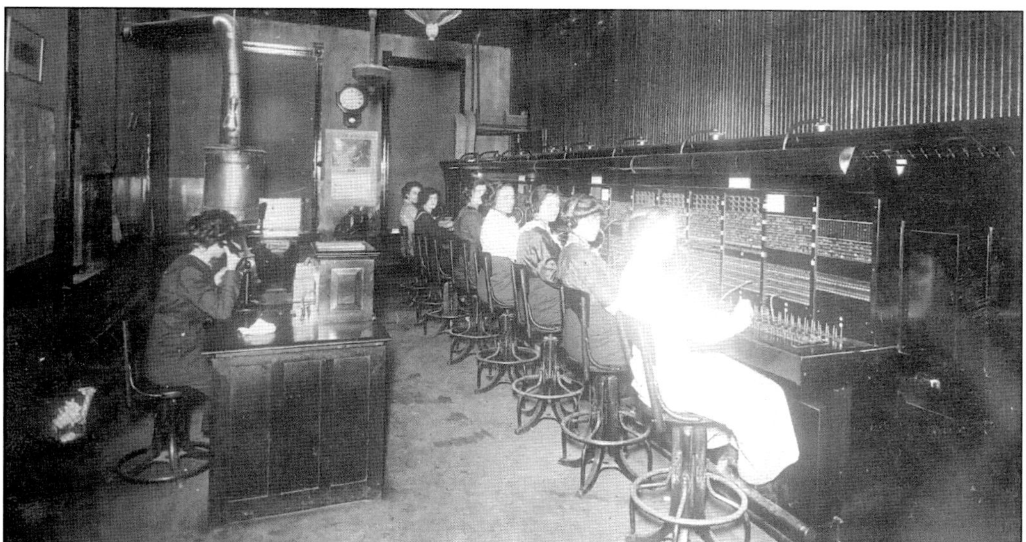

Guests at a local hotel who could access a telephone in the lobby, perhaps to call the Malone Theater, would have had their call handled by one the ladies operating this bank of switchboards c. 1910. Southwestern Telephone & Telegraph had bought the locally-owned phone company of Jonesboro in 1903. The ladies were working in the upstairs of a building located at what is today's courthouse square.

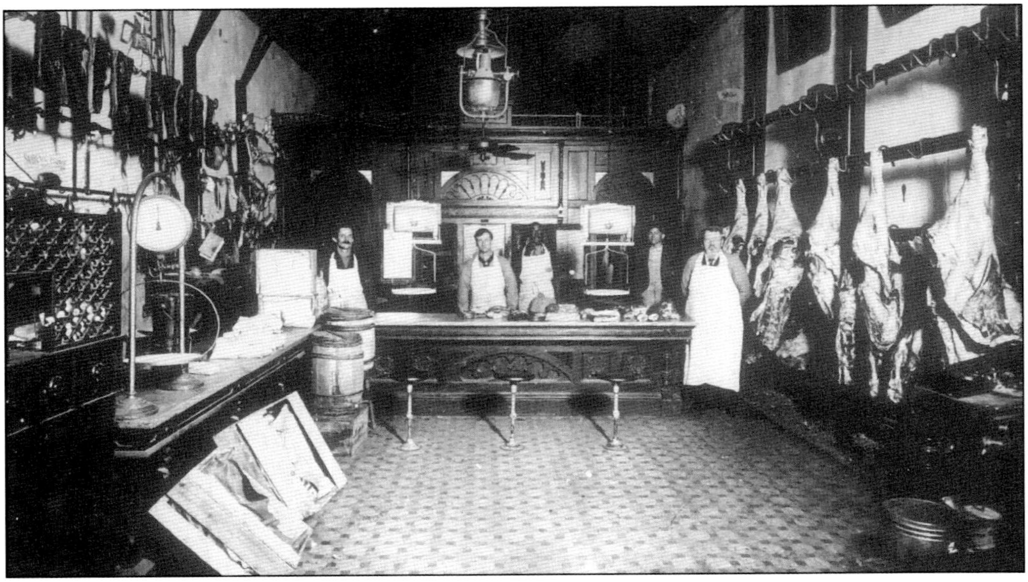

Among the rarer interior views of Jonesboro businesses at the turn of the 19th century are these two views from the ASU Museum collection. Though the exact addresses are not recorded, they reflect the nature of the small, personal service of shops of the era. At the butcher shop above, its white-aproned staff would have cut meat to specification from the carcasses hanging from hooks on the right, then wrapped it in paper near the scales to the left. In the photo below is seen what was likely a small grocery store. Notable are two prominent signs for Coca-Cola on the back wall, a mirrored tobacco case in the center, neatly stacked canned goods on the walls, and an overturned ice cream parlor-style chair on the floor. The jacket of the young man on the right is seen hanging from a nearby shelf, and both men are wearing their hats.

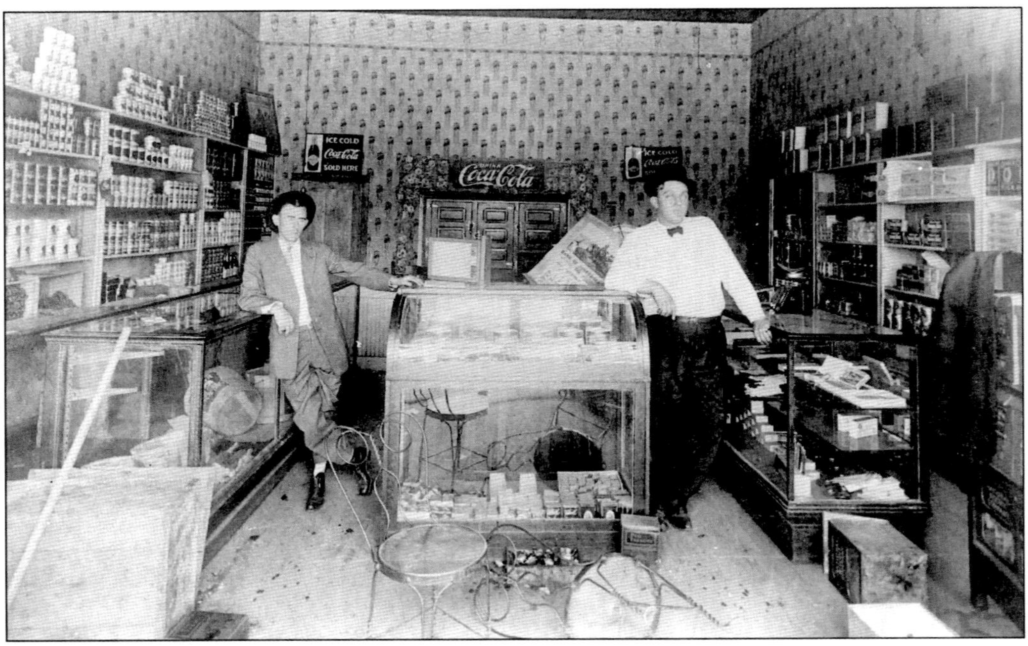

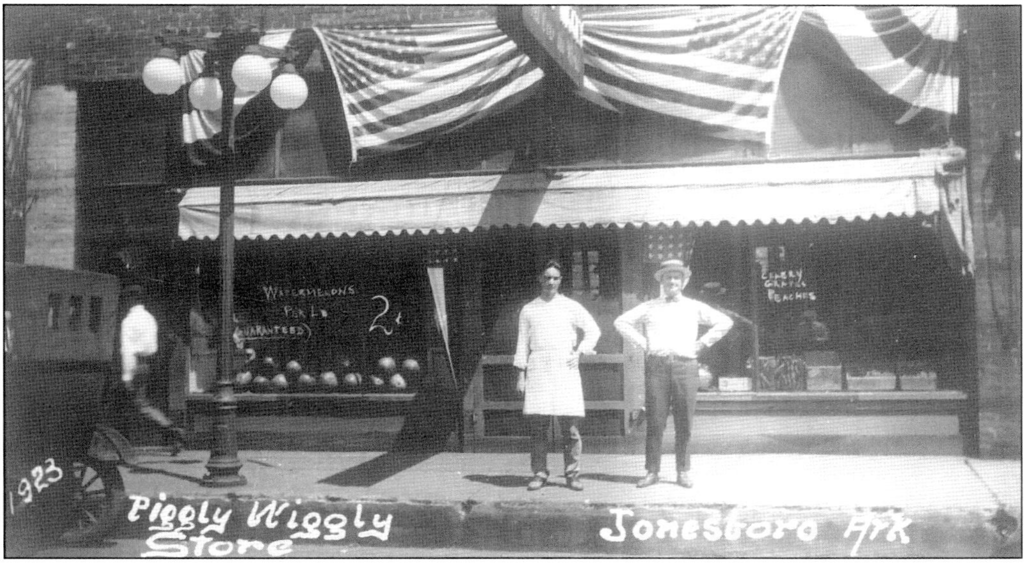

In contrast to the very small grocery store on the opposite page, Jonesboro also had what was becoming part of an early grocery chain, the Piggly Wiggly Store. Around 1920, Howard Stuck bought a recently-opened Piggly Wiggly, located at 234 South Main Street, out of bankruptcy. Though franchised, Stuck would soon own three Jonesboro Piggly Wiggly's. Likely, it is Stuck in front of the store, with hands on hips, in this 1923 photo; his store window advertises watermelons on sale for 2¢ per pound for the 4th of July, "guaranteed." Seen below c. 1911, Jeter Hardware did business at 403 South Main Street; the curved glass windows look out onto the recently bricked street. Founded by W.L. Jeter, the store reported annual sales of $37,000 at the turn of the century. Garden hoses, fans, axes, and other tools are visible, along with a woman looking through the screen door between the store's owners. Today the building houses the law offices of Ted Stricker and Charles Mooney Jr.

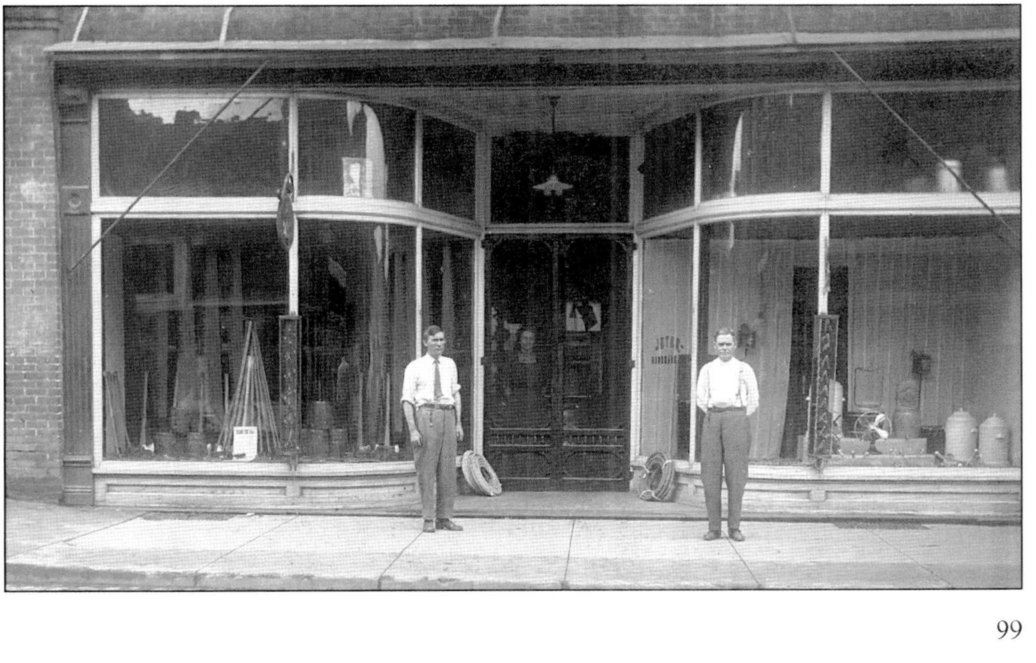

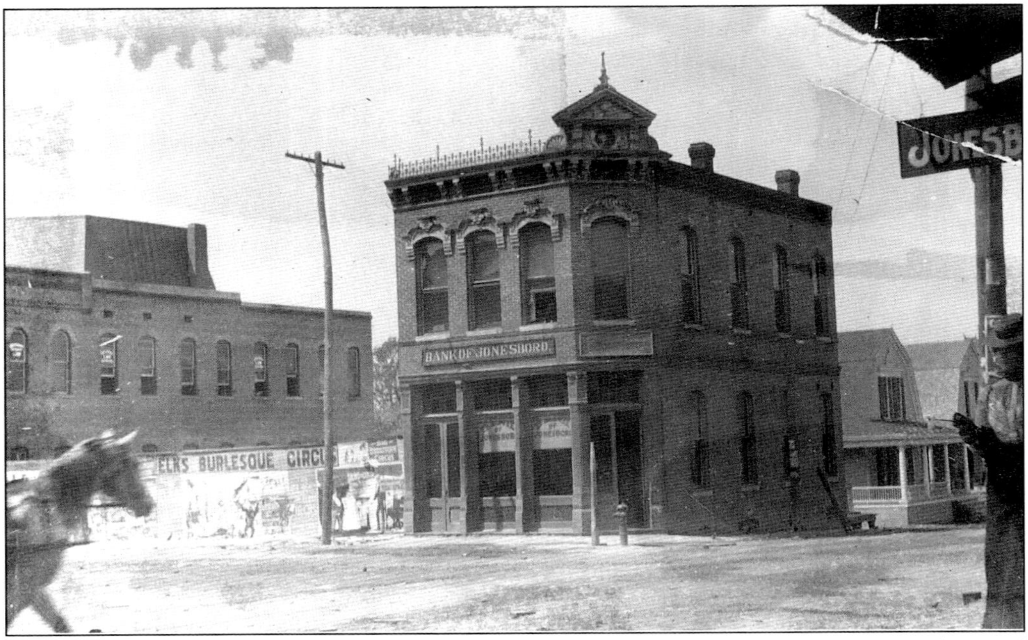

Many of the Main Street merchants did business with the Bank of Jonesboro, which had formed in 1887, with a capital stock of $25,000. Doing business from this building at 501 Union Street, the bank reported deposits on hand of some $600,000 and total resources of $1 million in 1900. Businessman G.W. Puryear, seen on page 90, was the bank's President. On the fence of the vacant lot next door to the bank can be seen signs advertising the "ELKS BURLESQUE CIRCUS," whose fliers were perhaps put there by City Bill Posters and Distributors (page 96).

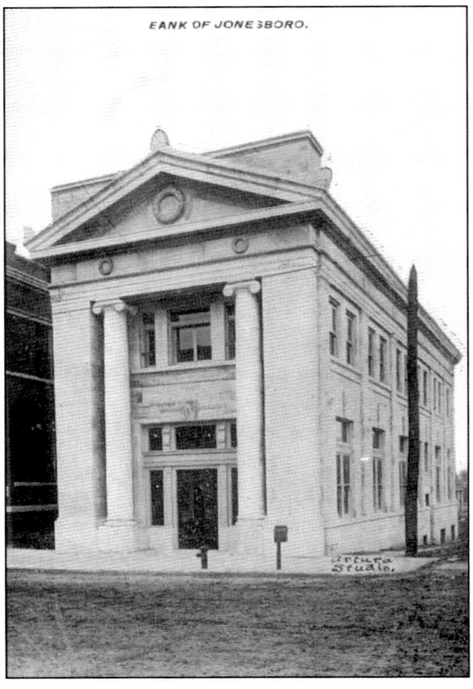

Feeling the prosperity of Jonesboro, by 1911 the directors of the Bank of Jonesboro decided to build a more modern home for the institution on the same location. The 1888 building was razed and—while conducting business from a temporary location—an imposing marble, stone, and terra cotta structure was built for less than $35,000. The opening coincided with the switching on of the "Great White Way" streetlights in 1912. Marketed as "The Strong Bank," it wasn't strong enough to survive the Great Depression and closed. In later years, the building served many functions, including housing a restaurant; today it is proudly restored.

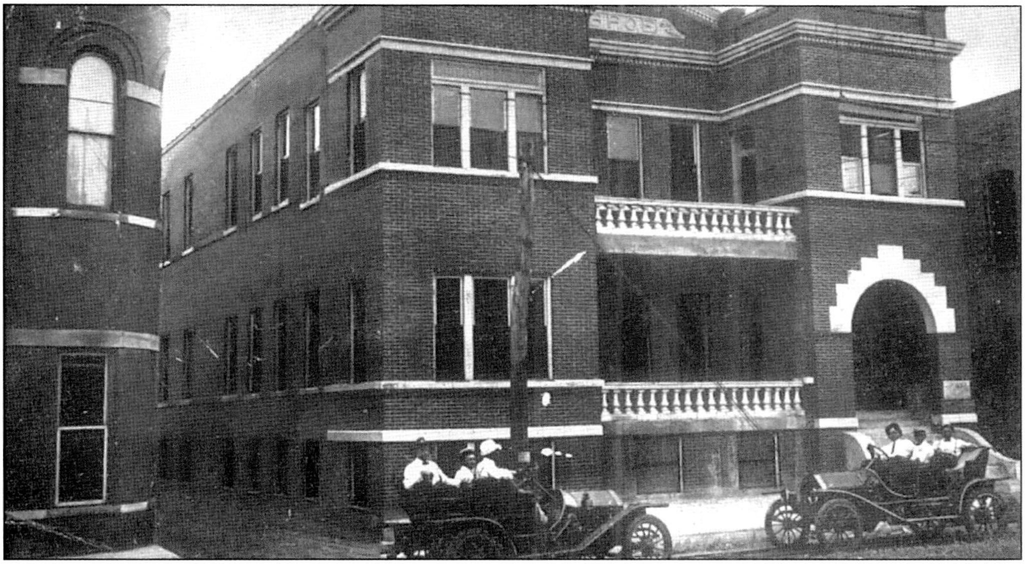

In this c. 1890 photo, the vacant lot (opposite) where the circus was advertised was filled with the construction of the Jonesboro Elks Lodge in 1910. The Jonesboro group had formed in 1899, and has been a presence ever since. The balcony of the Elks Lodge witnessed much history over more than 50 years; it provided a speaker's platform during the 1930s for Will Rogers to address those seated on chairs placed on Court Square. Others speaking from the balcony have included Arkansas Governors Carl Bailey, Francis Cherry, Orval Faubus, and Winthrop Rockefeller. The building was torn down in 1971, after the Elks had relocated to a new building on Southwest Drive.

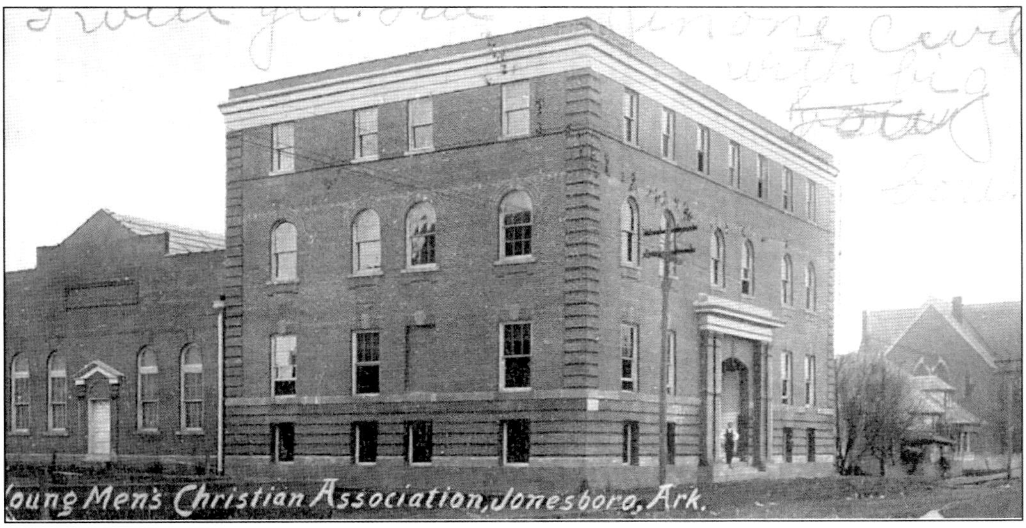

In 1907, Jonesboro got a YMCA building located at the southeast corner of Main and Jefferson Streets when Helen Gould, sister of tycoon Jay Gould, gave the money on the condition that the facility would serve the many railroad men stopping in the city between the trains they helped run. The building had an 18 by 40-foot swimming pool in the basement, an attached gym, a library, and sleeping rooms on the top two floors. The 1910 Jonesboro High graduate Berl Smith came to work at the "Y," and made it a center for organizing local boys' sports for years. The building was torn down in 1937, to make way for a service station.

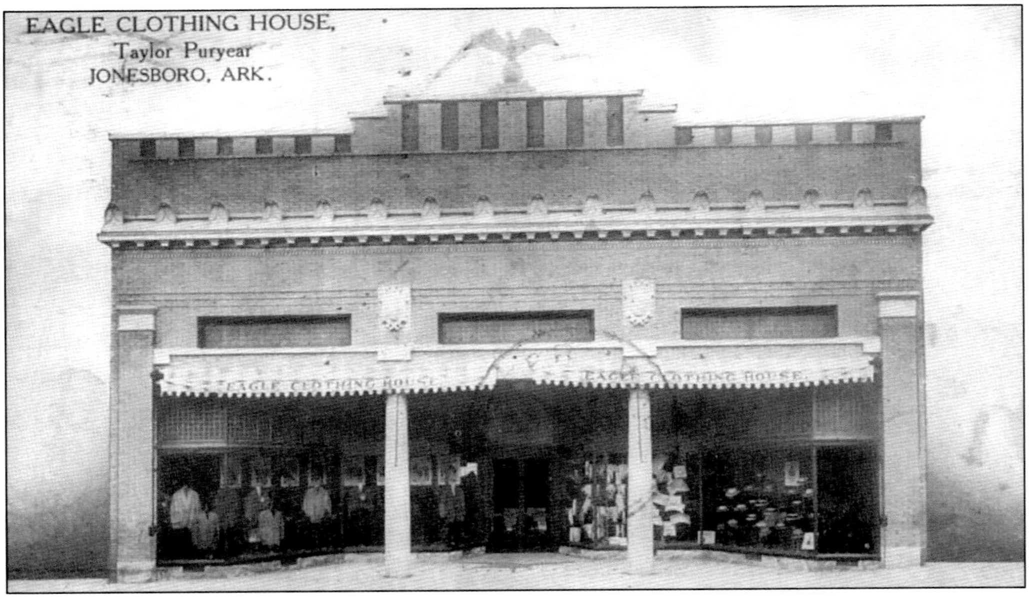

It is likely that many of the best-dressed Elks from the lodge on the preceding pages shopped at the Eagle Clothing House, located at 226 South Main. Owned by Taylor Puryear, the business opened in 1898. A promotional publication in 1903 stated, "In recent years the art of making clothing for men has reached a point where there is practically no excuse for a poorly tailored appearance. Fastidious dress is an American trait. The intelligent businessman and clerk has learned that by placing himself in the hands of a clothier who takes an honest pride in the dress and appearance of his customer, he can always be well dressed at small expense, well groomed and presentable.... Mr. Puryear takes an exceptional pride in making the clothes fit the fellow that is hard to fit, and he sells clothes to these sort of people." The brochure notes that Puryear sold some $30,000 worth of clothing a year, with a $15,000 inventory on hand. Visible in the exterior view—above—are window displays of suit jackets, spats, folded shirts, and jaunty hats. In the interior view—below—jackets, slacks, and suspenders are neatly stacked on tables, while shelves and glass cases with other items are topped by decorative palmetto plants. Though the Eagle is long gone as a business, the building still stands.

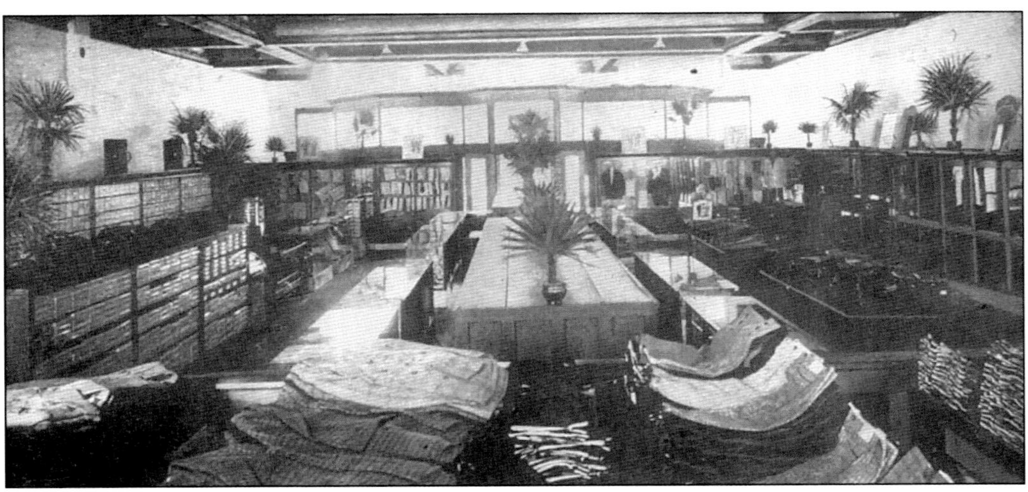

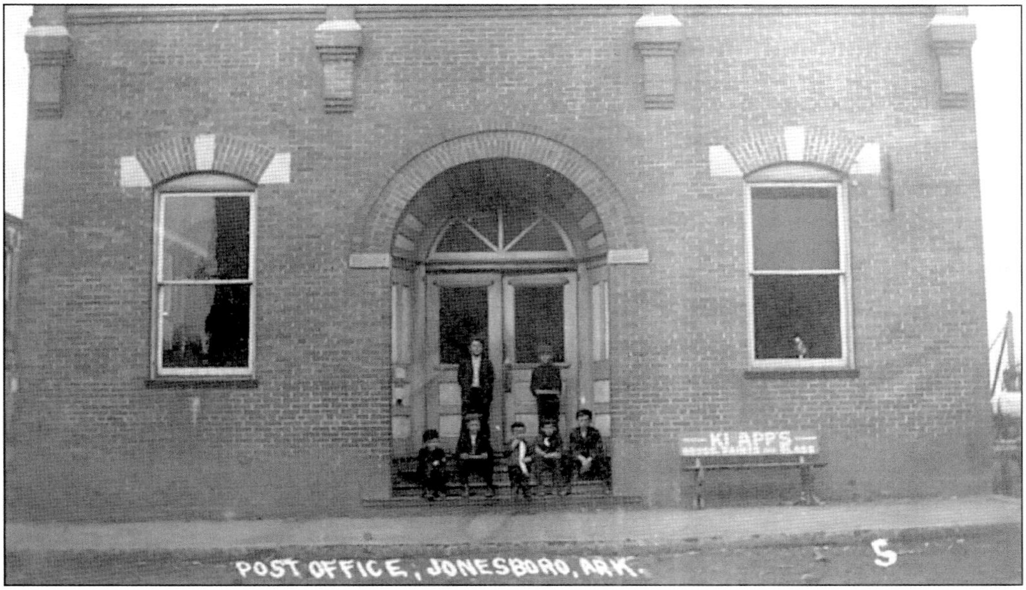

The Jonesboro post office at 110 East Huntington was a local landmark, as in most towns of the era. By 1908, when the above postcard was mailed, mail sorters such as those in the photo below would have handled hundreds of postcards each week, along with perhaps thousands of letters. Mailbags would have been labeled to both local and regional destinations; out-of-town bags would have gone to the train depot to be picked up for routing on to distant post offices around the nation. The Jonesboro Post Office moved in 1913; the original building later housed an automobile dealership. Though remodeled many times, the structure still stands. Of note in the 1908 view of the exterior of the post office is the bench with an ad for Klapp's Store, selling drugs, paint, and glass.

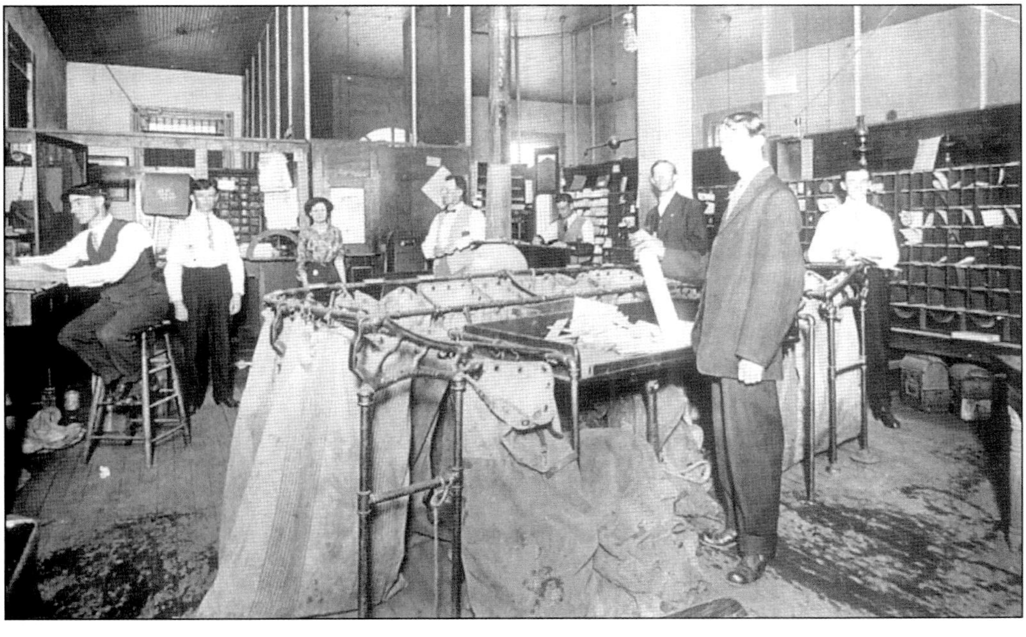

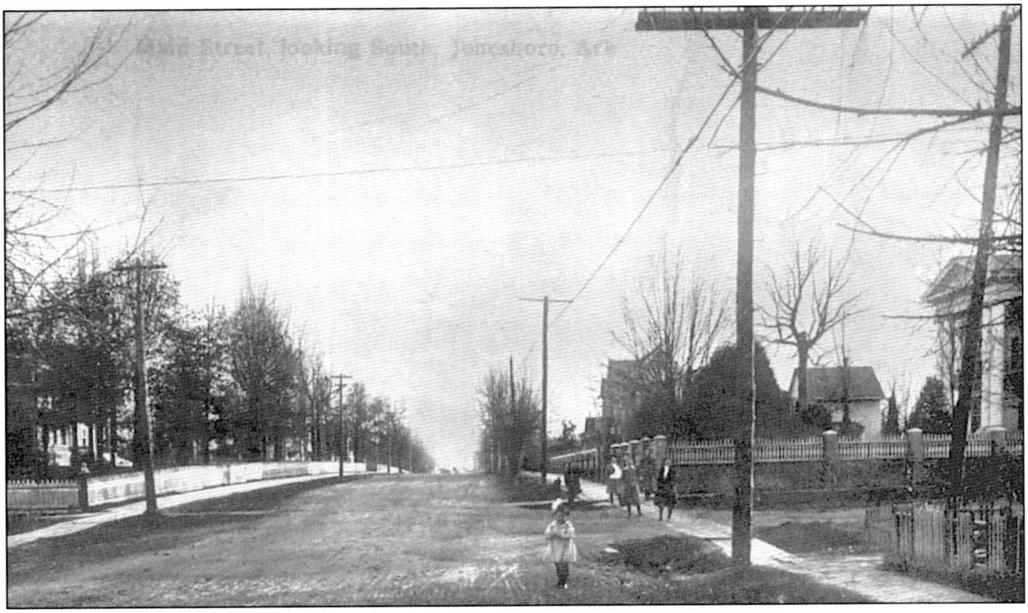

The hustle and bustle of the business district on Jonesboro's Main Street gave way a few blocks south, on the section of the avenue still unpaved, to large homes of the successful business and professional men of the town. The *c.* 1908 postcard above shows the broad dirt street with sidewalks, picket fences, and children at play. Visible to the right is a grandly styled front porch, belonging to the home seen on the *c.* 1910 postcard below. The home was built in the early 1900s for businessman Minor Millikin Markle, who had been named for a Union Army general killed during the Civil War. The son of a prominent Jonesboro family, Markle was an attorney and the owner of M.M. Markle Abstract Company. His business often advertised, "Loans on farms and city property without red tape." By 1930, the Markle home belonged to Central Baptist Church, which later demolished the grand old structure.

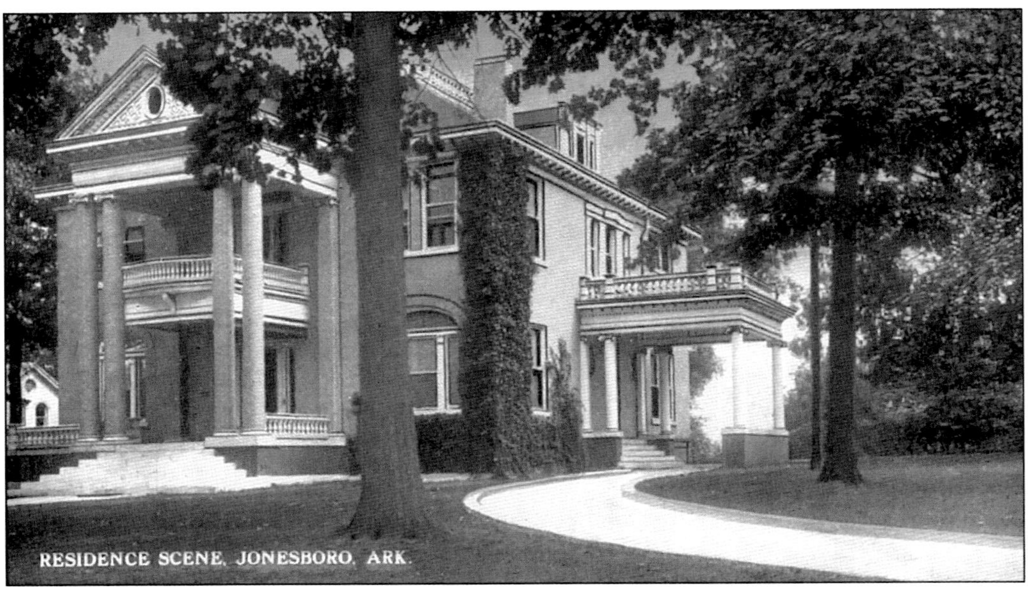

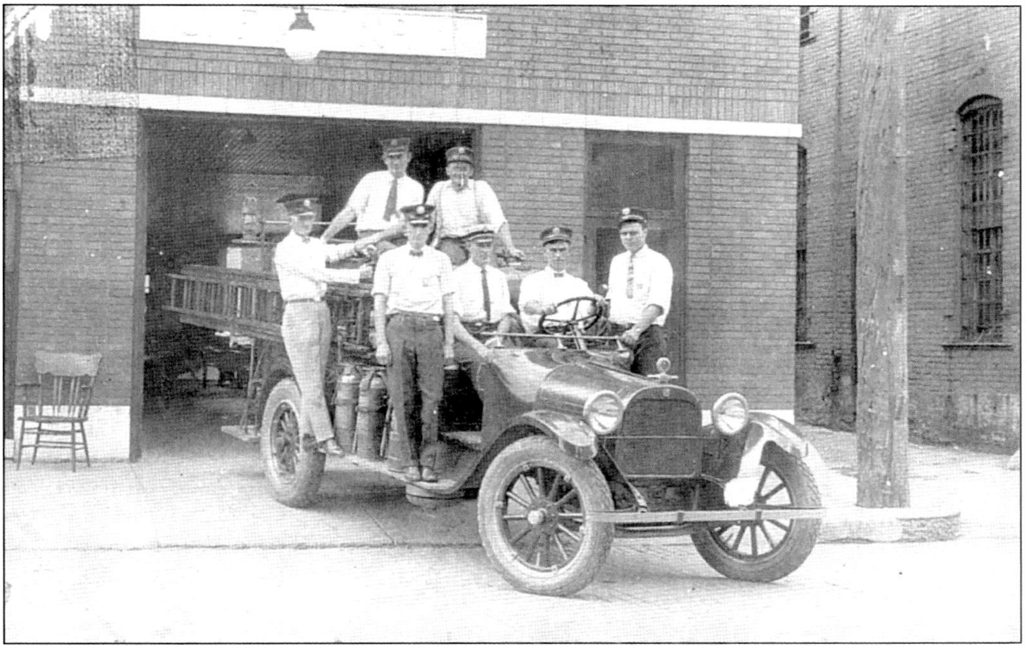

Jonesboro's first fire fighters belonged to a volunteer department formed in 1892, equipped only with ladders, buckets, and a man-drawn wagon of equipment. In 1899, the first city-employed fire department was created for the growing community. By the time of this c. 1915 photo, the city's Fire Station Number One was equipped with a motorized fire truck with hand-pumped fire extinguishers attached to the running boards and extension ladders ready to go.

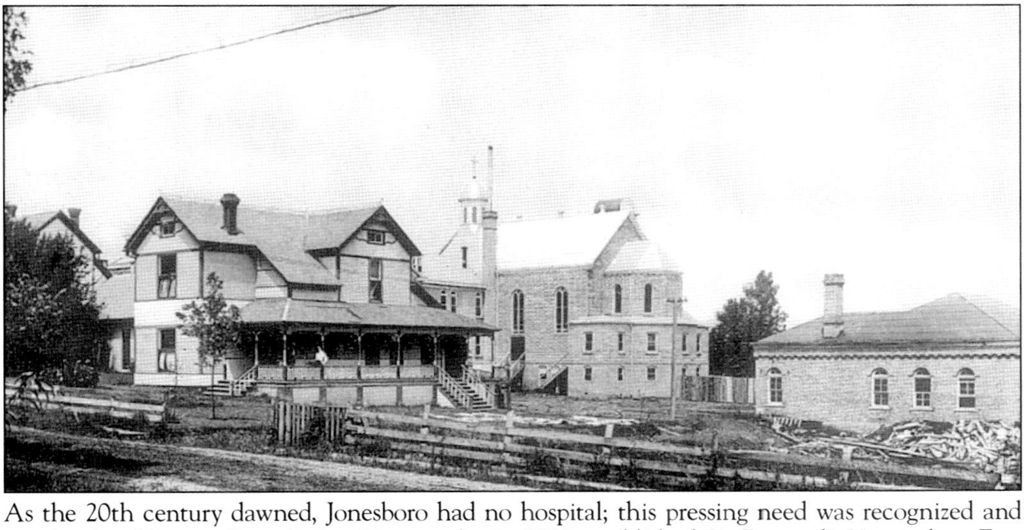

As the 20th century dawned, Jonesboro had no hospital; this pressing need was recognized and met by the Olivetan Benedictine Sisters, who in 1900 established St. Bernard's Hospital on East Matthew Avenue. The records of 1901 indicate a daily charge of $1 for a patient's room; physician fees could have added perhaps $3 a day, perhaps up to $5 for surgery cases. From this modest two-story medical facility—seen above next to the sisters' convent c.1905—has grown the largest medical center in northeast Arkansas, a century later. The Sisters' mission now, as then, is "To provide Christ-like healing to the community through education, treatment, and health services."

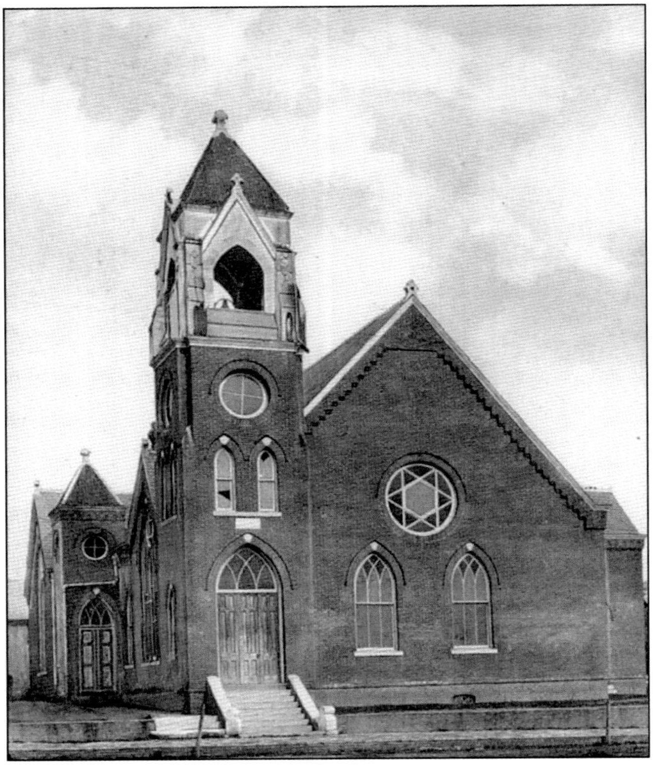

The first Baptist service held in what was later to become Craighead County was reported as early as 1839. In the late 1890s, the congregation of the Baptist Church in Jonesboro was described in the *Jonesboro Enterprise* as one of the wealthiest and most numerous in the city. In reporting on the town's various churches, the special edition advised that the building seen here was built in 1896 at a cost of $12,000, and that, "No church is now doing more to lift up and elevate fallen man." By the 1930s, First Baptist Church had moved to a new, much larger building that still stands; the building seen here is gone.

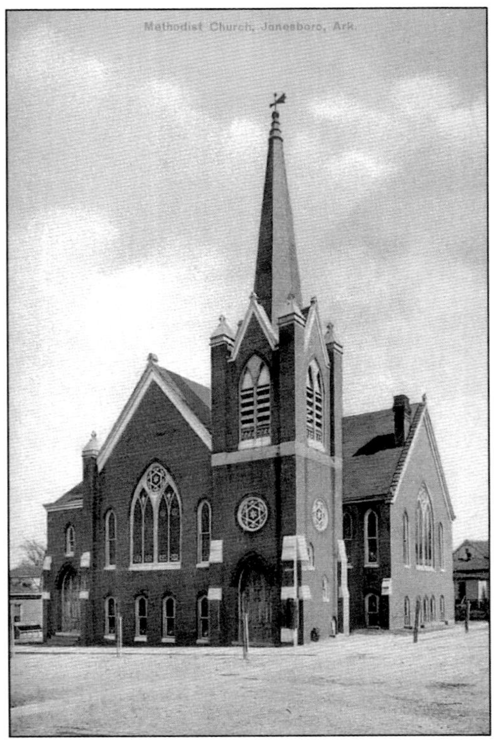

The *Jonesboro Enterprise* souvenir publication of 1903 said of the Methodist Church, "Its membership is composed of some of the city's wealthiest and most influential citizens." Indeed, the church at 724-726 South Main Street, which was erected in 1900 at a cost of $15,000, was reported to have 600 members. The pastor, Dr. Julian Brown, was said to be "a classical scholar, a profound thinker and logical reasoner.... He is considered the best preacher in the Methodist Conference, and for that reason, perhaps, he was sent to the best town in the Conference's jurisdiction." The church is gone today, replaced with a new and larger building in 1926.

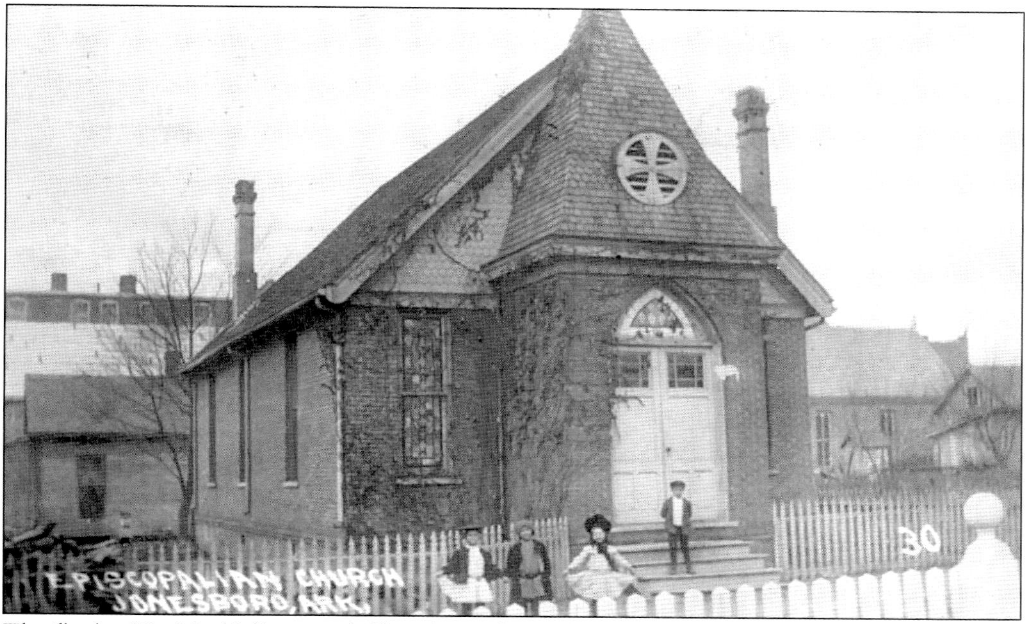

The flock of St. Mark's Episcopal Church worshipped in this ivy-covered building, at 703 South Church Street, from 1900 until 1952. Erected at a reported cost of $2,000, the building's funds came in part from "begging petitions" sent by the women of the congregation's St. Mark's Guild to other Episcopal churches around the nation. Today the church is at a new location; the site of this humble chapel where these children posed in 1908 is now a parking lot.

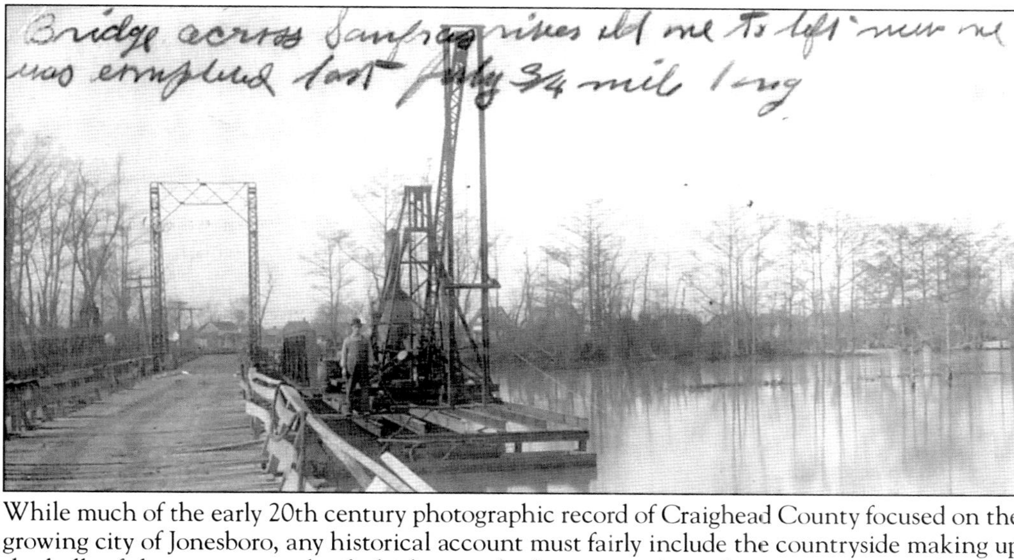

While much of the early 20th century photographic record of Craighead County focused on the growing city of Jonesboro, any historical account must fairly include the countryside making up the bulk of the county, much of which gave the large city a basis for its prosperity. Lake City, the county seat for the eastern district, was separated from Jonesboro by miles of swamps and waterways; these were traversed in one spot by a rickety wooden bridge near Lake City, seen here in 1913. The barge was equipped to do repair work, necessitated by frequent flooding. The note states the old bridge over the "Sanfrces river" [St. Francis] is seen here; "new one was completed last July—3/4 mile long."

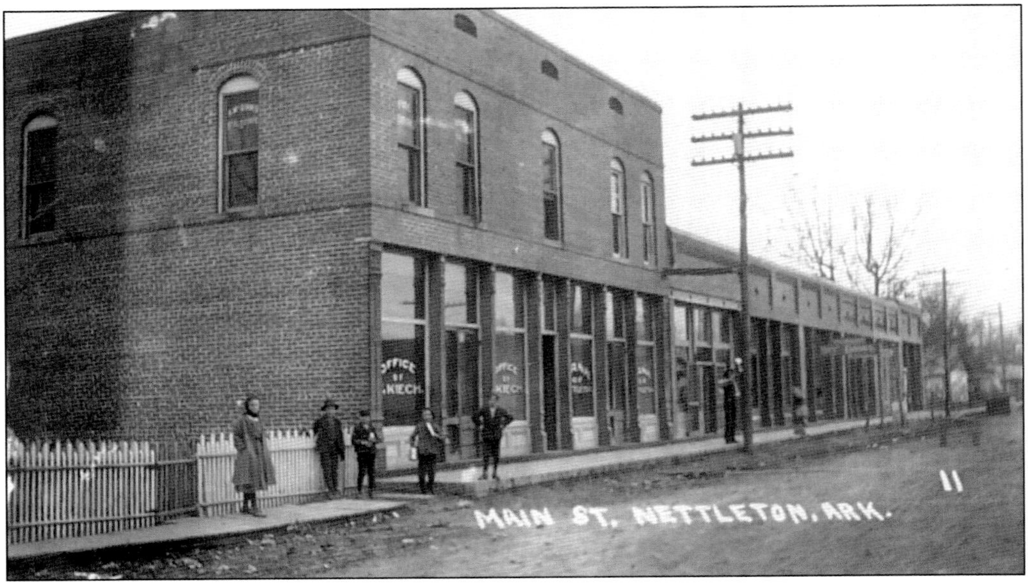

The Frisco and Iron Mountain Railways crossed tracks in 1893, near the heavily timbered bottom lands of the St. Francis River, some 5 miles east of Jonesboro. The intersection made a natural spot for a sawmill town; hence, the little city of Nettleton sprouted almost in the shadow of Jonesboro's population of 2,000. In the age before automobiles, with the hardship of traveling even short distances, Nettleton is a classic example of how thriving business centers sprang up so often near larger cities. At one time the town claimed two barrel stave mills and a large sawmill, along with a spoke factory that turned out wagon wheel parts. The *c.* 1905 view, above, shows the dirt Main Street, which was home to the Bank of Nettleton and the offices of F. Kiech Company, which owned 10,000 acres of timberland in the area around Nettleton. On a cold winter day, a few children were enticed to pose for the photographer. The 1913 view below, most likely taken from atop a water tower, looked out over a community of tract homes and dirt streets at a time when the former sawmill town was becoming a farming center due to the demise of the once bountiful timber supply.

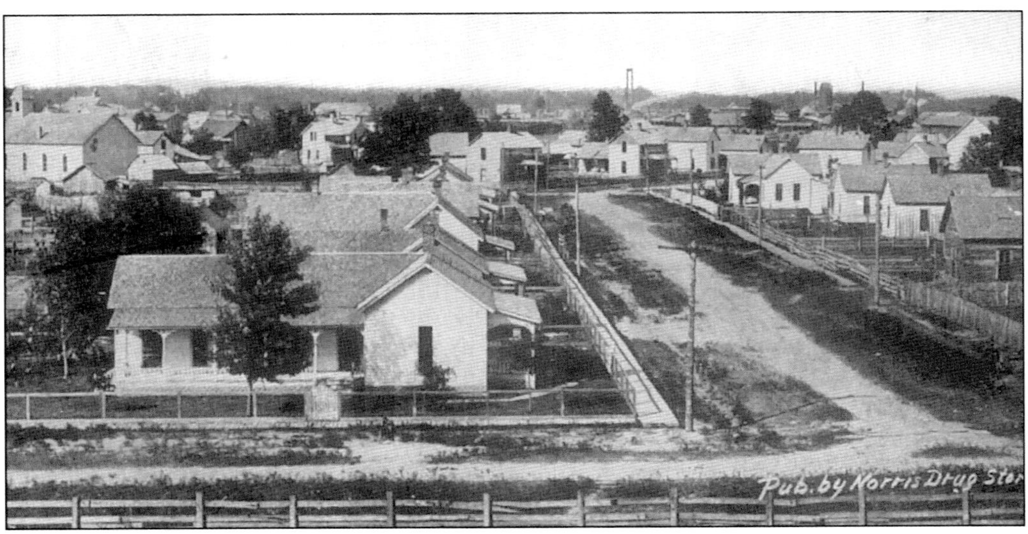

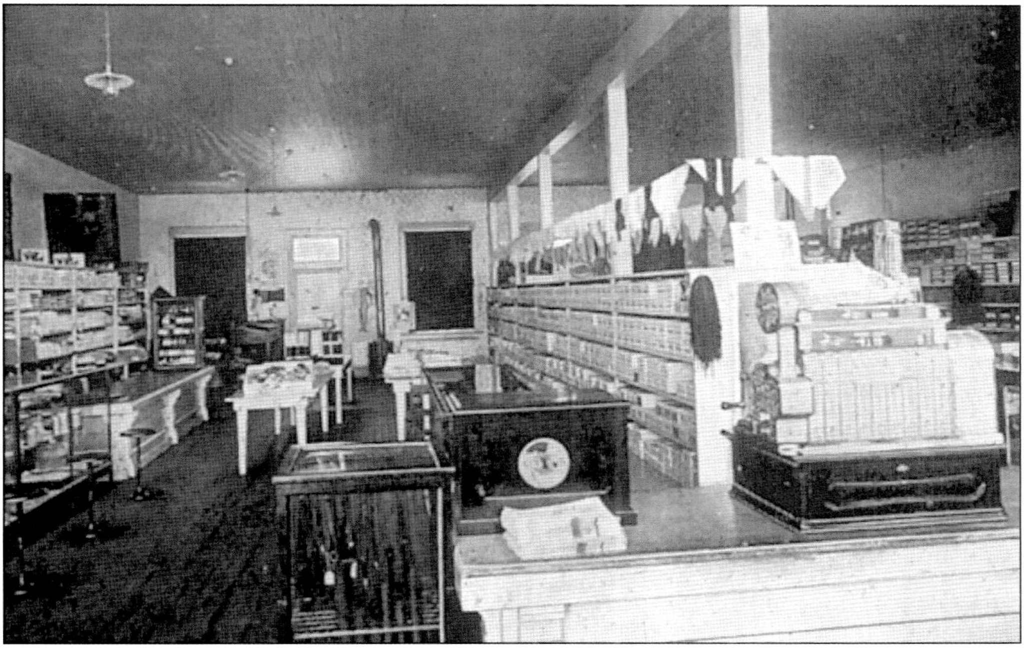

"Our appeal for your patronage is in our values. Know them." The card above was printed *c.* 1910 by Spencer Harris to promote his store on Nettleton's Main Street, proclaiming on the back, "Make this your store when in need of dry goods, clothing and shoes." A thriving business was possible because of the difficulty most residents would have had in reaching the larger stores of Jonesboro, some 5 miles distant. In 1958, the residents voted to be annexed to Jonesboro; the area has since been known as the Nettleton Ward of Jonesboro.

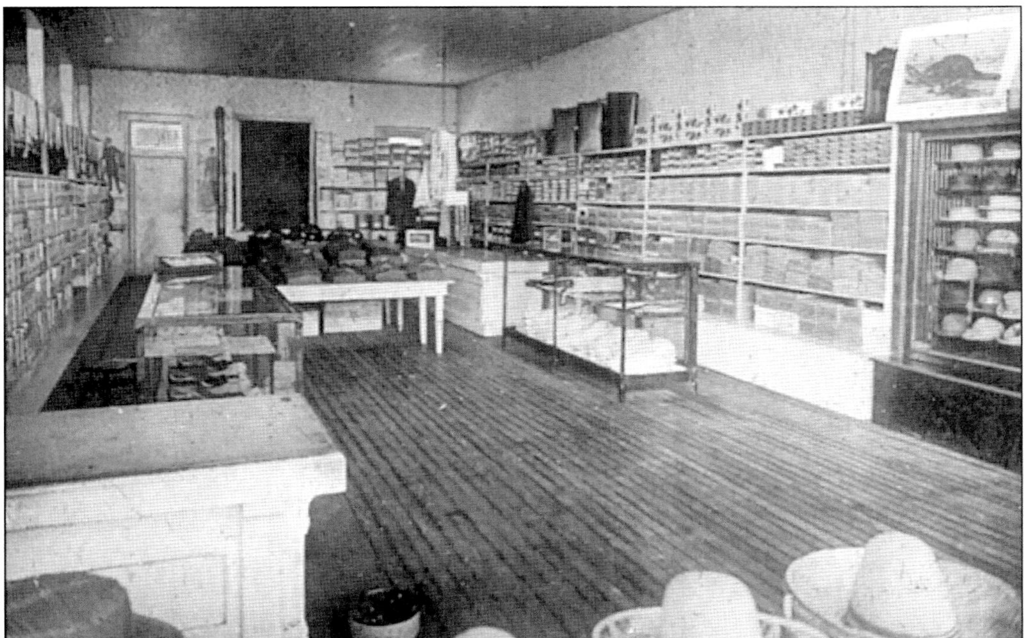

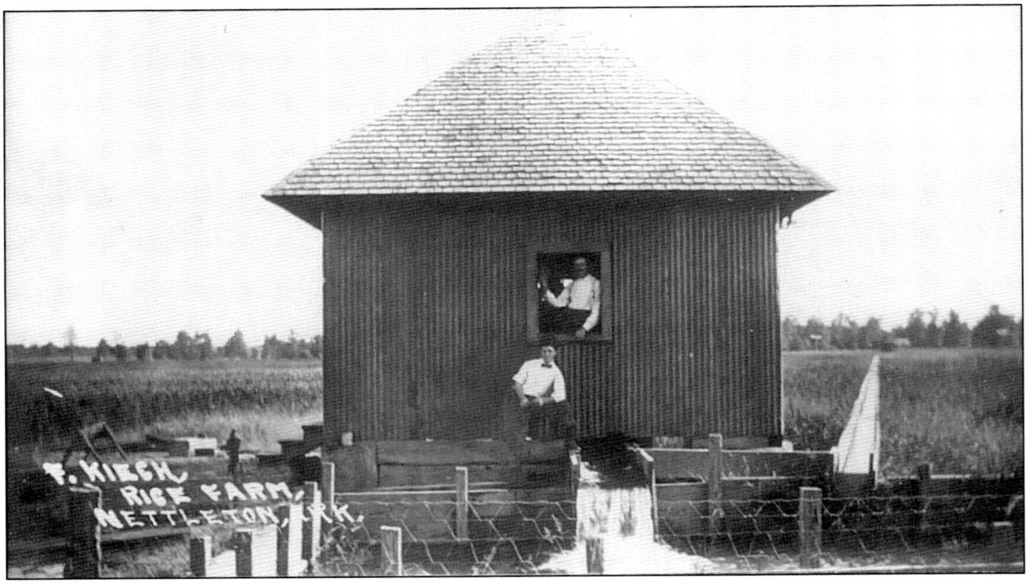

During the summer and fall of 1910, a steady stream of visitors came to watch the water pour from ground wells around Nettleton, as Craighead County agriculture entered a major new phase with the planting of rice. With rice having been successfully grown further south—around Stuttgart—some five years earlier, the farmers of Craighead County were eager to try the crop. In the card above, the farm of F. Kieck outside Nettleton displays the process of pumping the ground water that was needed to cover the crop during the growing season. With 10,000 acres of cleared timberland in his possession, the rice crop offered Kieck a new use for the land. Seen below on Kieck's farm in the fall, women and children look on as rice is harvested with the aid of mechanical equipment, which the larger landowners could afford. The rice would be transported to an area mill for processing and shipment by rail to distant cities. Today rice is a mainstay of the agriculture of northeast Arkansas, along with soybeans and cotton.

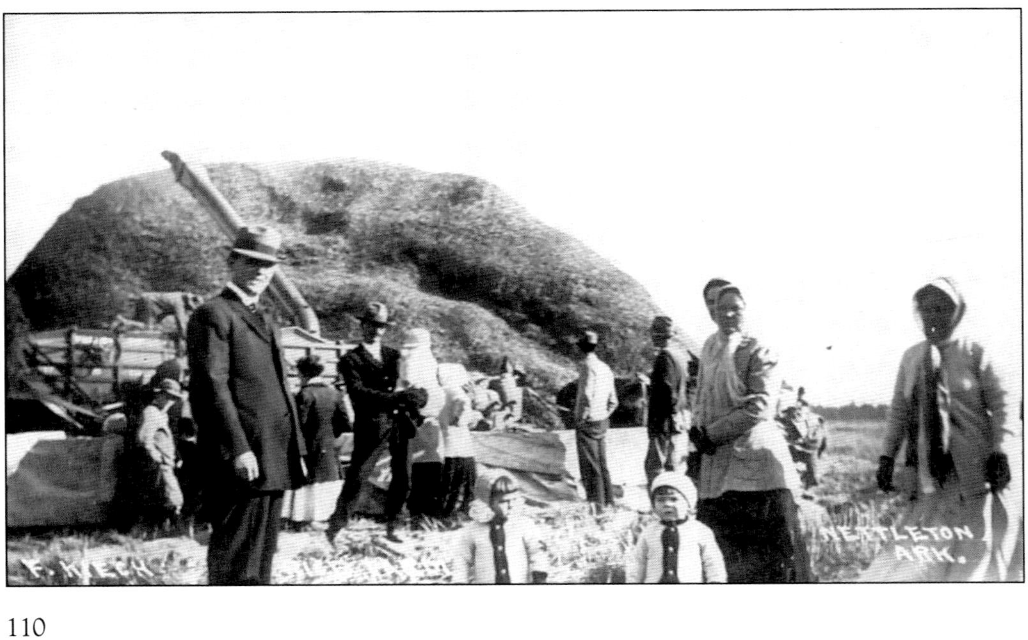

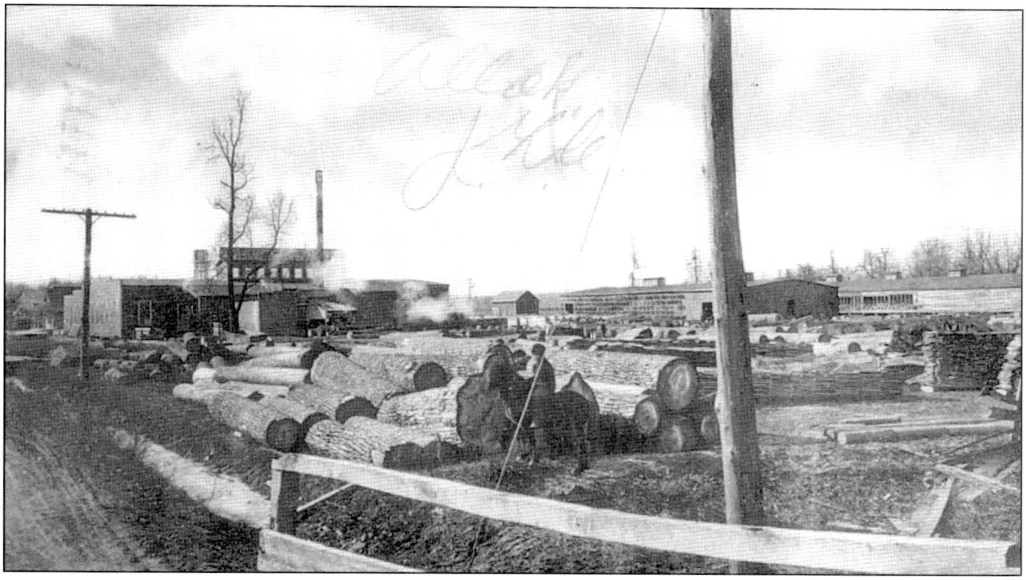

The once-bountiful, virgin hardwood forests of Craighead County supplied a variety of forest product industries with raw material and jobs for residents in the early years of the 20th century. Two of those mills were depicted on these 1907 postcards. Seen above is Pierce-William's Basket Factory—which began operation in 1903—manufacturing fruit packages, baskets, boxes, and crates. The large oak logs, today very rare, went into the mill where they were steamed until soft; the lumber was then peeled off in the form of thin strips of veneer. The finished products were shipped nationwide by train. The American Handle Company, seen below, was started in 1899, to turn hickory timber into handles for a wide variety of tools. For a number of years, the stated capacity of the mill was 600 dozen handles per day, with warehouses capable of storing 30,000 dozen handles. Unlike other mills using virgin, old growth timber, the handle mill specialized in processing "second growth" hickory trees unsuitable for other area mills.

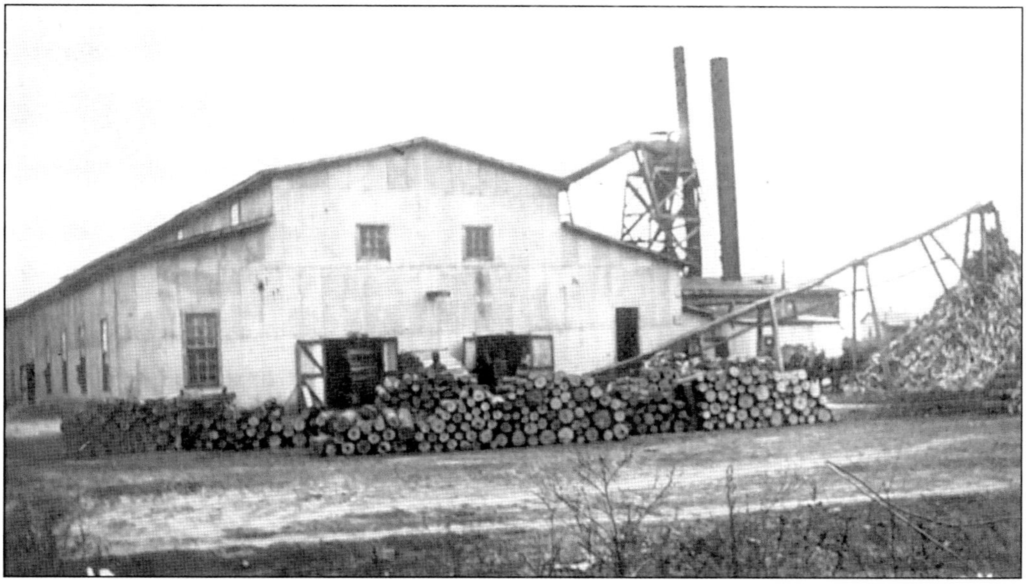

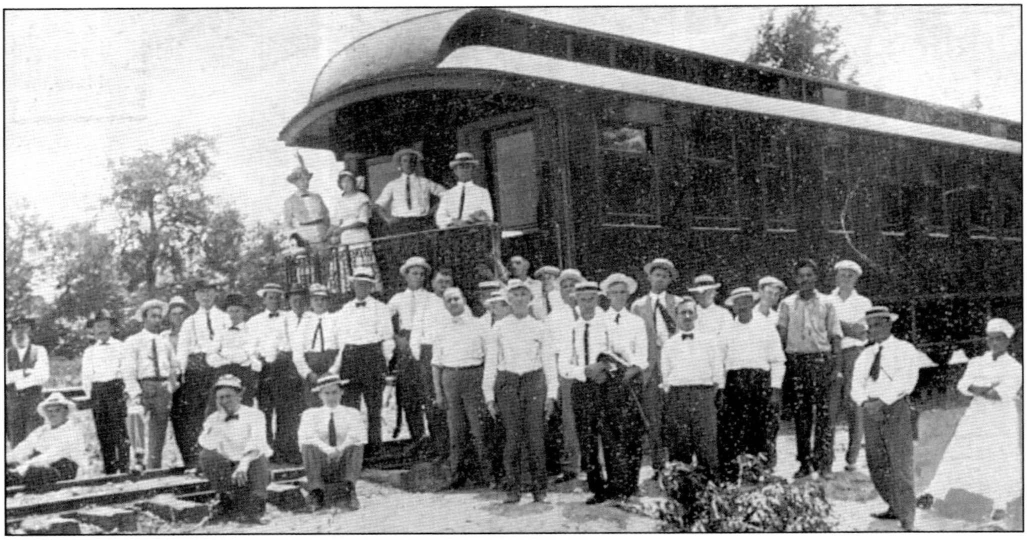

Today motorists traveling north on Highway 49 toward Jonesboro may notice the Otwell city limit sign but have little reason to slow down, a fate markedly different than that envisioned by Will B. Otwell when he laid out the town in 1913. Otwell and his partner Thad Brown were land agents from Carlinville, Illinois, who worked to bring in settlers for excess land owned by the railroads in undeveloped areas like southern Craighead County. The August 5, 1913 dedication of the newest "Farmer Boy Colony" found streets laid out on the planned town site, including a 70-foot wide Main Street. Squirrel stew was served to investors and potential residents, who turned out to hear of the great plans for Otwell's future. The postcards here came from that celebration; the one above stated that "leading farmers, bankers, editors, attorneys, surveyors, ministers, and railroad officials" spent the day on the site. "Don't you think it would be pretty nice to hitch up with a body of men like this and own a lot or two in our very own town, while it is brand new?" The card below read, "These young men look like the proper article. When 500 such sturdy specimens become interested in any one locality, something is bound to happen, isn't it?" However, the vision was not to be; with the exception of a couple of stores and a few homes, the little town 13 miles from Jonesboro never took off.

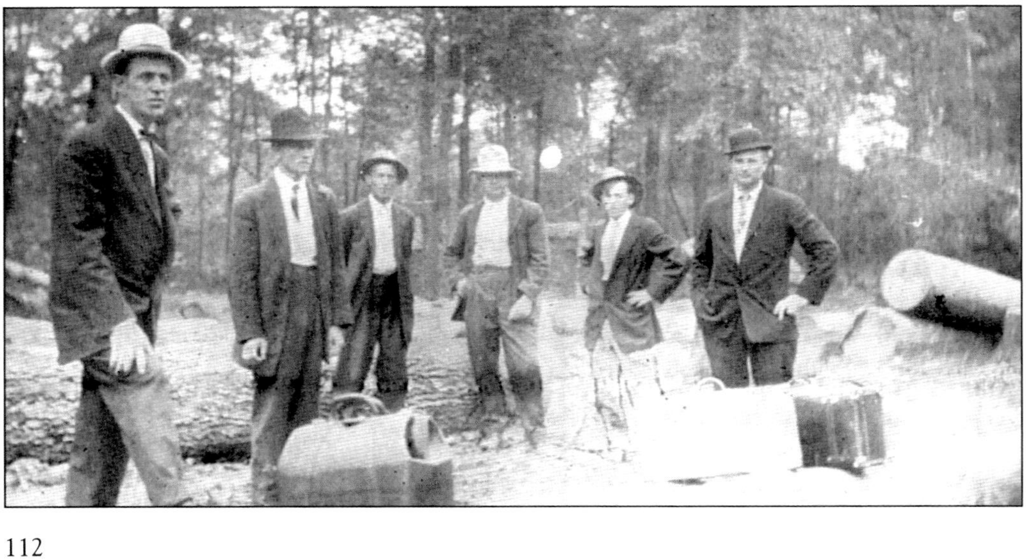

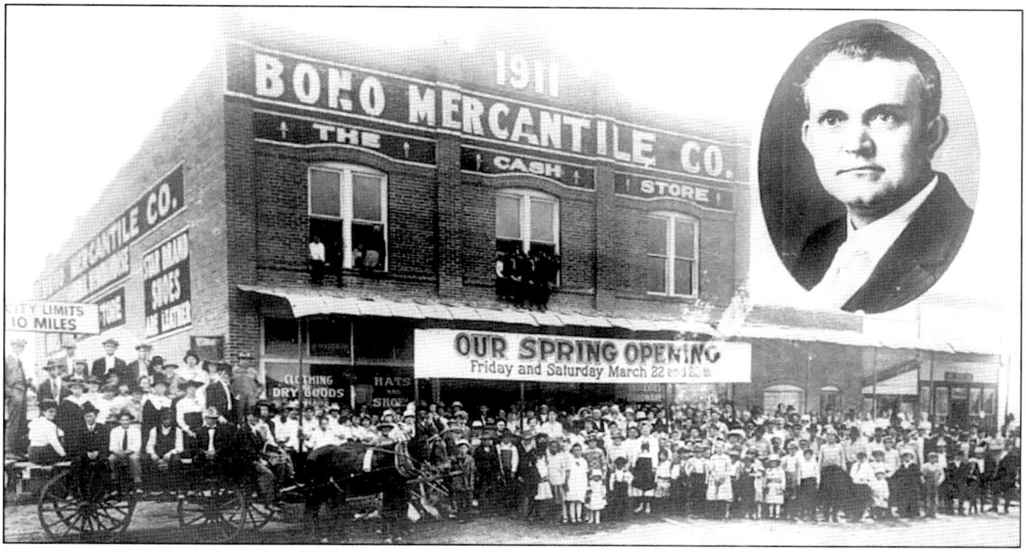

The Frisco Railroad came through Craighead County in 1883, seeking to establish a station to serve the Big Creek region northwest of Jonesboro. A successful farmer named Bonner offered to donate land for a rail depot and post office, provided it would be named after him—hence the birth of the town of Bonnerville. The U.S. Post Office complained, saying this town was often confused with Booneville in western Arkansas; the town residents picked a new name, Bono, in a contest. The Bono Mercantile had opened in 1903, and was seen here with a crowd for the opening of a spring sale. The top floors are gone today, but the rest of the building houses the IGA grocery store at 101 East College Street in Bono.

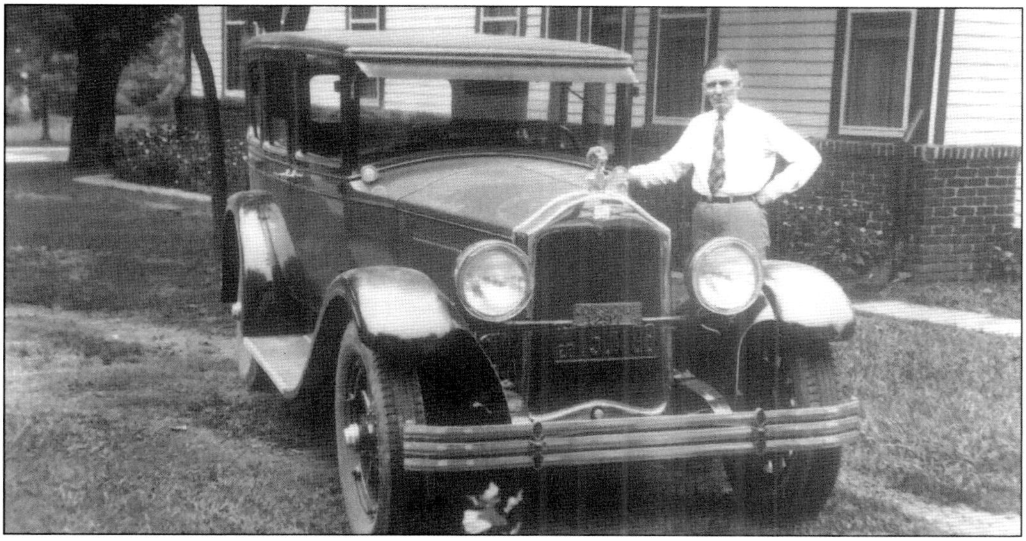

It's probable that the owners of the Bono Mercantile earned a fair but modest living from the tiny farming community. On the other hand, back in Jonesboro in 1925, J.T. Trice was photographed displaying a symbol of the success of his family's furniture business, a new Cadillac. The Trices were very successful owners of furniture stores, both in Paragould and on the 300 block of Main Street in Jonesboro. The car is seen to bear not only a license plate from the state of Arkansas, but also a Jonesboro city plate, #1297, at a time when the city also issued car tags.

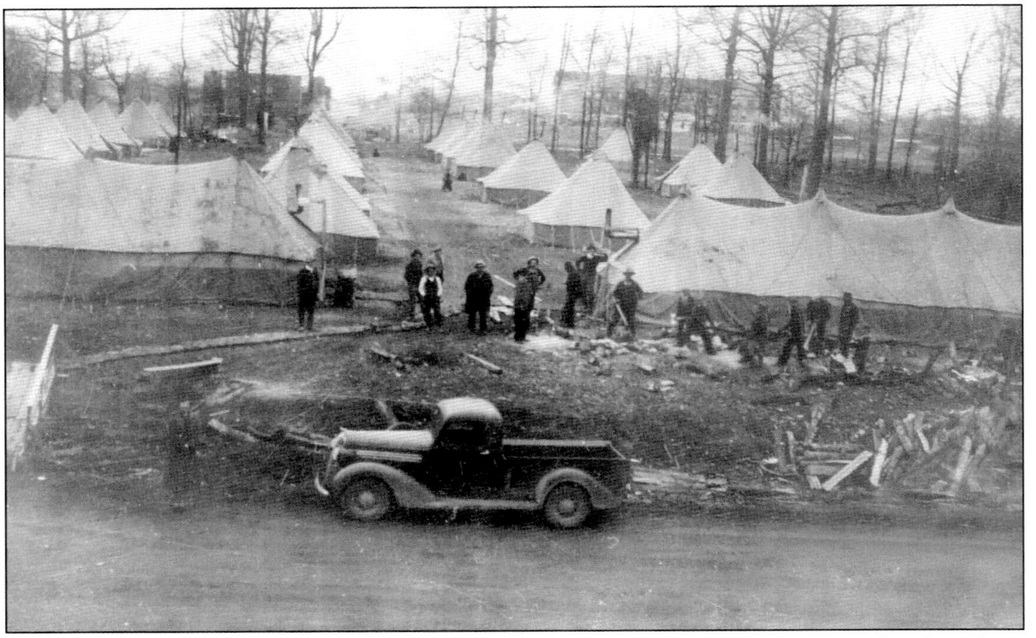

Craighead County and most of northeast Arkansas were susceptible to serious flooding from area streams, especially the St. Francis River, until the middle of the 20th century when extensive drainage and flood control programs began in earnest. Such projects began in the 1920s, but property tax revenue stalled with the Great Depression, and the county suffered the results. One of the worst floods was in 1937. A significant number of residents were forced to evacuate to emergency shelters, in a virtual tent city on the site of what is today the campus of Jonesboro High School.

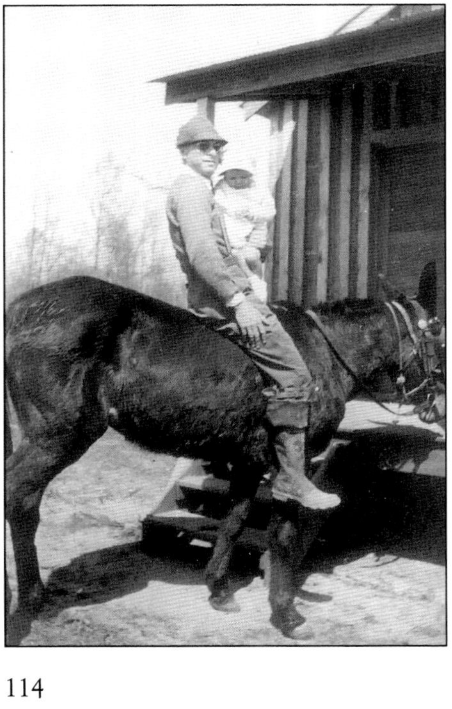

Herbert Sanderson, the lead organizer for the Red Cross relief effort, was among the stalwart citizens who turned out to help in the 1937 flood. Pictured here mounted on a mule, Sanderson later explained that in rescuing the baby from the rising flood waters, it was necessary to separate the infant from its mother for the trip out of danger. When he later tried to return the baby, the mother initially insisted the child wasn't hers and refused to accept it, but the family was eventually reunited. Herbert Sanderson later served as mayor of Jonesboro for 11 years.

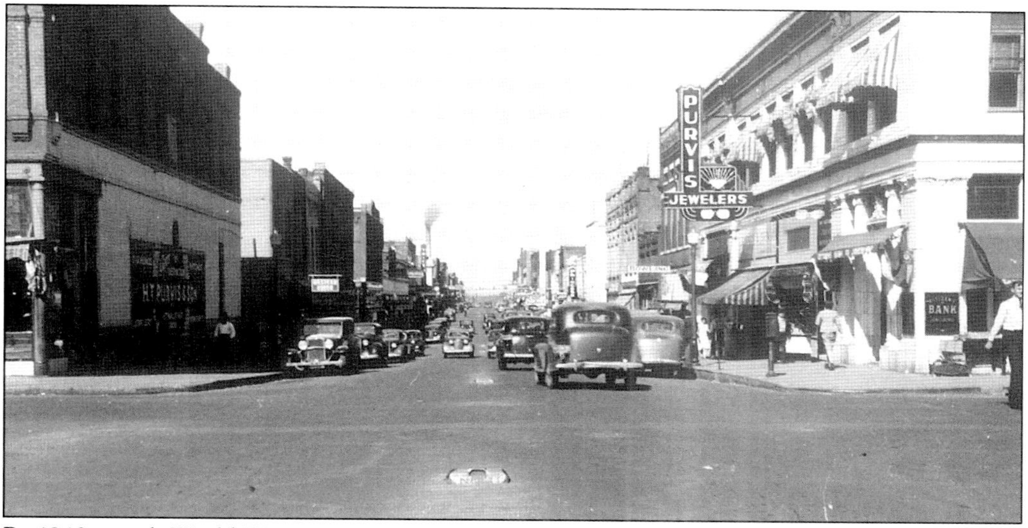

By 1940—with World War II nearing—Jonesboro recorded a population of almost 12,000; along with the rest of the nation, it had finally emerged from the Great Depression. The intersection of Main Street and Washington Avenue that year found much traffic and businesses such as Purvis Jewelry in the Citizens Bank building on the right; further down the street was the bowling alley. Purvis Jewelry had opened on the site c. 1900 and did business at the location for more than 50 years; the Purvis family advertised its store as having the largest stock of jewelry in northeast Arkansas.

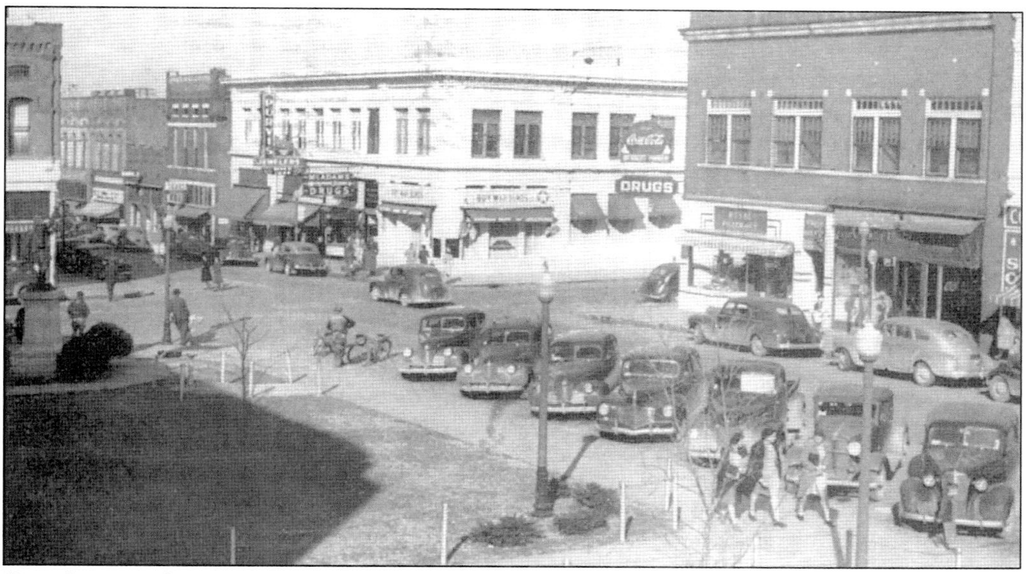

"Jonesboro is a fair town, small, not many soldiers. Only air cadets from State College, they're right next door," were the 1943 words of Pvt. Joe March Jr. of the 560th M.P. Company, P.W. Camp, Jonesboro, sent in the midst of World War II. The postcard he sent his Wisconsin family looked north from Court Square, toward Main Street and Washington Avenue. The American Trust Building, seen in the center of the photo with a "Buy War Bonds" banner, had replaced the Marcus Berger store building (page 94); today it is the local headquarters of the Bank of America. The buildings to the right, housing Royal Pharmacy, are now gone; the site today has a bank branch.

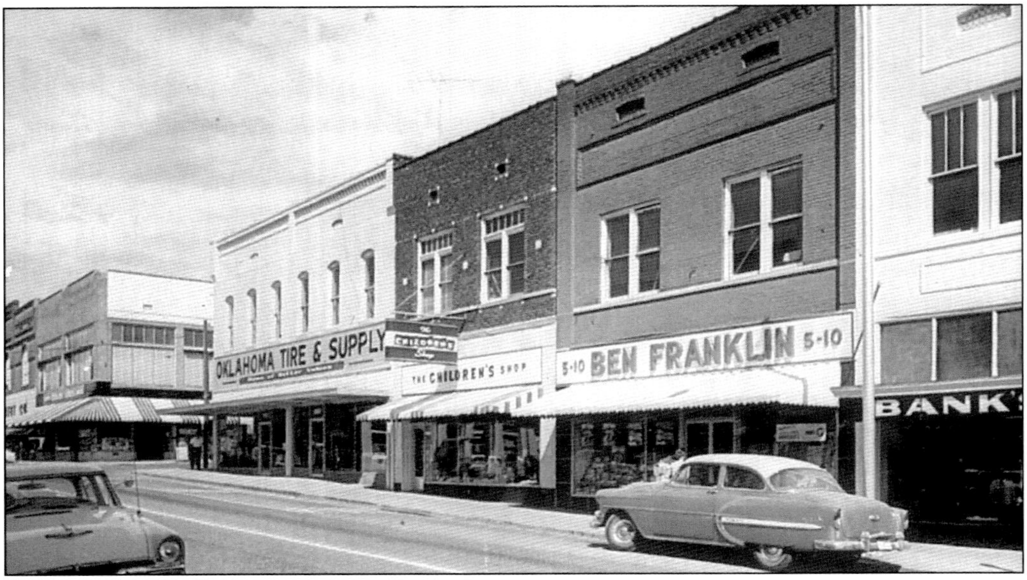

When World War II ended, young men returned to Craighead County and fed a pent-up drive for employment, housing, and other forms of security; the community responded with prosperity for many. By 1950, the population of Craighead County exceeded 50,000 people, with the city of Jonesboro home to some 17,000. By 1957, as seen above and below, Main Street was literally a postcard of 1950s America, with tail-finned cars and such former shopping bastions as the Ben Franklin 5 & 10, Oklahoma Tire & Supply (Otasco), McCrorys's, and Woolworth's. Local, homegrown retailers squeezed in amongst the national names and are also seen in these cards, such as Wahl's and The Children's Shop. The street banner in the card below promotes the United Way. Today the famous-name retailers are gone, replaced by shopping center names ending in "Mart," but Jonesboro's downtown has diversified and continues to be a center of business.

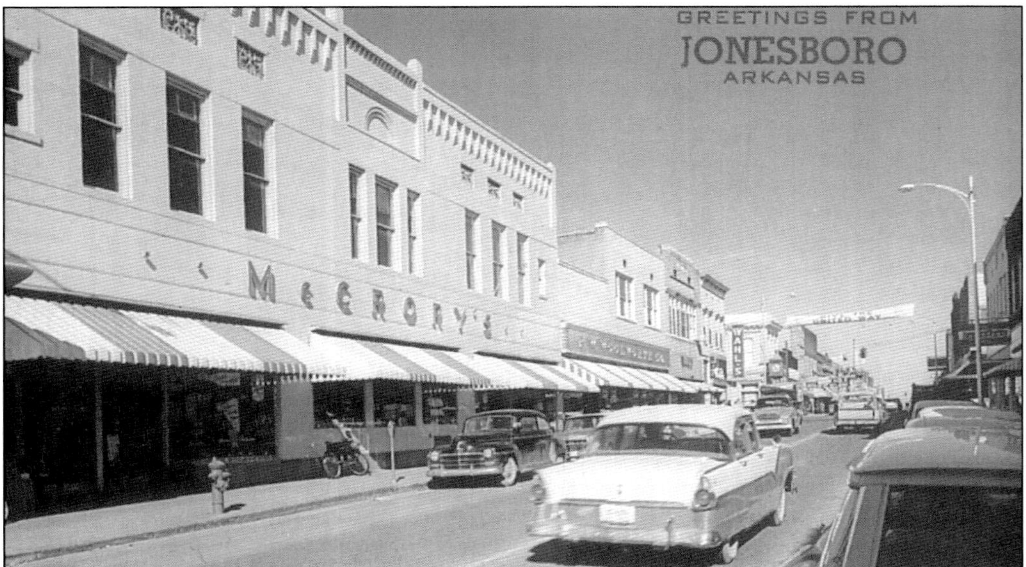

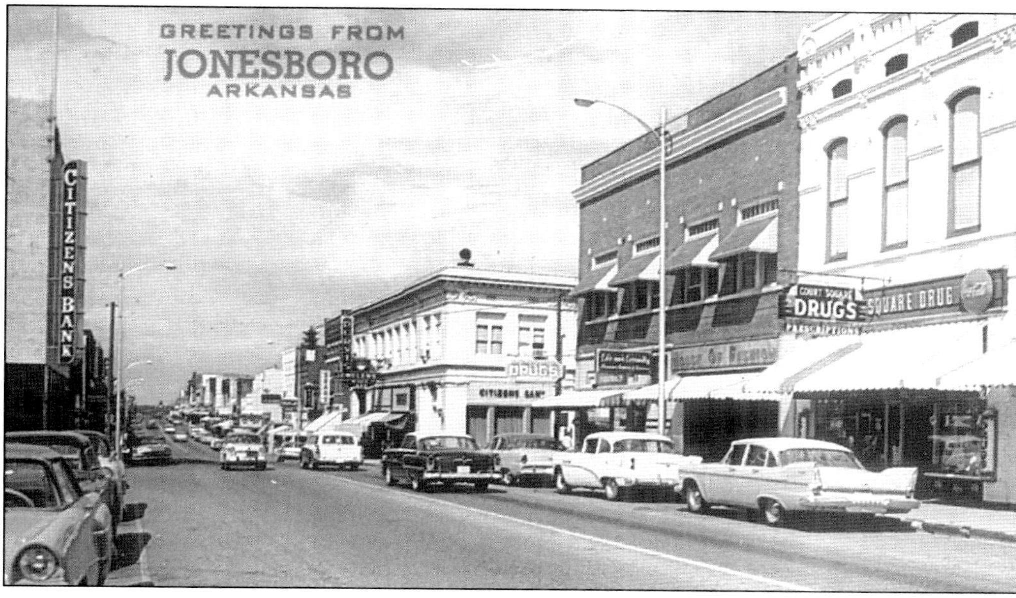

The c. 1957 card above looks similar to views seen on page 115, but was made some 15 years later; the venerable American Trust building still stands out, but houses the Citizens Bank. Court Square Drugs and the House of Fashion are seen to the immediate right. The back of the card proclaims Jonesboro to be "a land of friendly people, excellent schools, churches, and the home of Arkansas State College." Seen below about the same year was a lodging choice that had replaced the early 20th century hotels, for the age of the motel had arrived a decade or so earlier. Pete's Restaurant and Motel, owned by Pete Tyner at 3337 East Nettleton Avenue, "Phone Webster 5-2451" promised "old-fashioned, home-cooked, Southern food from 5 a.m. to midnight, 20 homey motel units, free TV and room service." Pete's was demolished c. 1980.

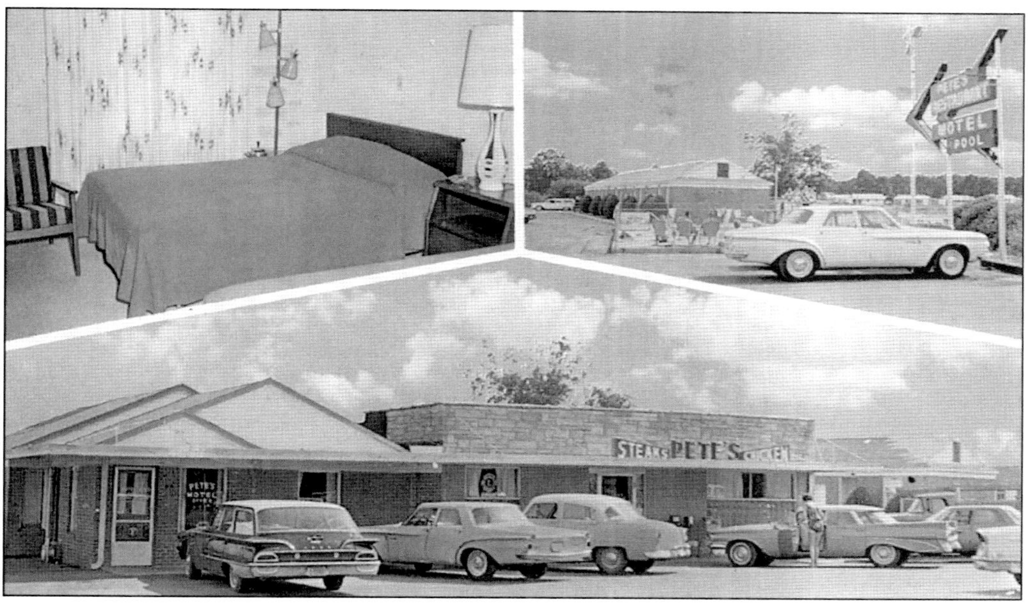

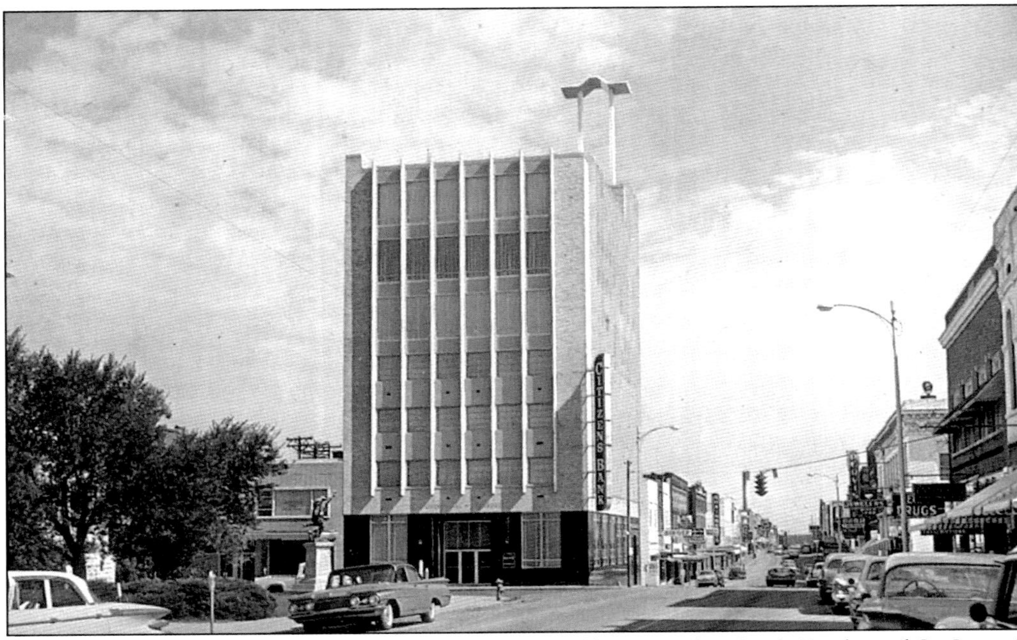

"The Building is the tallest in a triangular area framed by Memphis, Little Rock, and St. Louis," read the back of this card *c.* 1957, showing the Citizen's Bank building that was erected in 1955. The same intersection is seen *c.* 1910 on page 94, though markedly different. The unique "Torii" emblem, of Japanese design and meaning "Gateway to Security," was affixed to the top of the building in 1962. The symbol was removed in 1999, but the building still stands.

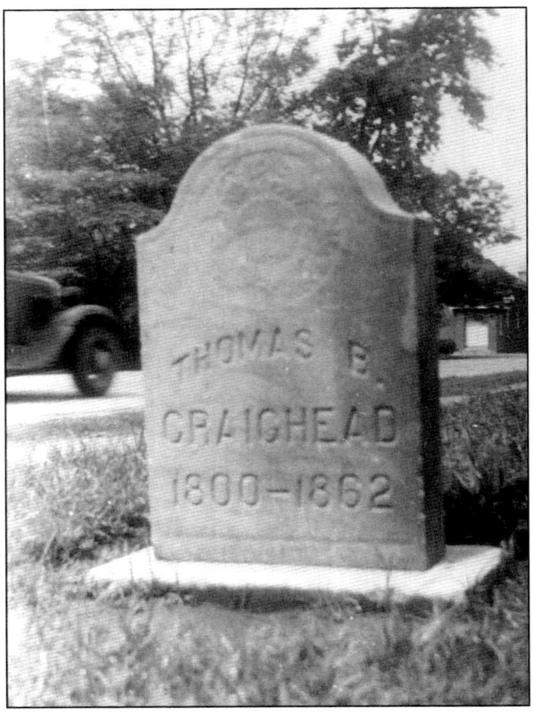

State Senator Thomas Craighead of Mississippi County died in 1862, at the age of 62, but three years earlier his name had been bestowed on the new county carved out of a wilderness. His grave, seen here in Osceola, Arkansas, is marked very simply in this 1930s photo. His real legacy, however, might well be the present-day county that bears his name, and the bustling city of Jonesboro, now some 80,000 strong and facing a bright future for industry and education. One can assume that, regardless of his initial protests, Senator Craighead would be rightfully proud.

Four

EDUCATION IN NORTHEAST ARKANSAS

FROM ONE-ROOM SCHOOLHOUSES TO ARKANSAS STATE UNIVERSITY

Arkansas, along with most of the South, was slow to develop a publicly funded system of education, owing to setbacks from the Civil War and rural poverty. As the 20th century dawned, however, the state started to confront the hard issues. The report of the state's Superintendent of Public Instruction lashed out in frustration with these words in 1904, at a time when Arkansas only spent $4.33 per student per year: "Much of our money is being practically wasted because of small schools and incompetent teachers, nepotism, and favoritism." Part of his feeling of despair was driven by the fact that the state had some 5,000 school districts (compared to 300 today); education was lost in a sea of under-funded parochial issues.

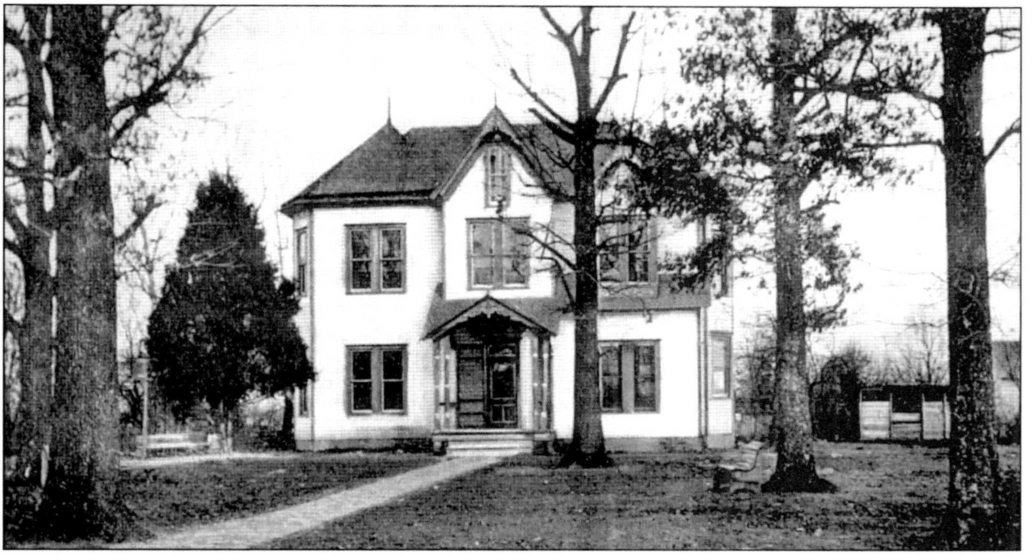

Jonesboro opened its first free public school in 1887; until that time, all schools had been private and funded by tuition for those who could afford it. By the turn of the century, the growing city had erected this two-story white frame high school, at a time when Craighead County alone had 77 independent school districts. Arkansas teachers, most of whom had little more than an 8th grade education, earned on average $166 a year. Without a state compulsory attendance law until 1909, attendance was erratic and few students graduated.

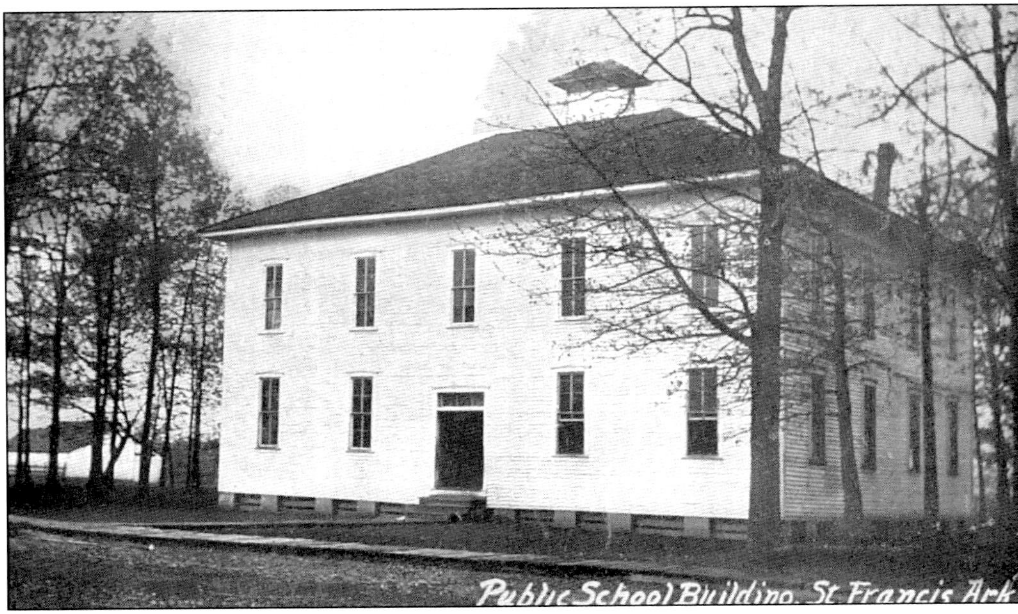

By 1910, timber, farming, railroad, and merchandising interests were expanding the population of northeast Arkansas; large or small, it seemed each community was trying to have its own school district. The two-story frame school built in a wooded clearing in St. Francis, seen above, was housing all grades at a time when working on the family farm allowed little time for schooling. Keeping children engaged for the 107-day school year was a huge challenge for the teacher, who earned less than $300 a year. The budding sawmill community of Nettleton on the outskirts of Jonesboro fared a little better, raising the sturdy brick school, seen below in 1909, at a time when the state contributed but $12 per student per year.

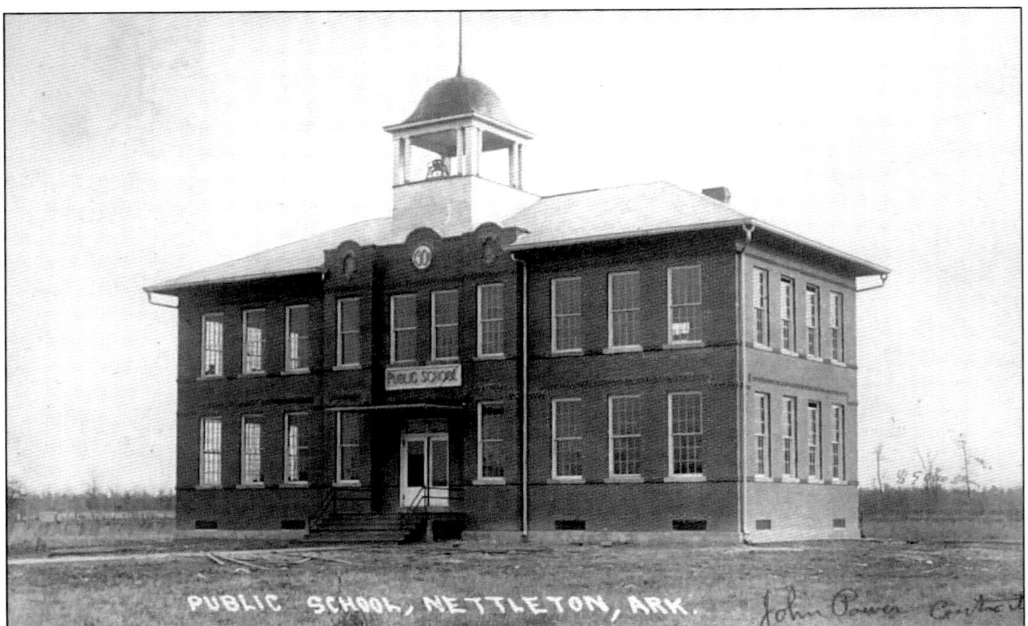

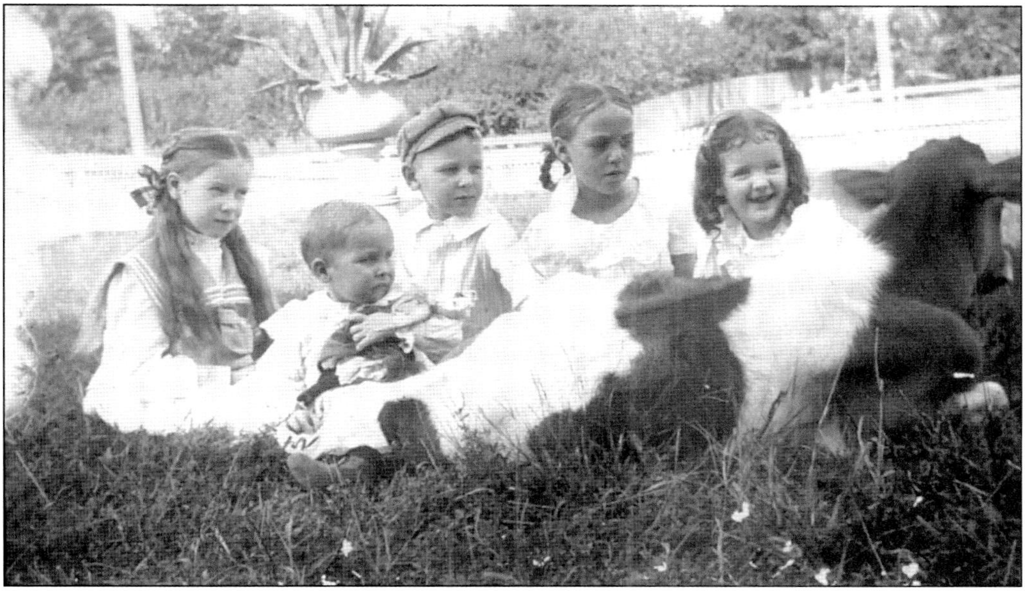

At the turn of the century, northeast Arkansas was very much a rural, agriculture-based area; the vast majority of the population lived not in cities like Jonesboro but on farms and in small hamlets. Around 1900, a young girl named Mary Rogers—seen on the far right—posed with a calf and her friends; the children were a part of the challenge of bringing the state up to the educational standards needed to face the emerging 20th century. The photo was taken in Craighead County, a decade before the state would enact even weakly enforced mandatory school attendance laws.

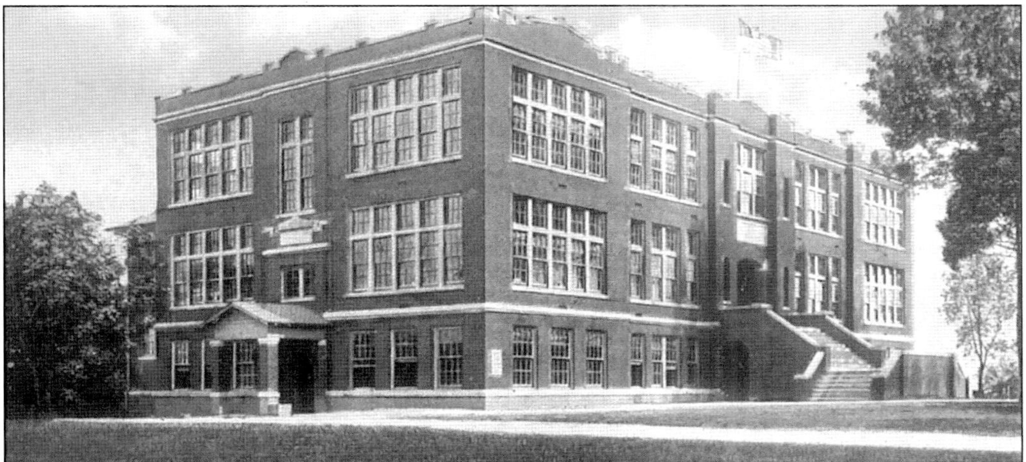

By World War I, Jonesboro had replaced its first wooden high school with this much more imposing brick high school, located at 1250 South Cherry Street. The imposing size of this school, compared to its predecessor, reflected the growth and prosperity of the community. Jonesboro's leaders clearly sought to include among its bragging points a high school deemed worthy of the community, which had almost 9,000 residents by 1920. The school building was later used as administrative office space, and was demolished in the early 1980s; the site today holds the Cambridge Court Condominiums.

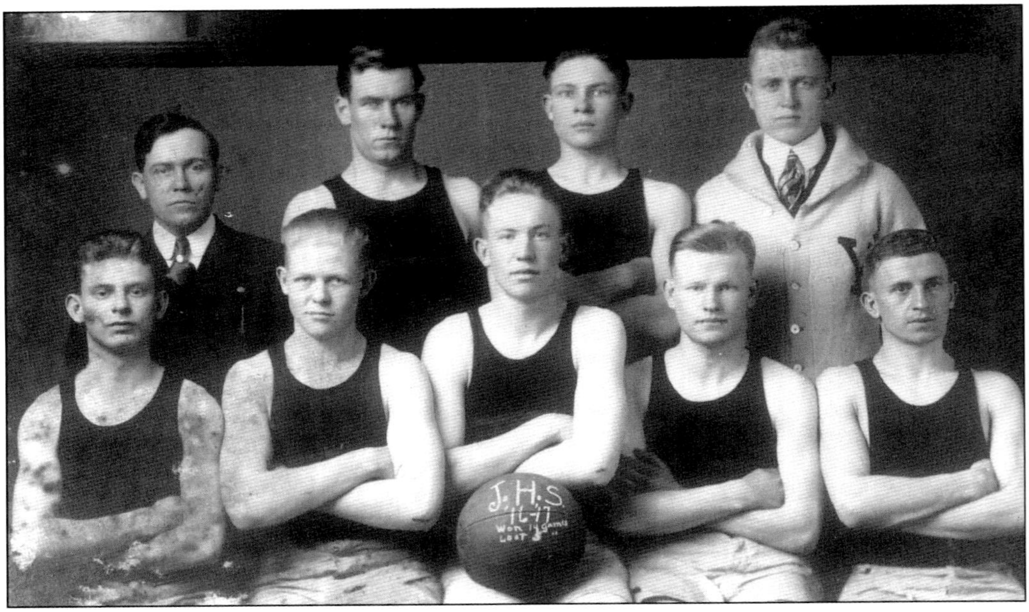

From 1910 and on, state and local officials were beginning the decades-long process of building a public education system for Arkansas, a struggle that continues still in the 21st century. Even then, high school sports were becoming part of the culture of small-town Arkansas, and Jonesboro was no exception. The high school basketball and baseball teams posed for their group photos, just as the school teams of today do. The basketball team of 1916-17 had completed its season, posting 14 wins and 5 losses after a 19-game season. They are shown with their coaches, while the baseball team included their batboy in their photo.

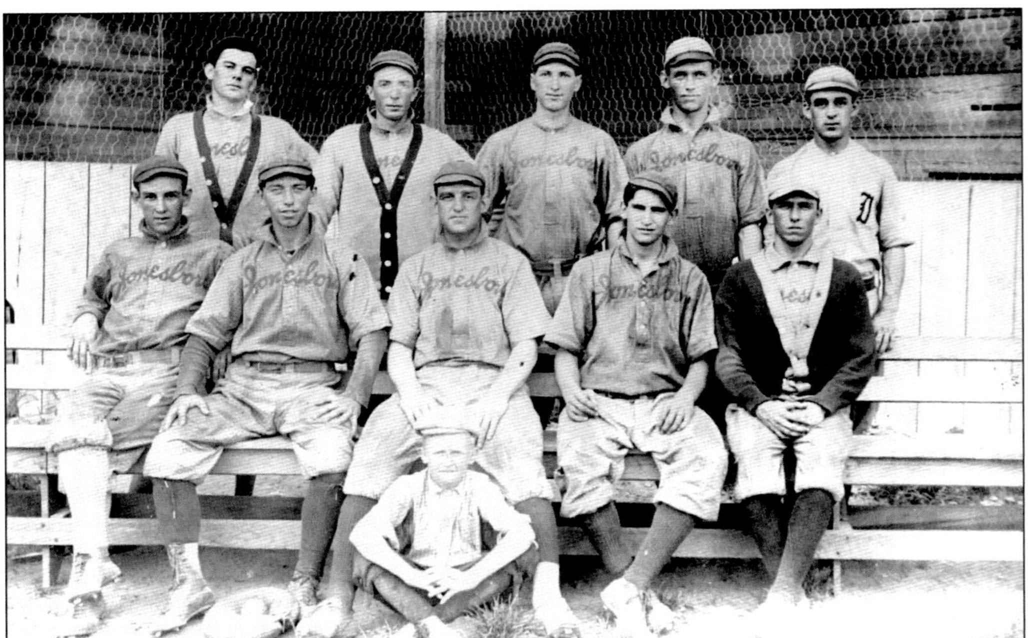

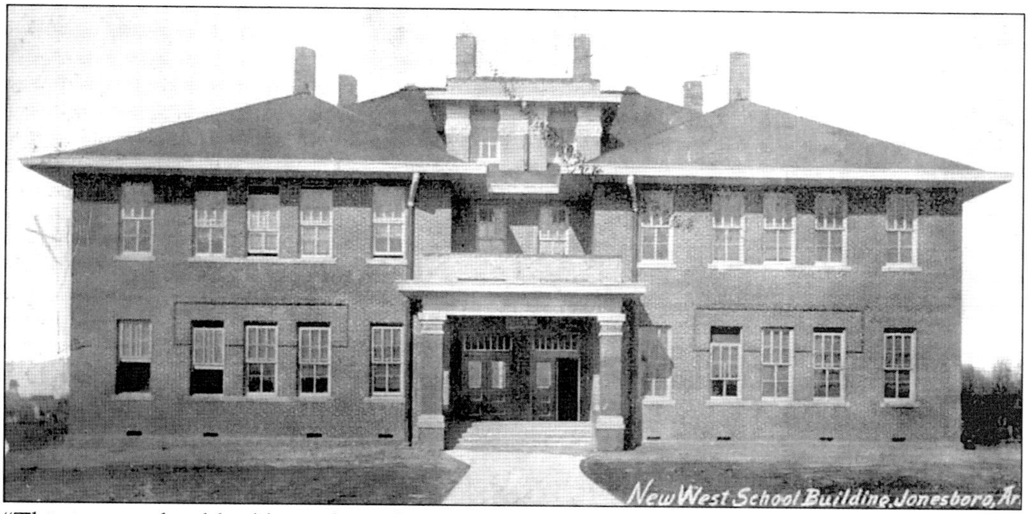

"This is our school building where the X is my room. You can't see Alleen's room, it is in the back, it is the largest in the town." These were the 1915 words of a student in the newly-erected West School in Jonesboro. The school, located between Washington and Monroe Streets, was for pre-high school age children. The second floor was removed in a remodeling during the 1950s, but otherwise the building still stands in use, three-quarters of a century after the young man sent this card to Irvington, Indiana.

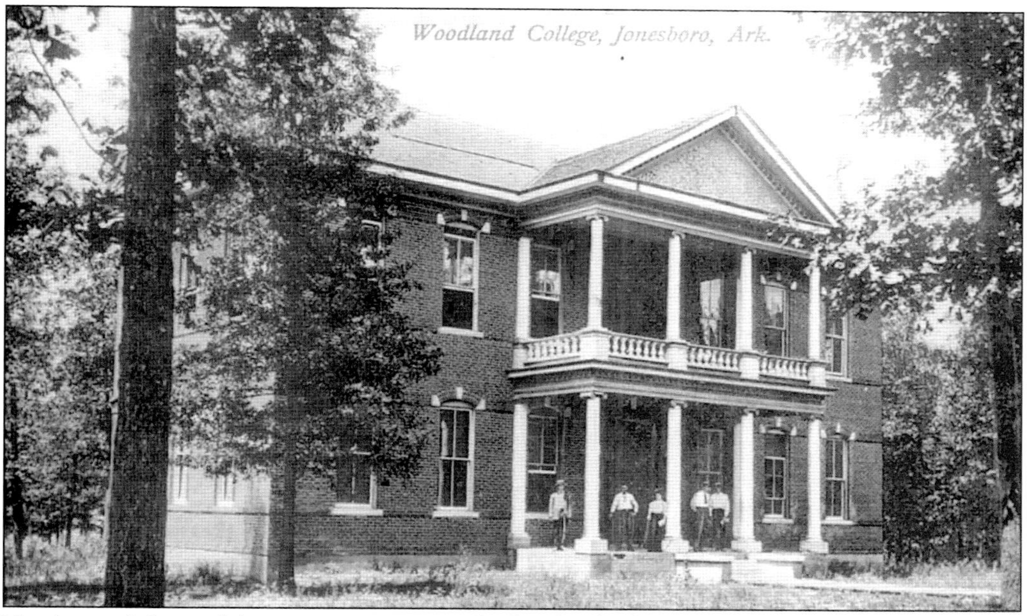

Northeast Arkansas' first attempt at a post-high school educational institution came in 1901, when the Mt. Zion Baptist Association moved to open what became Woodland College by 1904 in south Jonesboro. A newspaper at the time said of the course offerings, "The faculty of this school think that it would be worth very little to be able to jabber German or read Latin, while being unable to speak English, and yet Latin is not taught with greater care anywhere in the state." Failing finances caused the college to close in 1912; the property was later acquired by the Jonesboro school district, but the building shown here is gone today.

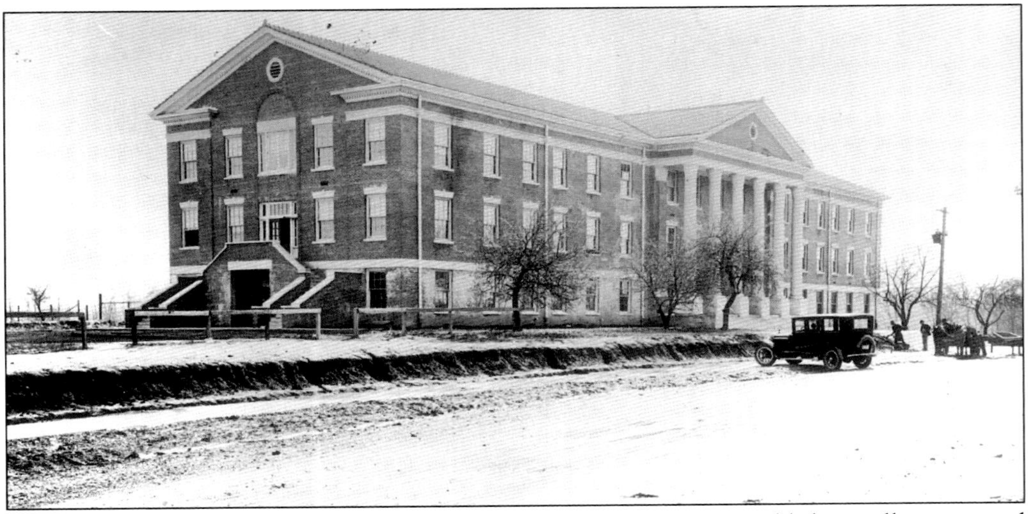

By 1920, northeast Arkansas Baptists were ready to try again to establish a college; ground was broken on the city's southern edge for the construction of Jonesboro Baptist College, with this large administration building erected first. With the promise of the state's Baptist "Home Board" to match locally-raised funds, classes began in 1924. Yet again, failure was the ensuing report card, for flagging financial support caused the school to shut down in 1934. The handsome building, which had opened with such hope a decade before, then became home to the Jonesboro High School for several decades.

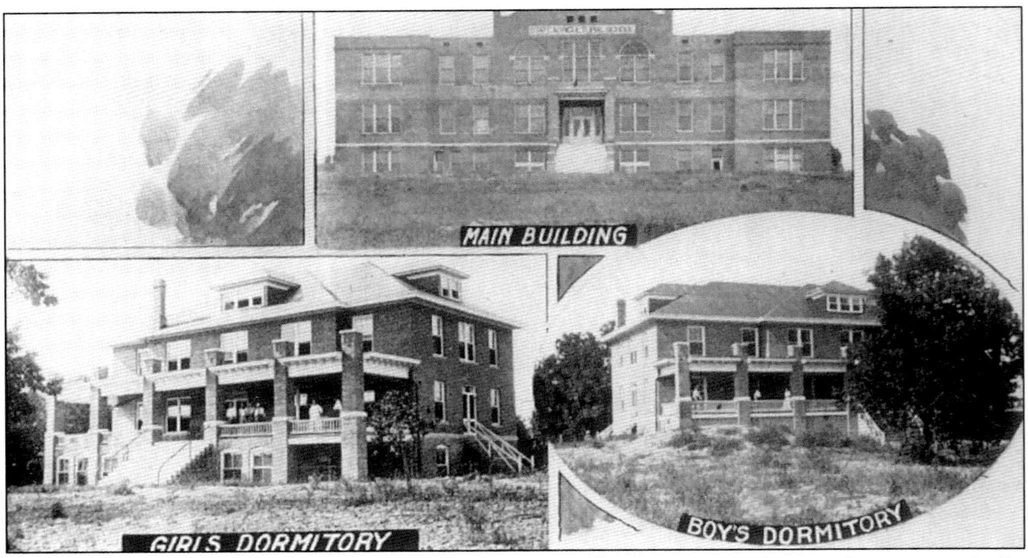

While the Baptists were struggling to establish a college, in 1909 the spark was struck for what would become the state's second-largest university. Area business interests successfully lobbied the state legislature to make Jonesboro the site of one of four newly-established regional agriculture training schools, intended to provide specialized high-school level study geared toward the farming industry. As seen in the top photo, cows soon grazed on the front lawn of the new administration building at the First District Agricultural School, which opened in 1911 at a cost of $30,000. The building to the left was Barnhart Hall, the girls' dorm, and on the right is Lewis Hall, which housed the young men of the school. These buildings are all gone today.

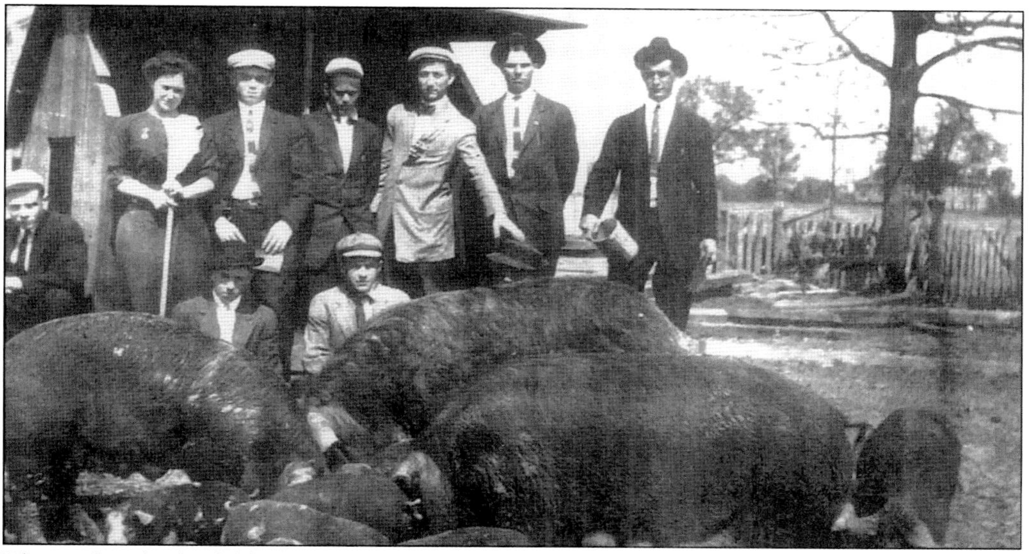

The student body, dubbed "Aggies" for the nature of their agriculture and mechanical school, were dedicated to exploring the field of knowledge in all facets of agriculture, a crying need in the expansive farm state that Arkansas was becoming with the clearing of once-great forests. This group of young men on campus was taking a class in how to best evaluate the quality of livestock; their instructor was the lone woman in the photo, named Zenobia Brumbaugh. One can only imagine, some nine decades later, the conversations this group had as they posed with these nursing hogs around 1915.

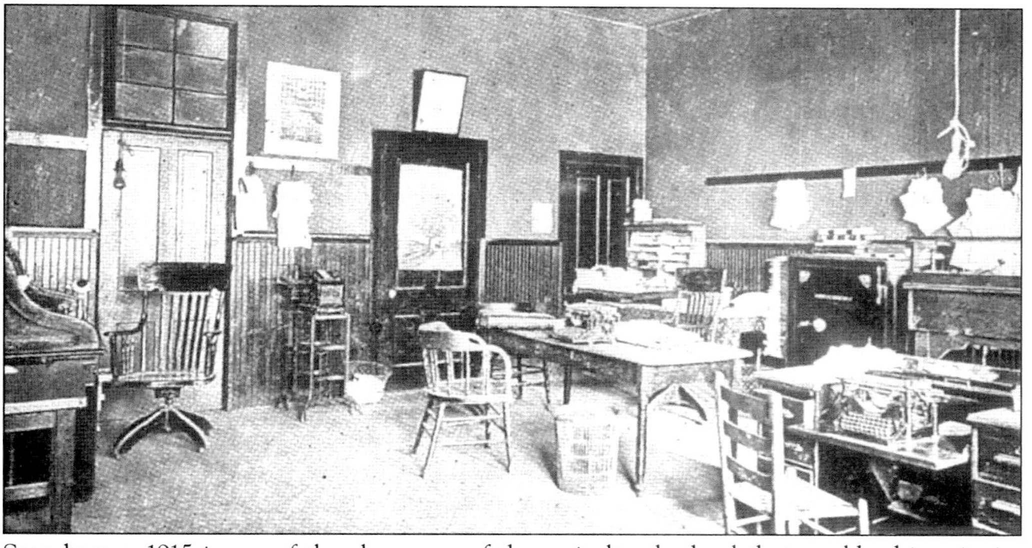

Seen here *c.* 1915 is one of the classrooms of the agricultural school that would achieve junior college status in 1918; the students who studied in this room knew little of what lay ahead for their school. Students of that day would have been inspired had they been able to look ahead to 2001 and read the words of ASU school President Les Wyatt, "We have produced over 50,000 graduates, who have taken their roles in leadership and economic development. We have populated the essential industries, and have created new wealth throughout the region. We have seen the children of children of children who attended ASU come back to their academic home."

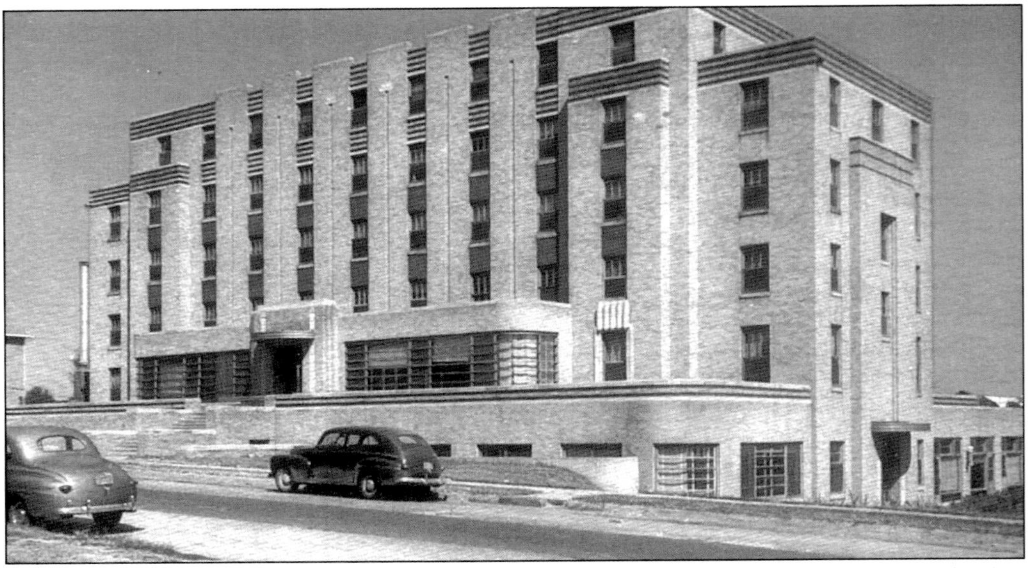

By 1937, with the nation slowly climbing out of the Great Depression, there was no doubt that northeast Arkansas had a college that was in business for the long haul. The school, granted junior college status in 1918, offered a four-year degree program in 1930; in 1933, the title "Arkansas State College" was established. The ASC Commons building went up in 1937, constructed from the top down to save cleanup efforts. The building housed a men's dorm, the college cafeteria, a lounge, and an apartment "for the matron of the building," according to the back of this *c.* 1940 postcard.

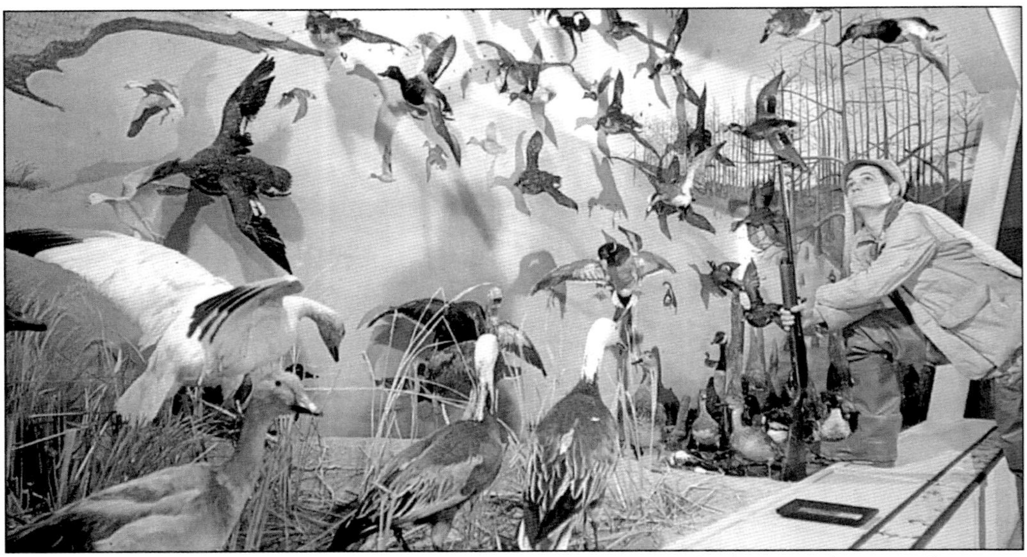

By the 1950s, Arkansas State College was not only producing leaders in education, business, and industry but was also showcasing the history of the school and the region with its Arkansas State Museum housed on the campus. Pictured here on a *c.* 1955 postcard was the Craft Memorial Exhibit of Arkansas Waterfowl. Showcasing exhibits on archaeology, minerals, military history, firearms, and pioneer artifacts, the museum was unique among Arkansas colleges. Its original vision has been fulfilled and surpassed, for today the museum is housed in one of the largest college library buildings in the South.

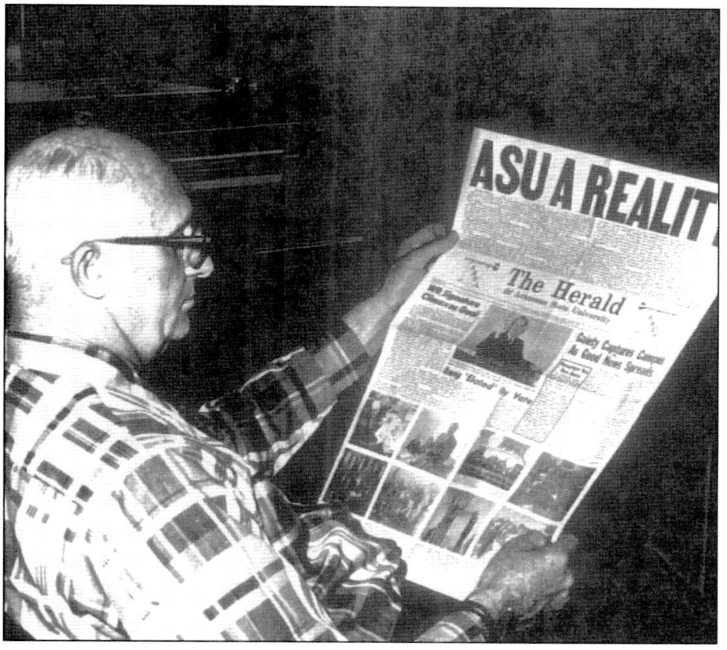

The school that began as a high-school level "cow college" in 1909 had the proudest day in its history on January 17, 1967, when, after more than a decade of political battle, it received full university status and the designation "Arkansas State University." Seen here is the banner headline on *The Herald*, the campus newspaper, being held by a man named Tex Plunkett. With the Arkansas General Assembly's passage of the bill making ASU a reality, the leading opponent, Fayetteville's Senator Clifton Wade, conceded defeat with grace. Wade took the podium and said, "Now gentlemen, I'm against this, have to be [as Fayetteville was home then to Arkansas' only state university], but I hear the bell ringing and the whistle blowing and I'm getting off the damn track."

Afterword

The authors chose to conclude this history of northeast Arkansas with a chapter on education, which is the key to the future success of the region, and which builds on the efforts of all those pictured in this work. We fittingly close with the thoughts of Dr. Les Wyatt, who has led ASU since 1995, and whose efforts are laying the groundwork for an even greater university of tomorrow.

"During the ninety-nine year history of our university, students traveling to and from campus have seen the places, people, and things depicted in the images in this book. In earlier years, those travelers could have hardly foreseen what the campus and the region have now become. Very few institutions have survived this passage of time. ASU is proud to have not only survived but to have flourished in its contribution and effect in Northeast Arkansas. From the first days when a few students crossed a dusty street to a makeshift lecture room to today's digitally-linked myriad of residence halls, laboratories, libraries, classrooms, and even distant campuses, Arkansas State University has been and is a powerful force for change and development of our region and its people. But ASU also represents the history of our place, as it has seen almost a century of progress.

What will the next century hold for ASU? We may speculate that our hometown will become larger and more significant to Arkansas and our multi-state region. To anticipate metropolitan growth, we have developed a campus in Greene County to more easily and efficiently serve students at both the northern and southern ends of the Paragould-Jonesboro corridor.

It will be a great future, as great as our past has been. The view back from the next century will be dramatic indeed."

Les Wyatt, Ph.D.
President, Arkansas State University
2001

Index

Photo Credits

ASU Museum pages 4, 84, 88, 91, 92, 94, 97, 98, 100, 118, 122, 124, 125, 127
Child Art Studio of Paragould 36, 37, 38, 42, 47, 49, 52, 58, 61, 62, 65, 69, 70, 73, 80, 87, 113,
Greene County Library 39, 41, 50, 53, 60, 67
Jonesboro Library 82, 84, 90, 93, 95, 103, 105
Arkansas History Commission 20, 46, 51, 59, 78
Jim Poole 30
Tom Mertens 76
Bob Meriwether 55
Chuck Haywood 18, 25, 27, 29
Herb Sanderson 114